Poverty in the Nonmetropolitan South

Poverty in the Nonmetropolitan South:

A Causal Analysis

George Thomas, Ph.D.

Lexington Books
D.C. Heath and Company
Lexington, Massachusetts
Toronto London

Published simultaneously in Canada.

Printed in the United States of America.

International Standard Book Number: 0-669-85357-7

Library of Congress Catalog Card Number: 72-9591

ACKNOWLEDGEMENTS

This document serves as a review of and commentary on the state of current knowledge about nonmetropolitan poverty in the South.

The work was supported by Grant Number 10-P-56015/4-02 from the Social and Rehabilitation Service, U. S. Department of Health, Education and Welfare. Interpretations and conclusions are those of the author and do not necessarily reflect those of SRS.

A large measure of appreciation is due Mrs. Marion Hutto for handling the nearly impossible job of typing the manuscript, Mrs. Merrilee Stewart for doing the lion's share of the library research and some preliminary writing of the text, and Miss Jo Callaway for preparing the bibliography. Through it all, Dr. Margaret Blenkner, Institute Director, provided the best possible working conditions by encouraging free pursuit of the topic to the limits of our imaginations and abilities.

PREFACE

Somewhere along the way in pulling together a vast array of facts and not-so-facts, I was reminded of the story of the three weather forecasters.

One forecast a warmer than usual winter for the eastern half of the nation and a colder than usual one for the western half. A second forecaster predicted just the opposite. The third, in trying to reconcile these seemingly hopeless contradictions, brightly concluded his report with the prediction that the coming winter in one half of the nation would be colder than usual and in the other half warmer than usual.

There is a strong inclination in working with theory and data on poverty to take the third forecaster's route: the simplest thing to do with this body of conflicting ideas and findings would be to raise it all to the next highest power of abstraction or generalization in order to achieve compatibility, a harmonious blend, an appearance of an integrated, meaningful totality. Indeed, this seems to be precisely the routine followed by various theorists who advance schemes of simultaneously interacting multiple causes and little else in their treatises on poverty.

However strong this inclination, I will attempt to avoid it by treating differing ideas and conflicting data not as contradictions to be resolved, but rather as independent perspectives on poverty having more or less support in the existing data.

The problem is specifically nonmetropolitan Southern poverty. Poverty in the nonmetropolitan South is not only a problem of major proportions because a very large share of all the poor live there, but also because currently it is believed that the rural South constitutes a "seed bed" for much of the poverty in other areas of the country, particularly within the Northern urban ghettoes (*Rural People in the American Economy*, 1966). Special emphasis is placed on blacks in this monograph because of the fact that they comprise a disproportionate share of all nonmetropolitan poor people in the South.

It is also important to state at the outset that one category of people in poverty is not dealt with in independent terms in this monograph, the so-called residual group. Within this category fall all those who suffer poverty primarily as a consequence of severe and perhaps irremediable (in an employability sense) physical handicaps and chronic health conditions.

Their poverty is considered residual in a causative sense in that it has occurred accidentally, that is, by virtue of unanticipated calamities such as auto accidents, industrial accidents, birth traumas, and similar events.

This is not to suggest that this is either an unimportant or minute segment of the poverty population. *The Manpower Report of the President,* for example, estimates that 5 million U. S. citizens are classifiable as physically disabled. Further, about 1.4 million males and 1.6 million females are considered handicapped by chronic health conditions. The effects of such impairments on the employability of the disabled are witnessed in the statistics showing only 11 per cent of 450,000 working aged blind persons employed, 50 percent of 60,000 working aged paraplegics employed, and 10 percent of 200,000 working aged cerebral palsy victims employed (April, 1967, 140).

The socio-economic consequences of brain damage in children stemming from a variety of events has also been frequently acknowledged, indicating children so afflicted as an important potential source of future numbers of poor persons (Birch, 1964, 132-199; James, 1959, 121-141; MacMahon and Sowa, 1959, 51-110).

The point can nonetheless be made that it is not necessary to contemplate the intergenerational effects of poverty resulting from such events. While such poverty can obviously be long term, in the life cycle sense, there is no necessary reason to suggest that most persons suffering such circumstances will somehow predispose their offspring to sustain similar disablements in the next generation. The intergenerational effect, an essential dimension of any general causal thesis about poverty, is therefore irrelevant in many—perhaps most—cases of poverty in this category.

Moreover, those physically and/or mentally handicapped persons who can be reasoned to transmit their conditions intergenerationally—as in the case of genetically caused impairments—are included in the various chapters dealing with causation. Hence, relatively few cases of poverty are omitted as being life cycle in length at most and accidentally induced in nature.

If degree of concern shown in the literature could be taken as reflective of our degree of knowledge about nonmetropolitan Southern poverty, we would indeed be well informed. But this is no adequate test as any cursory examination of the literature would reveal.

This monograph starts with the premise that we do not even know how much is known. As a state-of-the-art document, its chief purpose is to address that particular unknown in systematic fashion. No doubt the goal is overly ambitious, but the monograph will have served its purpose if it places some of the building blocks in the factual floor beneath our ignorance about poverty in the nonmetropolitan South.

TABLE OF CONTENTS

LIST OF TABLES

LIST OF FIGURES

Poverty in the Nonmetropolitan South

Chapter 1

THE SCOPE OF ANALYSIS

This chapter deals with problems in achieving acceptable definitions of basic terms, problems currently facing us in the methodology used to measure the size and duration of nonmetropolitan Southern poverty and problems in deciding on a model or scheme best suited to a meaningful presentation of materials.

These are problems facing any work of this nature, and for that reason alone decisions about them should be shared with the reader. But there are more compelling reasons. For one thing the limits inherent in any report should be clearly set forth. For another, and most importantly, the problems we face in defining terms, applying crude methodology, and constructing conceptual models are in themselves facets of the state-of-the-art.

The degree of trust we have in the materials presented, the extent to which we really know something about the subject of poverty in the nonmetropolitan South, is directly conditioned by the adequacy of our measurement techniques.

Working Definitions

Southern Region

The Southern region means in this monograph the eight Southern states comprising the geographical limits of our Regional Institute's concern. These states are Alabama, Florida, Georgia, Kentucky, Mississippi, North Carolina, South Carolina, and Tennessee.

Data unfortunately have not always been compiled for our convenience. In many studies, data on the South have been summarized for sixteen states and the District of Columbia. In others, six states are used as a base for aggregating data on the "deep South," and in still others, Florida is excluded from analyses as not being characteristically a Southern state.

In some cases the data could be easily reorganized to conform; in many others it is possible only to caution the reader that the data presented are drawn from a geographical base different than our own.

Rural-Nonmetropolitan

Organizing difficulties are compounded by the fact that data are often aggregated across states according to such categories as rural-urban, Metropolitan-Nonmetropolitan, and/or farm-nonfarm.

Moreover, definitions of the above terms often vary from study to study. The term *rural,* for example, has at least three distinct meanings as used in current literature: it is defined ecologically, occupationally, or socio-culturally (Willits and Bealer, 1967). The ecological definition rests on a notion of population distribution and density, the occupational definition links rural with agricultural and allied employment, and the socio-cultural definition associates rural with a Gemeinschaft quality of life and social organization.

Each definition is problematic in the sense that suburban sprawl has obliterated clear distinctions by population density, nonagricultural employment now exceeds agricultural employment outside urban areas, and the spread of mass media and other communications mechanisms are thought to have seriously altered the views and behavior of rural inhabitants.

Given these problems, we fall back on the principle that the simplest definition is the best. Therefore, for our purpose *rural* is distinguished from *urban* on the basis of population density (see: U.S.D.A., E.R.S. *Rural People in the American Economy,* 1966, 2). Also, insofar as possible, we will focus on the nonmetropolitan poor in the South, those residing beyond the boundaries of areas having at least one population center of 50,000 people or *more* (U.S.D.C., B. of C. *Consumer Income* C.P.S. P-60 No. 73, 1970b 3). The reader will note nonetheless, that rural poverty receives the most consistent attention simply because rural rather than nonmetropolitan has been the specific focus of most research efforts to date.

Poverty

Making an issue of what the word *poverty* means is akin to self-imposed punishment: one would like to avoid it, but on occasion it might be a necessary disciplining exercise. Definitions abound, but one's choice is important because, as Watts notes, one's choice

> affects not only the setting of priorities among anti-poverty programs but also the higher level assessment of the relative importance of getting rid of poverty *vis a vis* other objectives in society. (Watts, 1969b, 317. Also see: March 1967, 10-14)

Watts suggests that poverty definitions are of two general types: the economic definition which locates poverty in the person's condition and the socio-cultural definition which finds it in the person's character (Watts, 1969b, 316).

Those who accept an economic definition picture poverty to be the consequence of insufficient income to support a reasonable standard of living and good consumer practices (see: Lamale, 1965; Stinson, 1968). But an economic definition of poverty is not as simple as it appears at first glance. For example, concepts of basic needs upon which economic definitions rest are ill defined, costs of basic needs themselves may vary by size of the consumer unit and regional cost of living differences, and there is no agreement on where the poverty line should be set dividing the poor from those in poverty.

Banfield, for example, suggests four degrees of economic poverty:

> *destitution,* which is lack of income sufficient to assure physical survival and to prevent suffering from hunger, exposure, or remediable or preventable illness; *want,* which is lack of enough income to support essential welfare (as distinguished from comfort and convenience); *hardship,* which is lack of enough to prevent acute, persistent discomfort or inconvenience; and *relative deprivation,* which is lack of enough to prevent one from feeling poor by comparison with others. (Banfield, 1970, 116)

He adds that "the official poverty line obviously does not refer to destitution" (Banfield, *Ibid.*).

The closest thing to an "official poverty line" is the revised Social Security Administration (SSA) poverty index which is widely used in federal programming and evaluation. In this index a variable poverty line is derived adjusting for farm-nonfarm residence, age and sex of family head, and family size as shown in Table 1-1.

Seligman finds a concept of relative deprivation more attractive and concludes that the distinction between being poor and non-poor is largely in the minds of those who because of increased income come to feel "less oppressed, less tension in their lives, and [more] able to acquire those little amenities that make material existence less desperate" (*Ibid.*).

Support for an economic poverty line comes from those who view poverty more as an objective condition than an estimate of well being residing in the minds of the poor. They assert that from a policy standpoint the issue revolves around getting everyone above a fixed income line rather than around satisfying individual concepts of relative deprivation (President's Commission on Income Maintenance Programs, *Background Papers,* 1970, 27-28).

Finally, there are those who insist that no matter how the above issues are resolved, to be functional the adopted poverty line must be flexible over time so that it varies meaningfully with fluctuations in economic growth and cost of living (*American Statistical Association 1964 Proceedings,* 429-455; Friedman, 1965).

Were the matter to end here, it would seem possible to meet all demands for refinement in constructing an economic definition of poverty. Additional difficulties are encountered, however, among a large group of theorists who insist that any definition of

TABLE 1-1

Revised Social Security Administration Poverty Index for 1967 by Selected Criteria

Number of Family members	Total	Nonfarm: Total	Nonfarm: Male head	Nonfarm: Female head	Farm: Total	Farm: Male head	Farm: Female head
1967							
1 member	$1,669	$1,675	$1,750	$1,632	$1,440	$1,476	$1,382
2 members	2,149	2,168	2,178	2,110	1,835	1,841	1,754
3 members	2,640	2,661	2,674	2,573	2,256	2,264	2,168
4 members	3,388	3,410	3,412	3,393	2,906	2,907	2,882
5 members	3,992	4,019	4,022	3,984	3,431	3,431	3,438
6 members	4,476	4,516	4,517	4,497	3,851	3,852	3,808
7 or more members	5,486	5,550	5,562	5,433	4,719	4,720	4,667

Source: "Revision in Poverty Statistics, 1959 to 1968", *Current Population Reports Special Studies* Series P. 23, No. 28, August 12, 1969, p. 5.

Even though this index fulfills some of the previously mentioned refinements needed to establish a working economic definition, Seligman cautions that poverty lines themselves remain problematic in that "an increase of $50 or $100 a year over the official cut off line does not make a family substantially less poor than it was before" (1968, 39).

poverty must include sociocultural components to be meaningful. Consistent with this view, poverty as a term is often replaced with broader labels such as the "culturally deprived" or the "socially disadvantaged." These terms reflect a substantially different perspective, one which emphasizes the characterological and social inadequacies of the poor. The goal of economic adequacy and economic independence—if possible, is replaced with a goal of social adequacy and social independence—if possible (Goldin, 1970, 1-2).

In this view, poverty means much more than income insufficiency. It means poverty of power and political organization, poverty of social interaction and enrichment, poverty of basic services and opportunities, and poverty of heart as reflected in the apathy toward self and life among the poor.

These additions so inflate the meaning of poverty that it becomes difficult if not impossible to distinguish those in poverty from the larger group of poor people, the lower-lower class from the lower class in sociological parlance (see: Roach, 1965; Keller, 1968; S. M. Miller, 1964).

Bloating the concept in this way broadens its coverage to include everyone up through the fully employed but underpaid semi-skilled blue collar worker.

One thing is certain from all this: consensus on a working definition of poverty is beyond reach. This being so, we again opt for the simplest possible working definition, one which will avoid many of the useless entanglements found in the materials on cultural deprivation and social dependency. Therefore, insofar as possible the Orshansky index will be applied in defining the poverty population in this work.

The Persistence and Magnitude of Poverty; Measurement Problems

Persistence and size are the major dimensions of poverty, yet there are imposing roadblocks to accurate estimates of utilizing either current data or measurement techniques. Some of the more important roadblocks are discussed in this section.

Persistence is an extremely important concept largely because the view endures that there is a "poverty cycle" and that this cycle breeds substantial intergenerational poverty (President's National Advisory Commission on Rural Poverty, 1967a, 7ff.). Figures are occasionally cited purporting to show, for example, that 40% of current AFDC grantees were themselves raised in households which received some form of public income assistance (Seligman, 1968, 39). In contrast, others reason that poverty is not as persistent, supporting this contention with figures showing that the absolute number of persons in poverty over the last several decades is progressively declining.

While Kelly points out that current data bases for estimating persistence may be in error, he asserts that concern with persistence may be well taken. His data showed, for example, that of those who rose out of poverty only 25% remained within $500 of the poverty line, while 55% of those who fell into poverty fell more than $500 *below* the line (Kelly, 1970, 24). He concludes from these and other data that the poverty group is increasingly comprised of the aged, blacks, and female-headed households, categories of persons less likely to rise again once they become poor.

Another way that the question of the persistence of poverty has been tackled is by measurement of intergenerational occupational mobility among the children of poor families. Problems in the measurements of concepts such as occupation have probably contributed to mixed and often confounding results within and between studies which have rendered them less than useful in assessing persistence.

We need not belabor the quite valid question as to whether occupational titles can be ordinarily or intervally ranked for purposes of comparison in order to be receptive to Fried's equally powerful point that changes in job titles (e.g. from janitor to maintenance engineer) may reflect superficial rather than substantial intergenerational movement (Fried, 1969, 156 n. 43).

Kelly has demonstrated recently that these "attrition analyses" disclose little about persistence. He asserts that persistence cannot be estimated from declining stocks (absolute numbers) but only from flow analyses which compare rates of entrance to rates of escape from poverty over time. His study of poverty flows between 1965-1966 demonstrated

> a net decline of the number of poor families between 1965-1966 of 2.1%. However 35.6% of those classified as poor in 1965 became non-poor in 1966. In addition, some 34% were new arrivals; that is, they were non-poor in the previous year. Stated differently, about 6% of the non-poor families in 1965 became poor in 1966. Poverty flows over the 1965-66 period were over 15 times the magnitude of the changes in the stocks. Considerable variation is masked by simple analysis of stock data. The use of stock data to approximate flows is therefore inadmissible. (Kelly, 1970, 24)*

There is another way in which estimates of persistence become as much a function of labeling as a reflection of fact. Take, for example, the case of employability of AFDC mothers, and the associated notion that the unemployable likely will be more persistently poor. The size of the persistently poor AFDC population is a function of the criteria applied to them in assessing their employability. Too often such criteria do not reflect the labor market situation and thus are meaningless as estimates of persistence. For example, if we assume that employability is related to extent of education and past job experience, then increases in both categories among AFDC recipients over the past decade lead to estimating a progressively higher proportion of employable AFDC women (Levinson, 1970). If, on the other hand, such

*Kelly drew his sample of poor people from the CPS sample of 35,000 households conducted in 1966 and 1967 for the years 1965-66. He notes his sample was small and a 2-year period is inadequate for accurate flow analyses. A larger study of related phenomena is now underway under a 4- or 5-year plan at Survey Research Center, University of Michigan. See: Morgan and Smith, 1968. As yet no results are in publishable form. Of course, longitudinal studies themselves are open to substantial methodological error and biases in interpretation of data as discussed in Menkin and Sheps, 1970, 1506-1514.

factors as availability of child care and the effect of earned wage deductions from AFDC grants (marginal tax rates) are taken into account, the estimated employability of AFDC recipients declines, and presumably, persistence estimates go up (Hausman, 1970).

Finally, conclusions and assertions are often found in writeups of research and program evaluations which, intent upon convincing the reader of a project's worth, lead to distorted estimates of the persistence of poverty.

These impressions as Kunce, *et al.,* note in reviewing their own recent rehabilitation studies in St. Louis are often overly sanguine.

Citing their own work as an example, they show that 17 of 54 clients in their program were rehabilitated to full employment after undergoing program services. This represents almost a ⅓ success rate with a clientele defined as totally and permanently disabled by Social Security Administration standards. The temptation exists to leave it at that, the impression being that a large minority of very disabled people need not be classified as persistent poverty classes. In fairness, however, they note that the 54 clients were actually screened from a total area population of 1,070 who were receiving Social Security disability benefits. Thus, the success rate for this "hard core" population was actually on the order of 2%. Their overall review of findings from rehabilitation studies suggest that, at any one time, 5 to 10% of the current welfare population (all assistance categories) was actually rehabilitated (or rehabilitable) when correcting for selective sampling biases. Success rates and projections to total populations based on such findings were, by contrast, in most studies much higher than these percentages (Kunce, *et al.,* 1969, 35).

So much for problems in measuring persistence. On the matter of measuring magnitude only one example will be pursued, that of estimating under-employment in the rural South. We believe it illustrates how in a variety of ways present methodology leaves much of existing poverty undetected.

Rates of unemployment themselves are seriously misleading especially when applied to small areas or populations as White points out. This is so particularly because official rates are mathematical projections based on sample data gathered largely for insured unemployed persons. Domestic servants may not be insured, for example, but their rate of unemployment is projected from the rate of unemployment among insured workers in the same skills category (see: White, 1969, and for method U.S.D.L., *Handbook of Labor Statistics, 1969,* Ch. 1). Thus, unemployment among uninsured workers, who are a large number indeed in the rural South, is at best educated guess work.

Moreover, *underemployment* simply cannot be estimated with any logic at all from the available data and the procedures utilized in gathering it. Several studies have shown this to be the case (see: Galloway, 1969; Stinner and DeJong, 1969; Williams and Glasgow, 1968). White's study is of particular interest because he did a large field survey in rural areas of several Mississippi Delta counties in 1967 and compared his findings with official estimates of unemployment and underemployment for that year. His study disclosed underemployment to be as much as 6 times the official estimates (White, 1969).

These observations should forewarn the reader that features central to the study of poverty such as its definition, persistence, and magnitude are indeed very much open to debate and various interpretations. What we can presume to know about nonmetropolitan Southern poverty is clearly conditioned by this fact.

Organizing Schemes

Finally, how best to organize material into a meaningful totality? Two conventional approaches immediately presented themselves: the problem approach and the program approach.

The problem approach would focus upon reporting what is known about the health, housing, education, employment, and so on, of the poor in the nonmetropolitan South. This approach I felt to be sound only for preliminary work, that is, for reporting descriptive data. As such, it is utilized as a framework for Chapter 2, but rejected as a general organizing principle.

The program approach really is an effort to describe what government is doing, how well it is doing, and what its role is or should be *vis a vis* poverty in the nonmetropolitan South. Program description I felt to be beyond the scope of this work, and for that reason alone organizing materials around program categories was felt to be deficient. However, insofar as program evaluations produce data illuminating the nature and extent of nonmetropolitan Southern poverty, they were utilized.

By process of elimination, I was led to a more

FIGURE 1-1

Example of a Current Multicausal Model of Poverty

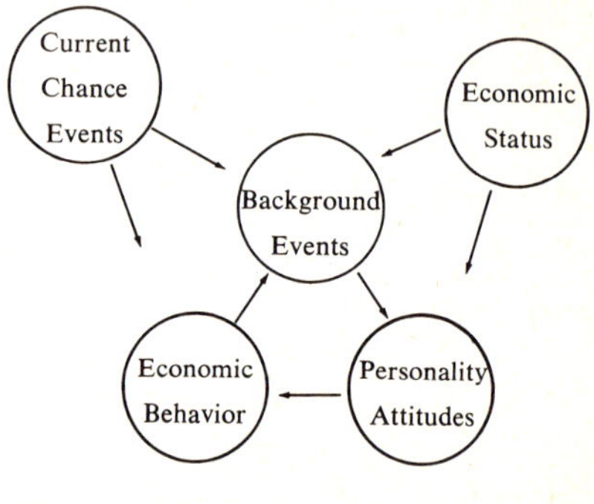

Source: James N. Morgan and James D. Smith, *A Palel Study of Income Dynamic's Wave 1,* Survey Research Center, Institute for Social Research, University of Michigan, 1968, 4-7.

theoretical scheme, that of organizing materials around various causal explanations of poverty (Rein, 1967). Two major pitfalls exist in this approach. The first relates to giving greatest weight to a single casual explanation of poverty attractive to one's beliefs, thereby manipulating the monograph to serve a pet theory. The second relates to organizing materials around a scheme which asserts poverty to be caused by and in turn to be the cause of a multitude of simultaneously interacting casual factors. This approach, the "everything causes everything else" approach, we felt would be more productive of confusion than clarity.

This latter approach, as illustrated below in the theoretical scheme currently being employed in a prominent piece of poverty research (Figure 1-1) is best at producing three — and perhaps more — equal and conflicting interpretations from any piece of data the research yields. The amount of academic debate the results may inspire is clearly no reflection of the amount of actual knowledge produced by the project.

We think we have avoided these pitfalls by isolating five causal explanations and attempting to give them equal treatment. The five are Genetic, Culture of Poverty, Opportunity, Maldistribution, and Scarce Resource explanations. Each is dealt with in some depth in Chapter 3. In organizing materials around these five causal explanations, we can begin to estimate what theorists and researchers assert to be known about the power of each in contributing to non-metropolitan Southern poverty.

Chapter 2

A DIGEST OF POVERTY IN THE NONMETROPOLITAN SOUTH

In 1970 the eight states in the region contained roughly 32 million people, or slightly over 15 percent of the nation's population. These figures show little change from 1960 when the region contained about 30 million people, 15.6 percent of the national total. While 73.5 percent of the nation's population was classified as urban by the 1970 census, about 43 percent of the population in the region remained rural. Although all states in the region experienced some population growth, only two exceeded national average for states, and only Florida surpassed the national average in percent of urbanized population.

Total rural populations in the various states did not change much: in five states the number of rural residents was roughly equal comparing between 1960 and 1970, while population losses were experienced in Kentucky (about 270,000), Mississippi (140,000), and Tennessee (slightly over 10,000).

Controlling for race and area of residence, some rough estimates of shifts in the black population over the last decade in the several states can be arrived at. Table 2-2 indicates that the states vary markedly in respect to changes in black population, the extent to which the black population is located in metropolitan areas (SMSA's), and the overall size of the black population of each to its total.

Of most interest in these rough approximations are the apparent shifts of blacks out of states where blacks remain, percentage wise, primarily rural in residence. Three states, Mississippi, North and South Carolina, all lost black population in the decade, and in all three states, blacks remaining continue to be heavily rurally located(or in this case, in nonmetropolitan areas). On the other hand, those states experiencing increases in black population were, for the most part, those with high proportions of their black populations located in metropolitan areas.

TABLE 2-1

Characteristics of the Southern Regional Population, by States (1970)

	*Total (Millions)	% Urban	Total Rural (Millions)	% Total State Change 1960-70
United States	203.2	73.5	53.9	+13.3**
Alabama	3.4	58.4	1.4	+ 5.4
Florida	6.8	80.5	1.3	+37.1
Georgia	4.6	60.3	1.8	+16.4
Kentucky	3.2	52.3	1.5	+ 6.0
Mississippi	2.2	44.5	1.2	+ 1.8
North Carolina	5.1	45.0	2.8	+11.5
South Carolina	2.6	47.6	1.4	+ 8.7
Tennessee	3.9	58.7	1.6	+10.3

Source: U.S.D.C., B. of C., *1970 Census of Population,* U. S. Series Pd (VI)-1 Table 2.
* Figures rounded throughout for ease of presentation.
** Represents rural-urban change, 1960–1970.

Population growth was hardly uniform for more heavily settled localities (here referring to cities of 25,000 or more), either within each state or across the various states. As shown in Table 2-3, many larger cities experienced population losses during the 60's, the percentage range of growth or loss dramatically pointing up the unevenness of the patterns of population change throughout the region.

North and South Carolina in particular experienced comparatively less dramatic urban growth in their larger urban areas. Examination of the data for several of the other states indicates rapid urban growth was highly selective, as in the case of Alabama where Huntsville's growth (+88.1) was substantially greater than that for any other large place, and, coin-

TABLE 2-2

Size, Change, and Location of the Black Populations in the Southern Region, by States (1970)

	Total Black Population (in Millions)	% Black to Total	% Change in Black Population 1960-70	% Black in Metro Areas to Total Black	No. of SMSA's
Alabama	.91	26.7	+2.6	53.8	7
Florida	1.05	15.4	— .8	67.6	9
Georgia	1.19	25.9	—1.2	47.1	7
Kentucky	.24	7.5	+4.0	54.1	6
Mississippi	.82	37.2	—8.7	14.6	2
North Carolina	1.14	22.3	—2.8	36.0	7
South Carolina	.79	30.4	—8.8	31.6	4
Tennessee	.63	16.1	+6.4	69.8	4

Source: Computed from: U.S.D.C., B. of C., *1970 Census of Population,* Series PC (V2) (for selected states), *General Population Characteristics.*

TABLE 2-3

Population Characteristics of Cities of 25,000 or More, by States (1970)

	No. of Cities 25,000+	No. Losing Population 1960-1970	Total Population All Cities over 25,000 (in Millions)	Range of Loss/Growth (in percents)
Alabama	13	8	1.11	—12.9 to + 88.1
Florida	28	4	2.65	—19.1 to +361.9
Georgia	12	3	1.24	—23.5 to + 73.8
Kentucky	8	5	.66	—13.9 to + 71.9
Mississippi	8	2	.41	—10.1 to + 54.5
North Carolina	15	2	1.14	— 8.7 to + 25.4
South Carolina	7	4	.37	—34.9 to + 14.6
Tennessee	10	1	1.53	—13.1 to + 51.8

Source: U.S.D.C., B of C., *1970 Census of Population,* Series PC (P3)-2, Tables 1 and 2.

cidentally, 8 cities declined in total population. The 361.9 percent increase in Boca Raton, Florida, a rather well-to-do locality, also far outstrips the growth for most large places in that state.

Data from the 1970 Census are not yet sufficiently refined to allow convenient interpretation of these apparent population shifts within the region. Comparisons among the states regarding rural populations show that every state had a lower percentage of persons defined as rural residents in 1970 than 1960. However, it cannot be determined from present data whether such losses resulted mostly from actual population shifts or from formerly rural areas being redefined as urban because of general population growth over the decade.

What we do know does not reflect well on the rural areas of the region. Selective growth of the larger population centers in the region can be coupled with the net population increase (mostly white) in the South* and the continued outflow of blacks (a high proportion who originated in rural areas) to suggest that, over all, the rural areas of the region continue toward more severe depopulation. Given the comparatively low population densities of the various states in 1960 — Massachusetts, for example, led the nation with 634.5 persons per square mile—one of the more sobering features of this analysis may be the increasing

*Here South includes 16 states and Washington, D. C.

TABLE 2-4

Percentage Differences in Rural Populations, 1960-70, by States

	(1) % Rural 1960	(2) % Rural 1970	(3) % Change 1960-70	(4) 1960 State Population Density
Alabama	45.0	41.6	—3.4	64.0
Florida	26.0	19.5	—6.5	91.3
Georgia	44.7	39.7	—5.0	67.7
Kentucky	55.5	47.7	—7.8	76.2
Mississippi	62.3	55.5	—6.8	46.1
North Carolina	58.8	55.0	—5.5	92.9
South Carolina	48.8	52.4	—6.4	78.7
Tennessee	47.3	41.3	—6.0	85.4

Sources: Col. 1-3, U.S.D.C., B. of C., *Census of Population Series* PC (V2) Selected States, *General Population Characteristics.*

Col. 4, U.S.D.C., B. of C., *Census of Population,* Part A. Inhabitants, Vol. 1, Table 12.

forlornness facing those who remained in rural areas in the region during the 60's.

Data suggest that two popular beliefs about the population in the rural South may be more myth than fact. One belief is that out migration has left a residual population in rural areas primarily composed of aging citizens. Beale's analysis of migration patterns during the 50's led him to conclude, to the contrary, that in many of the poorest rural Southern counties the median age of their populations was dropping dramatically. He was able to show that the median age for an aggregate of counties in the Mississippi Delta, the Black Belt, and the Coastal Plains was less than 23.0 years by 1960 while most counties with a median age of 35.0 or above were located totally outside the South. He attributes these trends to the higher fertility rates in these counties (Beale, 1969, 416ff.).

A second belief is that heavy out migration from the rural South was mostly spurred by the dearth of agriculturally related employment. This seems to be a selectively applicable belief rather than a generalizable one. For example, in Appalachia where 50 percent of the population was classifiable as rural in 1965, only 9 percent resided on farms (U.S.D.A., ERS-67, 1965). On the other hand, as late as 1967, it was estimated that about 20 percent of all employment in the poorest areas of the Coastal Plains remained agriculturally related, compared to 5 percent overall nationally (Nixon and Thompson, 1970).

For the moment, about all that can be concluded is that significant changes and shifts in the region's population seemed to occur during the 60's. Urban growth seems to be highly selective, and rural areas in general may have slipped. Common assumptions about the characteristics of the nonmetropolitan populations in the various states are clearly open to question, doubly so in light of the general population trends which have not as yet been definitely interpreted.

The Southern Regional Poverty Population

Poverty remains an abiding problem in the South: almost one half of the nation's poor resided in the South as of 1968, about the same proportion as was true in 1959 (U.S.D.C., B. of C., *Consumer Income,* C.P.S., P-60, No. 76, 1970c, 72). Estimates vary, but according to a fixed dollar line (1959 dollars), it has been agreed on that overall numbers of persons in poverty in the South have fallen during the decade. One estimate put 18.6 million Southerners (11.2 million white, 7.4 million black) in poverty in 1959, the figure declining to 11.9 million (6.7 million white and 5.2 million black) by 1969.*

Some selected features of part of the poverty population are shown in Table 2-5, controlling for some family characteristics and race.

However, estimates of overall declines in poverty numbers can be deceptive, particularly in reference to the nonmetropolitan South. For example, nonmetropolitan poverty in the South represented 58 percent of all nonmetropolitan poverty in 1959, but had grown to represent 62 percent by 1968 (U.S.D.C., B. of C., C.P.S., P-23, No. 33, 1970a, 72). Black citizens in the nonmetropolitan South are a particular source of concern: while they represented 37 percent of all the nonmetropolitan poor in the region in 1959, that figure rose to 43 percent by 1968 (U.S.D.A., B. of C., C.P.S., P-23, No. 33, 1970a, 74).

Unfortunately no way was discovered which would yield reliable estimates of the distribution of nonmetro-

*Throughout this section South means 16 states and Washington, D.C.

TABLE 2-5

Partial Breakdown of the Southern Regional Poverty Population, by Family Characteristics and Race (1969)

	Totals (in Millions)	Number in Poverty	% Poor	Total	White Number Poor	% Poor	Total	Black Number Poor	% Poor
All Families	15.8	2.3	14.8	13.2	1.4	10.8	2.5	.9	35.7
With Male Head	13.9	1.5	11.0	12.1	1.0	8.7	1.8	.5	26.1
With Female Head	1.9	.8	43.0	1.2	.4	32.6	.7	.4	62.0
All Unrelated Individuals	3.9	1.6	41.4	3.1	1.1	37.3	.8	.5	56.1
Male	1.4	.46	32.1	1.0	.3	28.5	.4	.2	40.9
Female	2.5	1.2	46.7	2.0	.9	41.7	.5	.3	69.0

Source: U.S.D.C., B. of C., *Consumer Income*, C.P.S., P-60, No. 76, 1970c, 49, Table 6.

politan poverty populations by states. While it has been estimated that roughly 13 of every 100 whites and 41 of every 100 blacks are poor in the South currently, no way was found to convert these general indicators to reflect variations between the states.

Again, blacks accounted for 45 percent of all metropolitan poverty in the South (1.9 of 4.2 million poor) and 43 percent of all nonmetropolitan poverty (3.3 of 7.7 million). Also, 63 percent of all blacks and 65 percent of all whites in poverty in the region resided in nonmetropolitan areas (U.S.D.C., B. of C., C.P.S., P-23, No. 33, 1970a, 73).

All of these "facts" are of little use in assessing the distribution of poor persons by race and type of residence, state by state. Most of the foregoing figures have been drawn from Bureau of the Census, Department of Commerce publications, which attempt to update our knowledge by projecting from surveys conducted during the time between national enumerations. Since these surveys involve relatively small samples (varying from 30 to 50 thousand), it is not possible to report on data on such small geographic units as states — let alone by metropolitan-nonmetropolitan areas within them — without hazarding monumental errors in estimates.

Yet, even if we had more specific data for individual states — which can be expected when more definitive analyses of the 1970 census are issued — we would not necessarily be able to determine the severity of the circumstances confronting the poor in the nonmetropolitan South, community by community.

Sutton illustrates this point in a recent study in which he attempted to determine from 1950 and 1960 U.S. census data, how many of the nation's rural poor actually reside in economically declining, isolated areas. Aggregating data for counties, Sutton classified each first as metropolitan or nonmetropolitan and then subclassified in terms of a predominance (over 50 percent) of urban or rural residents, and by whether each county was declining or not during the 50's according to absolute population change and Level of Living Index.

Reorganizing the data in these ways, Sutton was able to estimate that 28 percent of all rural poverty was contained within metropolitan-urban (SMSA) boundaries, 30 percent was located in stable, prospering nonmetropolitan but urban areas, and the remaining 43 percent* was found, consistent with the common belief, in isolated declining areas (Sutton, 1967).

These findings are instructive since they warn against general inferences about the access of the nonmetropolitan poor to metropolitan services, opportunities, cultural influences, and other important factors, from knowledge about where the poor are concentrated residentially. At the same time, it should be noted that Sutton's analysis is national in scope and based on rather ancient data; hence, its fit to the current circumstances of the Southern poor may be less than perfect.

At the moment, the more important features in the materials presented relate to the apparent growth proportionately of nonmetropolitan to metropolitan poverty in the South, and the increasing percentage representation of blacks in the region's overall nonmetropolitan poverty population over the decade of the 60's.

Clouds on the Horizon: Estimates of Persistence

In this section I will try to draw together a variety of indicators which illustrate the persistence of poverty in the region and perhaps partially explain the estimated growth in its nonmetropolitan poverty population over the last decade.

Some of the characteristics of the rural population in the region which do not bode well for an easy or rapid rollback in the incidence of poverty can be seen in Table 2-6

---

*Percentages do not add to 100 due to rounding error.

TABLE 2-6

Selected Characteristics of Rural Southern Populations, by States

	(1) Dependency Ratios*			(2) Terminal Fertility Rates**			(3) Illegitimacy Rates Per 1,000 Birth, 1968
	Rural Total	**Non-Farm**	**Farm**	**Rural Total**	**Non-Farm**	**Farm**	
United States	863	863	861	3.00	2.89	3.34	88
Alabama	938	945	920	3.52	3.39	3.84	124
Florida	831	832	818	2.84	2.81	3.21	130
Georgia	888	880	918	3.40	3.27	3.80	NA
Kentucky	897	926	840	3.37	3.37	3.35	70
Mississippi	1055	1022	1107	3.89	3.50	4.49	173
North Carolina	845	818	916	3.04	2.84	3.56	117
South Carolina	942	904	1070	3.39	3.12	4.24	143
Tennessee	834	841	821	2.98	2.88	3.19	112

* Ratio of persons under age 15 and over age 65 per 1,000 persons aged 20-64 years.

**Average number children ever born per every 1,000 women aged 35-44 years in 1960.

Sources: Column 1, 2, U.S.D.A., E.R.S., *Rural People in the American Economy,* 1966, 104, Table 15. Col. 3, Planned World Population for O.E.O., *Need for Subsidized Family Planning Services, 1968,* Table 1.

TABLE 2-7

Recent Trends in AFDC Caseload Size and Costs, by States

	(1) Average No. of Children per AFDC Case		(2) Percent Change 10/70 to 11/70 in:		(3) Percent Change 11/69 to 11/70 in:	
	12/60	**5/68**	**No of Recipients**	**Average Cash Grant**	**No. of Recipients**	**Average Cash Grant**
United States	2.95	3.05	+3.1	+1.9	+31.8	+42.4
Alabama	3.16	3.39	+2.7	+2.6	+34.7	+31.9
Florida	2.88	3.16	+2.0	+2.6	+26.3	+21.4
Georgia	2.88	3.03	+1.9	+2.1	+33.3	+34.3
Kentucky	2.69	2.84	+ .4	+ .7	+ 9.2	+12.0
Mississippi	3.05	3.48	+7.4	+7.7	+21.3	+24.6
North Carolina	3.07	3.09	+ .4	+ .3	+17.0	+20.0
Socth Carolina	3.15	3.18	+2.2	+2.3	+40.3	+40.3
Tennessee	2.82	3.04	+1.1	+1.3	+35.5	+41.5

Sources: Col. 1, President's Commission on Income Maintenance, *Background Papers,* 1970, Table 5. 2-3. Col. 2 & 3, U.S.D.H.W., S.R.S., N.C.S.S., *Public Assistance Statistics,* 1970a, Table 7.

These data show that not all states in the region are equally "bad off." However, an ominous note is sounded in observing that the states which include much of the Delta, Black Belt, and Coastal Plains within their boundaries (Ala., Ga., Miss., S. Car.) also cluster at the top in terms of carrying the heaviest burdens relative to the size of their rural dependent populations, overall size of families, and rates of illegitimate births.

The burden of a population growing younger, particularly in areas of states believed to be experiencing the most concentrated rural poverty, is in part reflected in trends being witnessed in AFDC caseload size and costs shown in Table 2-7.*

*No doubt the increases noted are also to some extent the result of liberalized policies as well as population changes and pressures. See: Meyers and McIntyre, 1969.

Thus, in association with some of the previous indicators which in part reflect socio-economic burdens within rural populations, we have case load sizes, growth trends in total cases, and overall payment costs for AFDC accelerating at greater—than national—average rates precisely in those states currently believed to be worst off in the matter of rural poverty. It should be added that the comparatively large increases in grant payments do not reflect an approximation of parity with the national average by the several states. Recent data indicate average monthly AFDC case payments in the region range from $47.30 (Mississippi) to $115.75 (North Carolina) compared to the national norm of $180.10 for equivalent sized families (U.S.D.H.E.W., S.R.S., N.C.S.S., *Public Assistance Statistics,* 1970a).

The meaning per capita income trends have for evaluating nonmetropolitan Southern poverty is also enhanced by making comparisons to national average trends. Unless this is done, some confusion arises as to how it is possible that per capita income has been rising rapidly in the nonmetropolitan South coincident with an estimated increase in the proportion of some groups in poverty in the region over the last decade.

The fact that per capita income rose 75% in the nonmetropolitan South during the decade and continued to accelerate at better than a 10% pace as of 1968 must be weighed by another set of facts showing that the region averaged only 64 percent of national average per capita income and represented only 7.42 percent of total per capita income in 1968. As Table 2-8 discloses, the growth rate *vis a vis* these national averages has not been striking.

It is now recognized that the South generally experienced a radical change in population trends in the 60's, becoming for the first time in this century a net gainer of population from migration shifts. It is also thought that this population gain is represented in the main by movement of relatively well educated and skilled employable and retired whites into the South (Barth, 1970; New York *Times,* 1971c).

If this is so, part of the per capita income increase is explained by this movement. This would also suggest that the poverty population outside the cities in the South is not directly benefiting by these apparent economic improvements.

The speculation that this conclusion is based upon is strengthened somewhat by examining the employment and employability characteristics of the working aged populations in the various states. Observations drawn from the data in Table 2-9 give some hint of the likelihood that the rural poor are benefiting substantially in terms of income gains through the avenue of employment.

With few exceptions, estimates for the states are that presently, the number of working aged persons in rural areas greatly exceeds the amount of employment available in 1960. Even if employment opportunities had advanced during the 60's to match the growth in numbers of employable persons—and this is questionable—such a growth rate would have produced only a marginal effect on employment for the already working poor.

In examining selective service rejection rates, we can gain something of a hint of the employment preparedness among working aged males in the various states. There is little consolation in the fact that rejection rates are mostly in line with national averages. This is so because if the employment picture is not overly sanguine in the rural areas of these states to begin with, the problem is compounded by adding the estimated 8 to 10 percent of selected service rejectees who would not be employable under the most favorable circumstances without substantial rehabilitation (see Kunce, *et al.,* 1969). It is probable also that a much larger percentage of rejectees need some sort of preparation to enhance their employability and that many of the rejectees are rural residents in the South.*

Taken together, these indicators lend the impression that much of rural Southern poverty is not going to simply evaporate as time marches on. They also point out some of the basic features of rural Southern life and its people which, in part, may explain why

TABLE 2-8

Per Capita Income Trends in the Southeast* 1959-1968

	% of National Income			% Increase	Average Annual Growth Rates (%)			% of Total U. S. Per Capita Income	
	'59	'65	'68	1959-68	'50-'59	'59-'68	'67-'68	1929	1968
SMSA's	91	91	92	61	7.47	7.58	11.37	5.58	9.13
NON-SMSA's	58	62	64	75	5.05	7.61	10.20	5.89	7.42

*Includes 12 Southeastern states, excludes Washington, D.C.

Source: Regional Economics Division Staff, "Personal Income in Metropolitan and Nonmetropolitan Areas," *Survey of Current Business,* L (May 1970) 22-36.

*This conclusion is based on findings which show comparable selective service rejection rates for rural men in eastern Kentucky and South Carolina. See: Menach 1969.

TABLE 2-9

Job Replacement Ratios and Selective Service Rejection Rates, by States

	(1) Rural Job Replacement Ratios for Working Age Group 20-64 Years, 1960-1970			(2) Selective Service Rejection Rates 7-1-69 to 12-31-69 at Preinduction & Induction (in Percents)	
	Total	**Non-Farm**	**Farm**	**Preinduction**	**Induction**
United States	177	184	160	45.4	18.5
Alabama	210	217	196	48.1	14.5
Florida	168	169	161	48.5	19.6
Georgia	224	235	197	45.4	6.9
Kentucky	203	234	160	48.1	18.3
Mississippi	207	210	203	54.0	13.5
North Carolina	235	248	213	49.4	17.6
South Carolina	279	288	255	46.7	18.2
Tennessee	197	221	165	48.1	16.3

Sources: Column 1, U.S.D.A., E.R.S., *Rural People in the American Economy,* 1966, 104-105, Table 15. Column 2, U.S. Congress, *Semi-Annual Report of the Director of Selective Service,* 1970, 44-45, Table 4-5.

poverty has persisted on a large scale in rural areas of the region over the last decade.

Southern Population Movements and Poverty

There is no doubt that all the states in the region experienced substantial population shifts during the 50's, but there the similarity ends. Some states lost a fair percentage of total population by migration, others seemed to hold their own over all, and Florida experienced very high growth.

Again, as witnessed in Table 2-10, population losses were experienced—with the exception of Florida

TABLE 2-10

Southern State Net Migration Rates 1950-1960, by Sex, Race, and Metropolitan—Nonmetropolitan Location

	White			Non-White			State Total	
	Total	**Male**	**Female**	**Total**	**Male**	**Female**	**White**	**Non-White**
Alabama								
Metro	5.5	5.3	5.7	— 9.1	— 9.4	— 8.8	— 5.9	—18.6
Non-Metro	—13.3	—13.6	—13.0	—25.7	—25.6	—25.8		
Florida								
Metro	69.6	70.2	69.1	25.1	27.4	22.9	59.6	12.9
Non-Metro	43.2	42.1	42.5	1.4	— .2	— 2.6		
Georgia								
Metro	12.7	12.4	13.0	.9	.6	1.1	— .2	—15.3
Non-Metro	— 9.8	—10.0	— 9.6	—23.9	—23.9	—23.8		
Kentucky								
Metro	3.4	2.9	3.9	2.8	2.8	2.8	—11.6	— 6.5
Non-Metro	—17.5	—17.1	—17.9	—14.3	—13.5	—15.1		
Mississippi								
Metro	18.2	17.3	19.1	— 8.7	— 9.7	— 7.8	— 8.1	—26.0
Non-Metro	— 9.9	— 9.8	—10.0	—27.1	—27.1	—27.1		
North Carolina								
Metro	6.9	6.4	7.4	— 2.5	—17.8	—18.4	— 3.4	—15.2
Non-Metro	— 6.4	— 6.4	— 6.4	—18.1	— 5.2	— 7.6		
South Carolina								
Metro	12.0	14.4	9.6	— 6.5	— 5.2	— 7.6	— .2	—20.7
Non-Metro	— 5.9	— 5.8	— 5.9	—24.6	—24.6	—24.6		
Tennessee								
Metro	1.8	1.2	2.3	— 1.2	— 1.5	— .8	— 6.8	— 8.8
Non-Metro	—12.0	—12.2	—11.7	—19.8	—19.8	—19.9		

Source: G. K. Bowles and J. D. Tarver, *Net Migration of the Population, 1950-60, by Age, Sex, Color.* Population Migration Report II, U.S.D.A., E.R.S., 1965.

—in all nonmetropolitan areas across both sexes and races. While metropolitan areas in the states generally gained population, the gains made may have been largely due to shifts in the white population: metropolitan areas in four of the states actually lost black population through migration.

Importantly, some of the population loss in metropolitan and nonmetropolitan areas, and perhaps some of the overall state losses, represents a shift of population *within the region* even during the 50's, rather than a wholesale flight to other areas of the country.

Tarver and Beale show this clearly in their analysis of population changes in the 50's among 762 places in the South having between 2,500 and 9,999 population as of 1950. They were able to show that small towns grew on the average of 16.5 percent nationally during the 50's while in the South the average growth rate was 21.3 percent (Tarver and Beale, 1969, 13).

Average growth for all small towns in each state in the region exceeded the national average with the exception of Mississippi as shown in Table 2-11.

In the same article, Tarver and Beale suggest that the growth of small towns in the South may be the consequence of the migration of persons seeking employment coupled with the natural increase among elderly persons in such places. This latter factor is emphasized in showing that towns grew on the average of only 942 persons for every 1000 persons becoming 65 years of age in such places during the decade (Tarver and Beale, 1969, 23; H. Sheldon, "Destribution of the Rural Aged Population," in Youmans, 1967).

These specific migration patterns were occurring within an overall out-movement of an estimated 1.5 million persons from the South* during the 50's. Beale has suggested, in concert with Barth, that this flow has radically declined in the 60's estimating that between 1960-66 only 164,000 people vacated the 4 East South Central states (Beale, 1969,420).

As recently as December 29, 1970, Beale continued to assert that migration patterns had altered radically during the 60's—so much so, that he was prompted to conclude that "most of the current further increase of the urban population is coming from natural increase rather than migration" (Beale, 1970, 15).

He suggests in the same article that fundamental policy shifts can be expected as a result of these changing migration patterns:

> The period when policy support for programs to benefit rural blacks — and thus perhaps retard migration — could be obtained from urban sources on a self-interest basis was rather brief in its life span. Cutbacks in rural-urban movement now — when the supply of migrants has been somewhat depleted — would be unlikely to have major beneficial effects . . . [on urban life]. (Beale, *Ibid.*)

Given the "weight of the evidence," more than mild surprise must be registered in response to Herman P. Miller's quoted comment in a recent copywrited article by Jack Rosenthal (New York *Times,* 1971c, 1, 20). Miller, Director of Census Population Studies in the Bureau of the Census, indicated that preliminary 1970 Census data revealed that migration from the South during the 60's very closely approximated the rate of outflow for the 50's.

It is currently estimated that 1.4 million blacks left the South during the 60's, three fourths of whom relocated to five large Northern states. All 11 states of the Confederacy lost population during the decade, with Mississippi losing 279,000 and Alabama 231,000, to lead the pack.

*South here includes 16 states.

TABLE 2-11

Population Growth for Small Towns in the South 1950-60, by States

	*Number of Towns	Number Losing Population	Number with Less Than 20% Growth	Number with 20% + Growth	Average % Change 1950-60
Alabama	52	4	20	28	+28.0
Florida	41	1	4	36	+51.8
Georgia	64	4	29	31	+23.8
Kentucky	44	13	19	12	+10.0
Mississippi	36	5	14	17	+21.3
North Carolina	63	15	27	21	+19.7
South Carolina	48	6	27	15	+17.3
Tennessee	45	7	21	17	+20.3

*All towns in 1950 with populations 2,500 to 9,999.

Source: J. D. Tarver and C. L. Beale, "Relationship of Changes in Employment and Age Composition to the Population Changes of Southern Nonmetropolitan Towns," *Rural Sociology,* XXXIV (March 1, 1969), 18, Table 1.

Noting these figures and the soaring welfare costs in Northern states, Secretary of Commerce Maurice Stans was moved to comment, in the same article: "I have no doubt that higher welfare benefits in the North are a factor." But, he added, "greater job opportunities [in the North] would be the chief motivating factor" (New York *Times,* 1971c, 20).

Secretary Stans' comments imply that the poor comprise the bulk of those who continued to migrate South to North. But the extent to which the rural Southern poverty population contributes to these movements, in fact, remains problematic. Studies are just beginning which will provide needed information on the relationship between migration and poverty among rural Southern residents.

Bacon, for example, recently completed a study using a good sized national sample* which indicated that a substantial number of rural Southerners are non-mobile. Fully 61 percent of all adult blacks and 26 percent of all whites interviewed were found to be residing in a rural residence in 1967 less than 50 miles removed from place of origin (Bacon, 1970, 15-17).

Among those who had ever moved, a high proportion had done so *within* the South. Among blacks, for example, 58 percent of those who had ever moved, moved from one rural place to another in the South, and an additional 35 percent had moved intra-regionally from rural to urban environments. Only 14 percent of the total sample of persons of rural origin had migrated directly from the rural South to the urban North.

Overall, Bacon estimates 7.1 million adults living in the North in 1967 were of Southern origin while 4.3 million adults living in the South had migrated there from the North. Twelve percent of the former and 9 percent of the latter were estimated to be living in poverty.

On the basis of this analysis, Bacon concludes that 9 percent of all whites and 20 percent of all blacks originally from the South and now living in the urban North are currently in poverty. These estimates led him to observe that much of Northern urban poverty is home grown, that concern with the Southern rural contribution to Northern urban poverty derives from the visability of the transplanted rural poor in the cities rather than from sheer numbers (Bacon, *Ibid*).

Utilizing the same data source, Ritchey recently found that rural migrants often exhibit multiple relocations before winding up in major metropolitan areas (Ritchey, 1970, 16). He found that of the estimated 18.4 million rural to urban migrants in the U.S. as of 1967, 58 percent had moved 2 or more times before settling in their current urban locations. Further, about two-thirds of all multistage migrants had urban experience prior to selecting their 1967 residence. Among one-stage migrants (the 42 percent who moved directly from rural to urban settings) preference was exhibited for larger sized urban areas with only 26 percent of this group found to be residing in nonmetropolitan urban areas in 1967 (Ritchey, *Ibid.*).

Since Ritchey was using a national sample, the small percentage of people he found who by 1967 had moved from rural to smalltown locations may indicate different migration patterns in rural areas of the rest of the nation from those found by Tarver and Beale for the South. On the other hand, his data could reflect changes in migration patterns among rural people between the 50's applicable to the South. Currently, there is no clear way of determining the correct interpretation.

In any case, rural blacks seem to be contributing disproportionately (in numbers) to migration patterns, whatever their changing directions. The estimated monumental decline in out-migration in the 60's was no doubt partly prompted by other recent estimates that black population in major Northern cities is on a slight decline and that much of the black in-migration that continues constitutes the shift of persons from one urban setting to another, not a rural South urban North shift (See: Barth, 1970; Ritchey, 1970, Census reports quoted by same).

If there is any accuracy to the estimates that blacks comprise 43 percent of nonmetropolitan Southern poverty and that 61 percent have never left their rural place of origin, the immensity and persistence of poverty in such areas takes on staggering proportions. Again, possible changing migration patterns among rural Southerners suggest that the South might expect to absorb ever increasing numbers of its own as they shift from rural to urban settings.

If these patterns are validated by subsequent research, and if the recent estimate that 62 percent of all nonmetropolitan poverty is located in the South is accurate, then it is fairly clear that cities of all sizes in the South should prepare to experience more severe poverty problems in the immediate future. One thing that is not clear is where the black and white nonmetropolitan poor are relocating within the South. One might guess that poor whites are contributing more to the population growth of small towns and poor blacks more to the populations of larger cities. But this is pure guess work.

It is possible, however, from available data to suggest that smaller towns and cities are becoming "staging areas" for poor rural people in the South, stopping off places on the way from or back to rural residences. In any case, it would appear the South must now begin to shoulder directly much of the burden of its uprooted rural poor as well as those who remain entrenched in the hinterlands.

Upward Mobility among the Southern Poor

Informative as migration patterns and changes may be, they do not in themselves shed much light upon upward mobility among the nonmetropolitan Southern poor. It cannot be assumed, for example, that geographic relocation works magic in lifting families and individuals out of poverty.

*Survey of 35,000 persons aged 17 or older conducted under contract by the Bureau of the Census for OEO in 1966-67, commonly referred to as the SEO.

Ritchey recently examined the relationship between rural South to urban North migration patterns for their bearing on poverty. He found that poverty tends to decline as length of urban residence increases. For example, only four percent of all persons of rural Southern origin who migrated before 1940 were poor in 1967. By comparison, about 10 percent of all migrants with similar backgrounds who migrated since 1960 were poor in the same year (Ritchey, 1970, 18). This decline was noted, however, only for whites in the 12 largest metropolitan centers nationally. Thus, the likelihood of remaining poor upon migrating to the urban North is greatest for recently arrived persons and for blacks generally.

Kelly's work on poverty flows yield estimates showing that the South is doing well in the matter of poverty reduction. He suggests that 26.9 percent of the poor in the South in 1966 were nonpoor in 1965 (new entrants), whereas 45.4 percent of those poor in 1965 were no longer poor in 1966 (escapees). These favorable ratios, of course, may be a function of the fact that data were aggregated in this study for 16 states and Washington, D. C. It is probable, based on previous data, that these ratios would not be representative of the poverty flows in the 8 states in the region as we define it.

His data also show that rural Southern farm residents had more escapees and fewer entrants than did non-farm rural residents, and that blacks are outperforming whites especially in the rural South, as shown in Table 2-12.

TABLE 2-12

Southern Poverty Flows, by Race and Residence Area between 1965-66 (in Percents)

Race and Residence	Poverty Entrants	Poverty Escapees
White Metropolitan	12.9	9.1
White Nonmetropolitan	11.3	20.8
Black Metropolitan	1.6	4.5
Black Nonmetropolitan	1.2	11.0

Source: Kelly, *Technical Studies,* 1970, 48.

But this is a superficial reading of the data. If one recalls that a high proportion of nonmetropolitan blacks are already in poverty, he can see that the low rate of entrants may be simply a function of a lack of potential entrants. At the same time, the rate of escapees among blacks is below that of whites comparing the progress of the races in both metropolitan and nonmetropolitan locations.

In any case, these flow rates are computed according to a fixed dollar poverty line (the Orshansky Index) and therefore tell us little about how rising costs of living in the South are actually affecting the material existence of the poor who are experiencing some income growth.

Income has risen in the South in the 60's along with cost of living, as noted elsewhere. However, income has risen selectively, both according to race and occupational skills categories. The income gap between the poor and non-poor, and between whites and blacks in the South actually seems to have widened in the 60's.

Fried, for example, estimated that by 1966 three times as many whites were earning $7,000 a year or more compared to blacks in the South whereas the ratio was 3:2 elsewhere in the nation (Fried, 1969, 143).

Trend data suggest that the income of blue collar blacks in the South remains much lower than that for whites with similar occupational skills, and that this differential remains even when controlling for the age of the earner as shown in Table 2-13.

The data do suggest that blacks, at least in this skills category, have closed the income somewhat over the last decade; however, the major improvement in in earnings seems to be for metropolitan black workers by and large.

Black craft workers in nonmetropolitan areas consistently earned less regardless of age than the average for all blacks similarly employed in the South in 1960, and they continued to do so in 1970.

These data suggest that even for this most skilled category of blue collar workers, those who profited the most by income trends in the last decade were whites in metropolitan areas of the South. Further, regardless of race, younger workers appeared to make greater income gains during the decade.

These income gain differentials favorably weighted toward white, metropolitan, and younger workers, dampen optimism about the role employment has played in recent years in improving the lot of low income Southerners.

Enthusiasm is further undercut by examining trends in the comparative increase in numbers of craft workers among blacks and whites in the South during the 60's. Table 2-15 shows a percentage decline in craft occupations among older working whites throughout the South and even in nonmetropolitan areas of the South. Older blacks so occupied also declined in number, but far less proportionately.

Percentage declines among older white wage earners may well reflect upward mobility into either white collar or allied positions. The reasoning applied to blacks would yield the conclusion that blacks are not moving up in similar proportions. Younger blacks do seem to be entering this skilled occupational category in proportionally greater number than similarly aged whites; however, the percentage differences are not great. These data lend further weight to the impression that blacks in the South did not move up out of low income conditions at an overpoweringly impressive rate during the 60's, at least in craft occupations.

TABLE 2-13

Average Yearly Income for Craft Workers
in the South, by Age Cohorts and Race, 1960-1970
(in Dollars)

Age Cohort (Year Born)	3/1970 White	3/1970 Black	1960 White	1960 Black	% Earnings Increase for Decade White	% Earnings Increase for Decade Black
1906-15	6600	4200	5800	3000	14	39
1916-25	7600	4800	6100	3400	24	41
1926-35	7500	4900	5700	3200	32	52
1936-42	7400	5300	4000	*NA	86	—

Source: U.S.D.C., B. of C., *Consumer Income* C.P.S., P-60, No. 73, 1970b, Table 1.
*Not computed, base smaller than 75,000 earners.

TABLE 2-14

Average Yearly Earnings of Southern Black
Craft Workers, by Area of Residence and Age Cohorts,
1960-1970
(in Dollars)

Age Cohorts (Year Born)	3/1970 All Black Craft Workers in South*	3/1970 Nonmetro Blacks	1960 All Black Craft Workers in South	1960 Nonmetro Black Craft Workers
1906-15	4100	3200	2700	2200
1916-25	4600	3500	3000	2100
1926-35	4900	4200	3100	2100
1936-42	5200	4500	2400	**

*South = 12 Southern states
**Base smaller than 75,000 earners.
Source: U.S.D.C., B. of C., *Consumer Income,* C. P. S. P-60, No. 73, 1970b.

TABLE 2-15

Growth of Workers in Craft Occupations
by Race, Age, and Area of Residence, 1960-70
(in Percents)

Age Cohorts (Year Born)	White Total South	White Nonmetro	Black Total South	Black Nonmetro
1906-15	— 31	— 27	— 3	*—
1916-25	— 8	+ 18	+ 20	—
1926-35	+ 14	+ 21	+ 28	—
1936-42	+144	+168	+182	—

*Base less than 75,000 Workers
Source: U.S.D.C., B. of C., *Consumer Income,* C.P.S. P-60, no. 73, 1970b.

Unfortunately data are incomplete in the sense that this conclusion cannot be applied as specifically as we would like to conditions in the nonmetropolitan South. The employment situation, and assumptions about the income employment is yielding, can be addressed after a fashion, however, by examining a recent study by Williams and Glasgow on the extent of *underemployment* in the rural South (Williams and Glasgow, 1968).

These authors aggregated 1960 census data for the 92 State Economic Areas (SEA's) in seven Southern states (Alabama, Arkansas, Georgia, Louisiana, Mississippi, North and South Carolina). National median yearly incomes were computed for a variety of occupational categories adjusting within each category for such factors as educational level, percent labor force participation, age, employment status, and civilian-military status of the work force.

Similar adjusted medians were derived for the 92 SEA's. These medians were then compared to national medians with the differential considered to be the extent of underemployment in an adjusted occupational category within the Southern SEA's. Another formula was then used to convert differentials in median incomes into the number of man years being underutilized in the Southern rural labor force by sex and race. Some of the results, totaled over all 92 SEA's, are shown in Table 2-16.

national median incomes. This in turn reflects the estimated extent to which the employed labor force in the rural South is underemployed in the sense that employment is underpaid by national norms.

The situation is clearly most acute among males generally and particularly among blacks. Finally, breakdowns between rural non-farm and rural farm employment shows that underemployment is especially pressing in farm related employment (Williams and Glasgow, *Ibid.*).

We can also see here how official unemployment rates may under-estimate the actual situation for rural low income groups in the South. Unemployment in the various states of the region for 1968 ranged from 2.9 percent (Florida) to 4.6 percent (Mississippi-Alabama) (President's Commission on Income Maintenance Programs, *Background Papers,* 81). Current reasoning about the state of the economy reflects the opinion that unemployment rates within this range are not cause for undue concern. But in the rural South, Williams and Glasgows' data suggest that massive underemployment is buried within the *employed* sector of the labor force. Coupling underemployment with unemployment does not yield a rosy picture of economic conditions in the rural South.

The overall picture of income-employment lags among the rural Southern population raises the question of whether there is indeed any way up except by getting out for many low-income persons and families in the region.

TABLE 2-16

Estimated Underemployment in the Employed Rural Southern Labor Force, by Race and Sex for 1960 (in Man Years)

	Totals			**White**			**Black**		
	Both Sexes	**Male**	**Female**	**Both Sexes**	**Male**	**Female** *	**Both Sexes**	**Male**	**Female**
# Man Years	800,000	743,000	57,000	455,000	455,000	—	346,000	289,000	57,000
Rural South (Total Available man-years at full equivalence of U. S. median 15% Less Than Full Utilization)	531,000	494,000	40,000	257,000	257,000	—	274,000	237,000	37,000

*White rural females omitted because they are, of all groups, being utilized generally at national median levels or better.

Source: T. T. Williams and R. B. Glasgow, "Developing Estimates of Economic Underemployment for the Rural Labor Force in Seven Southern States," *American Journal of Agriculture Economics,* L (December 5, 1968), 1435, Table 1.

The figures in row 1 indicate number of man years of labor available in the rural South according to adjusted national median incomes for aggregated occupational categories. Row 2 indicates the number of man years which could be utilized now by paying *15 percent less* than the national median income across all occupational categories. In other words, of 800,000 man years available in the rural South, 531,000 could be utilized for 15 percent less than

Analysis of the data suggests that the picture may not be as bleak in rural non-farm employment, especially for the young, as it is for other rural Southerners, especially those in agriculturally related employment. Smith recently reported an intriguing study of social class structure in the rural farm South which illustrates how little potential for upward mobility there is in farm related employment in the South (T. L. Smith, 1969).

Utilizing a series of criteria for separating social classes in the rural South according to land ownership, land management, and land labor, Smith proposed a 5 class model. Data from both the 1959 and the 1964 Census of Agriculture were aggregated by counties and states in the South, each earner's social class location being computed according to the above mentioned criteria: relationship to the land, attendant income, etc.

Table 2-17 presents the social class distribution in rural farm areas of the states in the region arrived at through these procedures.

With few exceptions, the data indicate that the states in the region differ from the national distribution in important ways. First, a very tiny group of persons control ownership of the land in the South. Second, and most importantly, middle management occupations in agriculturally related employment are scare in the South (comparing upper-middle and middle-middle class groups to national percentages). Finally, agricultural employment in the South is characterized by an overwhelming majority of persons who exchange unskilled labor for wages on a day-to-day basis.

Clearly, the route up from unskilled labor to skilled labor, management, and perhaps ultimately ownership, is narrow indeed in Southern agriculturally related employment.

Whether changes in migration patterns among rural Southerners reflect movement of rural farm persons toward more attractive rural non-farm employment in the South or not is problematic. Should this be the case, however, pressures on rural non-farm employment opportunities would obviously be intensified. Such pressures could undermine comparative — if not overly bright — gains that have been made in rural non-farm employment in the last decade and drive increasing numbers of the rural poor directly into major metropolitan areas in the South.

Given that this is speculation, the weight of the data presented in this chapter about the people of the nonmetropolitan South and their socio-economic conditions suggests that it is worth pondering. It would be unwise to overlook some apparent trends in the data and their consequences for the years ahead. The rural dependent population is on the increase, being swelled by larger numbers of the very young and the very old, the South seems to be absorbing ever larger numbers of its own uprooted rural residents, and avenues to upward mobility in the rural South for such people do not look overly bright. These are some of the sobering features of the current scene.

TABLE 2-17

Social Class Structure in Rural Farm Areas of the South, by States

(in Percent Distributions)

	Upper-Class	**Upper Middle Class**	**Middle-Middle Class**	**Lower-Middle Class**	**Lower Class**
United States	2.1	14.5	26.6	25.7	31.1
Alabama	0.6	5.0	14.7	41.8	37.9
Florida	2.6	7.4	11.9	22.5	55.6
Georgia	0.9	9.1	19.2	28.4	42.4
Kentucky	0.2	5.6	25.6	38.8	29.8
Mississippi	0.7	3.3	11.5	34.2	50.3
North Carolina	0.3	6.3	28.0	27.8	37.6
South Carolina	0.5	4.8	16.6	31.3	46.8
Tennessee	0.2	3.8	20.3	39.5	36.2

Source: T. Lynn Smith, "A Study of Social Stratification in Agricultural Sections of the U. S.: Nature, Data, Procedures, and Preliminary Results," *Rural Sociology*, XXXIV (December 4, 1969), 506, Table 1

Chapter 3

CAUSAL EXPLANATIONS

Theory about poverty is in a sorry state. It is confusing, if not confused. The best efforts often dissolve into a fog of multicausality and simultaneous interaction begging off any hard and testable ideas, obscuring the value premises upon which they are based in the bargain.

Much poverty may very well result from multiple and simultaneously interacting causes. But to leave it at that deprives those who must deal with the poverty of meaningful insights which would enhance research and programing activities. Multi-causal "explanations" often do not yield estimates of the relative importance of one causal factor *vis a vis* another; thus they cannot assist in defining useful research targets or in setting priorities in program planning. Further, such approaches obscure the crucial fact that identifiably different values and assumptions about poverty and program effectiveness in dealing with it adhere to separable causal explanations. Finally, most research data in their interpretive emphases tend toward support or refutation of a dominant causal explanation even if the projects were clothed initially in concepts of multicausality.

For these reasons, we have proceeded to isolate five identifiable causal explanations which have conceptual integrity. The five are Gentic, Culture of Poverty, Opportunity, Maldistribution, and Scarce Resource explanations.

The five causal explanations were derived from a review of the literature which proceeded to treat each work uniformly according to the following routine:

1. First, we were concerned with extracting the dominant cause of poverty as reflected in open statements or implicit biases.
2. We then proceeded to isolate those measurable variables within the work to flesh out the definition of dominant cause.
3. Following this, the work was examined for assumptions about the reversibility of poverty once it had been produced by exposure to or experience of the dominant causal phenomena, within the life cycle and over generations. This exercise told us something about the assumed potential for upward mobility of the poor viewed from the standpoint of the dominant causal explanation.
4. Finally, a search was made for assumptions about why poor people migrate and the contribution geographic migration was thought to make to inducing or reducing poverty.

This approach enabled us to arrive at impressions of how each causal explanation is theorized to contribute to the development and persistence of poverty. In turn, the brief statements of each causal explanation which follow provide both an overview of causality and separable packages of descriptive standards around which research data is organized and assessed in subsequent chapters.

I. The Genetic Explanation

General Statement

Genetic concepts rest on the primary notion that poverty is a predictable outcome of a variety of physiological defects or inadequacies. The genetic thesis asserts that poverty is the consequence of the transmission of inferior genetically influenced traits (e.g. low intelligence and physical deformity) over generations.

This line of reasoning places the cause of poverty directly and wholly within the make-up of individuals who are poor. It has the conceptual "virtue" of being able to explain poverty perfectly—that is, why poverty persists, why some get out, and why others fall in, according to the concept of drift. Simply put, water seeks its own level. More elegantly, those with superior endowments will rise on the socio-economic ladder while those inferiorly endowed will fall—regardless of socio-economic position at birth—to the bottom of the heap.

Since the common characteristic to be explained is poverty, all forms of social and psychological inadequacies—from alcoholism to unemployment—which might contribute to poverty are interpreted to stem from physiologically determined inadequacies. Even those most clearly in the residual category, those who suffered severe physical loss owing to auto or industrial accident, can be handled within this approach. All that is necessary is to compare all those who rose socio-economically to all those who did not following onset of similar afflictions. Those who sustained such losses and became poor in the process can be clearly understood to derive from inferior stock.

This view infused with certain value judgements such as the poor are inherently lazy, stupid, and/or morally weak, is often reputed to be the layman's explanation of poverty. True or not, the view has found favor from time to time in our nation's history among respectable groups of theoreticians. It is perhaps best identified with the Social Darwinist movement of the turn of the century. It is not, however, to be treated as ancient history as it continues to be encountered in the works of some behavioral geneticists, research psychologists, and newspaper editorialists, among others.

Assumptions About Reversibility

Clearly, poverty is an irreversible condition in this line of reasoning. Any appearance of reversibility, as in the case of the AFDC mother who gains economic independence following vocational training, is simply an incidence of previously undetected superior endowments.

Preventative techniques, such as geographically relocating and dispersing the poor to break up the gene pool and its potential for perpetuating poverty through inbreeding, seem to be among the means for eventually eradicating poverty. Meaningful reductions in poverty over time cannot be obtained through interventions designed to improve the socio-economic lot of the poor. Increases in income to the presently poor would statistically reduce poverty but could not induce greater self sufficiency and social contributions among this generation of poor people or economic independence in the next.

Assumptions about Geographic Migration

It also follows from this view that the poor migrate in search of life supports. Since the poor are by definition incapable of coping with life's major vicissitudes, they will relocate in the absence of adequate social supports in their native environs nearer families, friends, or similarly afflicted others in search of shelter, protection, and care. Either by choice or because of social pressures generated by families, friends, social agencies, and other sources, the poor drift to these protective repositories. Wholesale movements create visible accumulations of poor people in overcrowded neighborhoods, skid rows, custodial and treatment institutions, and so on.

II. The Culture Of Poverty Explanation

General Statement

The Culture of Poverty Thesis suggests at its heart that poverty is caused and sustained by a life style common to the vast majority of poor people. This life style is composed of a set of behavioral norms deviant from those of the dominant better off majority which is guided by a highly integrated set of attitudes reflective of apathy, defeatism, hopelessness, reliance on chance, and concern with short-term gratifications.

These attitudes support matriarchal patterns of child-rearing and family decision-making, enable the poor to live without reflection upon filth and violence in their environs, and provide the base for accepting deviant and criminal modes of making a living as proper.

As these attitudes and norms proceed toward integration, they develop into a comprehensive frame of reference for understanding life and making sense out of miserable conditions. Finally, this frame of reference constitutes the substance of "social heredity" and is passed on intergenerationally through the primary relationships of child-rearing and peer associations.

The existence of a highly integrated network of attitudes and behavioral norms, and social patterns insuring their preservation over long periods of time, both inspires the use of the term *culture* and explains the existence and continuation of poverty on a grand scale.

Assumptions about Reversibility

It is clear that patterns of belief and behavior so ingrained and habitualized as to be capable of transmission over generations are not easily overturned. Hence, it is commonly assumed that even if all the material trappings of poverty were to be removed now (e.g. poor housing, low income, etc.), the behavior patterns productive of social deviancy, political apathy, poor child-rearing, and so on, would persist. While such measures would improve the physical conditions of the poor, they would not alter present behavioral patterns of the poor or prevent the next generation from duplicating them.

Thus, poverty is conceived as reversible only to the extent that program interventions are aimed at altering the behavior and attitudes of the poor. The poor must be remotivated to compete for success defined by prevailing dominant values, they must be educated to become good consumers, and they must be trained in the social and vocational skills needed to assure successful competition. Efforts short of these would not permanently retrieve the poor.

Assumptions about Geographic Migration

While not often acknowledged, it follows from this thesis that the poor migrate more for reasons of seeking life supports than for reasons of seeking the means to upward mobility.

As in the Genetic concept, a powerful motivating factor is the need to affiliate with similar others and obtain confirmation for an established life style from accepting outside sources. Hence, migration is stimulated by the need to reside in surroundings populated by persons with similar life styles.

Factors undermining the life style of the poor in the area of origin (such as the break up of tenant farming in the South) are reasoned to lead to flight to avoid the implications for life style changes these factors carry with them. Regrouping in new surroundings (such as urban ghettoes) helps protect against influences threatening to their basic views of life. Reliance upon family as the basic resource for coping with new environments and the sending for kin are part and parcel of this process.

III The Opportunity Explanation

General Statement

Poverty is held to be a major consequence of a multitude of social policies and other social practices exercised by the better off majority to arbitrarily exclude groups of people bearing a common characteristic or status from opportunities to acquire a fair share of society's goods and services.

Persons discriminated against are of two major types: those with obviously different physical characteristics such as skin color, speech defects, physical deformities, and so on, and those who are stigmatized by a social status or category held in low regard such as delinquents, felons, welfare clients, mental patients, hillbillies, and so on. Often these characteristics and statuses overlap in the same person, compounding the number of ways he is excluded from improving his circumstances.

Generally, the bulk of the poverty problem is understood to derive from various forms of exclusion and injustice in matters of law and justice, political participation, credit and purchasing power, choice of housing, social and health services, education, employment, and governmental benefits.

Assumptions about Reversibility

Poverty conceived as the consequence of unjust restrictions on opportunities and access to existing goods and services (including income) would yield to the creation and imposition of a social structure capable of producing equal opportunity.

Importantly, this view implies that the poor are now capable of advantaging themselves of any widening in the avenues to upward mobility. The poor, in short, are not viewed as habitualized to a unique and deviant way of life, but rather are viewed as persons trying to achieve success in accord with the values of the better off majority within a severely restricted opportunity structure.

The decisions poor people make governing their behavior are understood to be rational and pragmatic. The fact that they lead to behavior deviancy is a consequence of an absence of alternatives. Such behavior is inadequately understood if it is reasoned to stem from limited intelligence, defeatism, or poor consumer orientations. For example, the unemployed father who deserts his family is not often an escapist. He is better understood to be making a pragmatic choice which might allow his family to become eligible for AFDC support. Lacking other alternatives, he does the best he can to fulfill his legal and moral obligations to support his family.

Reasoned in this way, poverty is assumed to be eminently reversible in direct proportion to the extent to which equal opportunity is realized.

Assumptions about Geographic Migration

The Opportunity Thesis makes a clean break from previous causal explanations on this matter. Holding that the poor are rational, pragmatic decision-makers supports the logic that the poor migrate in the main to seek environments which hold out greater employment, education, and other opportunities for themselves and their children. To the extent to which greater opportunity really exists in the place of destination, migration is conceived to be one mechanism which contributes to the reduction of poverty.

IV. The Maldistribution Explanation

General Statement

Affluence is assumed a fact of life in the sense that existing resources could, if redistributed, end poverty. This holds true however broadly poverty is defined. If poverty is stretched to cover factors beyond income such as health, housing, and so on, its elimination could still be achieved by enlarging and diversifying the planned mechanism for redistribution in concert with the definition.

Socio-economic resources (e.g. means of production, investment capital, skilled manpower, etc.) are currently maldistributed in two ways: by geographic area and by socio-economic strata. Maldistribution probably has its roots in historical and/or geographical accident. Maldistribution among persons may in part be the result of their or their predecessors having been in the right place at the right time. Geographically, discovery of exploitable natural resources no doubt played a role in the comparative affluence of some areas to others. In any case, this initial imbalance clearly has led to a competitive edge in attracting a disproportionate share of resources over time among certain persons as well as certain geographic areas. Unplanned economic and population growth have thus led not only to monumental national affluence but, in the process, have intensified the degree of maldistribution.

In its most radical form, this view argues for a total leveling out of all forms of resources across people and areas. A simple redistribution of income, for example, would not be successful in ending poverty because in the matter of monetary resources those who have income stockpiled (in various forms of savings and capital for investment) would remain at an unfair competitive advantage. Others who hold generally to the Maldistribution Thesis view income redistribution in itself as an effective key to an end of poverty.

Assumptions about Reversibility

Opinions vary on this matter, perhaps largely on the issue of how much the dominant majority would tolerate in terms of resource redistribution, either by areas or by persons. It is commonly assumed that existing resources are sufficient to achieve the goal. It seems also commonly assumed that assuring equal opportunity to the access of resources, by persons or areas, would not achieve the goal simply because equal opportunity is a myth when areas or persons are ill equipped to compete on an equal basis. Resources must be reasonably distributed before equal opportunity takes on meaning.

Insofar as existing political, social, and economic systems are open to redistributions of power, status, and income (or insofar as the poor can organize to achieve these ends themselves), to that extent poverty could be reversed now.

Assumptions about Geographic Migration

It would be consistent with this view to reason that the poor move primarily for economic reasons. However, it is not necessarily assumed, as it is in the Scarce Resource Thesis, that the poor generally migrate from stagnant to high growth economic areas. Rather, it would seem assumed that the poor move because they believe there *might be* greater command of resources in the place of destination than place of origin, whether the place of destination is experiencing growth or not.

V. The Scarce Resource Explanation

General Statement

Essentially, this thesis holds that affluence is a myth. Regardless of how rapidly our productivity expands, two forces—population and rising expectations—keep pace or, more likely, increase more rapidly than productivity.

Poverty thus is understood to be the end result of not enough to go around. There is both an absolute and a relative sense in which this is reasoned to be the case. In an absolute sense, population is simply expanding faster than productivity with the end result that the consumer base outstrips goods and services available at any given time.

In a relative sense, as affluence grows in a society, past luxuries tend to be converted to necessities. This results in a broadened base of goods and services defined as basic to minimal well being in a society. Health care may be one of many examples of services which are moving out of the luxury class (available only to those who can afford them) toward the basic needs class (adequate health care is necessary to minimal well being for everyone).

For these reasons, and because our current value system supports notions of private property and the right to retain accumulated personal wealth, the present distribution of socio-economic resources is best seen as a distribution of scarcity. By definition, a group will exist at the bottom of the ladder, and they are in a relative and absolute sense the people of poverty.

Assumptions about Reversibility

Serious questions arise within this view about the extent to which planned redistribution mechanisms will work. Resources are scarce in the sense that it is not feasible to conceive of redistributing existing resources at a level required to end poverty. Feasibility is limited by what the better off majority sets in terms of what it will allow to be taken from it for purposes of redistribution. At higher socio-economic levels it is probable that a great variety of luxuries have been redefined as basic necessities required to retain the established standard of living. This being so, there is little affluence (unneeded resources) which the better off majority would view as the proper source of redistribution.

Hence, reversibility is conceived in the first place to be a function of economic growth. Economic growth has the twin advantages of allowing employment opportunities to expand and "trickle down" to lower socio-economic levels and enabling government to obtain increased revenue for the expansion and enrichment of income and other programs for the poor without raising taxes or applying massive redistribution schemes.

At the same time, some theorists suggest that the population base must be controlled and expectations kept from escalating in some way in order to maximize the impact of economic growth on poverty in either an absolute or relative sense.

Assumptions about Geographic Migration

The poor are understood to relocate in this view primarily for reasons of seeking greater economic advantages in areas of destination. There is the implication that migration is tied to a pattern of movement from stagnant to high growth areas. Migration itself could only slightly reduce poverty and only for early arrivees. A continuing influx of the poor would simply intensify scarcity since it can be assumed that even under conditions of high growth a large share of growth is absorbed by the better off majority.

Comparisons and Summary

Each thesis presents poverty from a different perspective. Genetic and Scarce Resources explanations may be considered the poles on a continuum of causal explanations extending from the individual to society. The Genetic concept locates the causes of poverty wholly within individuals who are poor while the Scarce Resources Thesis posits cause wholly within the outcomes and mechanisms of societal processes. Both theses have the advantage of conceptual simplicity but by the same token their explanatory power is limited: neither firmly confronts the interaction of individual and societal influences or attempts to estimate the relative importance of one to the other in producing and sustaining poverty.

Finally, both theses are extremely difficult to measure and test in the context of social reality, one because of its monumental sweep and the largeness of the order of its important variables and the other because its proofs lie literally within the most deeply recessed and microscopic components of individual existence.

The three theses in the middle of the continuum have by contrast most of the advantages lacking in the two more extreme views. They draw upon the interaction between the individual and social processes in explaining poverty, and for the most part, the variables they employ to define poverty and its causes are much more accessible to measurement and test.

At the same time, each has its limitations which take the form of the assumptions each must make about the other two in order to make it a complete conceptual entity. The assumptions each must make in order to stand apart from the others are as follows:

1. *The Culture of Poverty Thesis* to make sense must assume that the distribution of resources is adequate and opportunity is sufficient to make them accessible. Thus, the key factor in

poverty is the inability of the poor to grasp what exists.

2. *The Opportunity Thesis* must assume, on the other hand, that the culture of poverty doesn't exist and that resources indeed do in quantity sufficient to end poverty. The key factors in poverty are the arbitrary social and other barriers that separate the poor from goods and services.
3. *The Maldistribution Thesis* must assume, by comparison, that the culture of poverty is a myth and equal opportunity meaningless (prior to adequate redistribution). The key factor in poverty is simply a maldistribution of existing goods and services which the poor could readily utilize if placed at their disposal.

Having come this far, we are now ready to apply existing data and opinion to this format as a way of assessing what we actually know, presume to know, and need to know about the nature, extent, and persistence of nonmetropolitan Southern poverty.

Chapter 4

ASSESSING THE GENETIC THESIS

Most of those who have invested careers in the scientific study of man's heredity are cautious in applying the knowledge gleaned from such work to developing generalizations about the role of genetics in creating and sustaining human poverty.

This is understandable for at least two reasons. First, actual research in genetics is still in the developmental stage. While it has been over a century since Mendel introduced his probabilistic model of the inheritance of certain traits, the great majority of research in the field has actually been undertaken in the last 2 or 3 decades. Hence, generalizations from such partial findings would be hazardous in many cases (Borgaonkor and Shak, 1970).

Secondly, genetic arguments are not often well received by egalitarians and those with bitter memories of how eugenics was politically applied during the Nazi era. Some of the geneticist's reticence in making public pronouncements no doubt stems from an anticipated outcry and barrage of accusations that he is attempting to foist the concept of Master Race on contemporary society through a smokescreen of scientific rhetoric and fact (Crow, 1970).

It is safe to say that of all the causal theses, the genetic thesis evokes the most heated debate: an unabashed loyalty among its advocates confronted by the unabated fury and intransient rejection of its detractors. It takes no great wisdom to suggest in cases such as this that the truth probably is to be found somewhere in between. Even so, the whole truth, whatever its nature, is not likely of establishment at this juncture in history. The excruciatingly slow pace of evolutionary process assures that the debate itself will endure for some time to come. If we have to wait for natural selection to prove either side right or wrong, the debate may last as long as man himself.

Major Assumptions

In order to increase the reasonableness of the proposition that heredity is the dominant cause of poverty, the major assumptions underlying it must be extracted from the cauldron of debate. Three major assumptions seem to recur in the literature.

1) First, and most obviously, poverty is assumed to be the consequence of the transmission of inadequate genetic endowments. Inadequate endowments predispose the receiving individual toward poor socioeconomic performance over his life cycle. Many behavioral manifestations—from poor learning skills to criminality—which may be productive of poverty are believed to be traceable in one manner or another to a genetic source.

On the societal level certain social and geographic factors and constraints inhibit the process of eliminating recessive genes in a population through natural selection. These factors and constraints create artificial selection which, in turn, increases the probability that persons with matching recessive genes will mate and perpetuate unfavorable or undesirable characteristics in the population.

Chief among these factors are assortive mating and the geographic isolation of small populations. Assortive mating results both from social conventions which prevent natural selection as in the case of taboos against mixing of the races,* and from social preferences which lead persons of similar economic, cultural, and educational backgrounds to mate with one another (K. Davis 1966). In geographically isolated small populations, lack of numbers imposes constraints on the choice of mates, and the level of variation in the gene pool may well be below that of the population at large. Hence, intense inbreeding may lead, over time, to the fixation (e.g., the irreversible transmission of recessive genes unless the population is infused with new members from the outside) of unfavorable traits and the extinction of desirable traits in such populations (Emery, 1968).

Additional but less common ways by which unfavorable traits may be introduced or continued in a population relate to consanguineous mating—or mating within one's own blood lines; random mating—or the "accidental" mating of persons with matched recessive genes in a highly mobile society; and mutations, stimulated by parental exposure to atomic radiation, certain drugs, and other factors (Glass, 1966, 31 ff.).

Importantly, no society has perfected (i.e. fully controlled) assortive mating, nor is it likely that many small populations are perfectly isolated. For these reasons transmission of undesirable traits is not wholly restricted to isolated populations or the lower socioeconomic ranks. Rather, what is suggested is that the probability of transmission is much higher in these groups than in any other.

2) Secondly, the concept of social drift is introduced to describe the process by which those with

*Although it has been argued that genetically based instinctual preferences actually produce racially segregated choices. See: G. D. Darlington, *The Evolution of Man and Society* (N.Y.: Simon & Schuster, 1970).

inadequate genetic endowments accumulate at the bottom of the socio-economic heap. Social drift according to Roman and Trice, represents the downward movement of people from a previously achieved socio-economic position. They suggest an alternative view, labeled social selection, which represents the inability of the individual ever to achieve or surpass the socio-economic level of his parents (Roman and Trice, 1967, 45-49).

In any case, these concepts are limited to accounting for shifts between socio-economic strata, and it is not necessary to tie such shifts to genetic influences. Some genetic theorists have taken a broader view which accounts both for such shifts and for those who never go beyond their lower socio-economic strata of origin. They suggest that the aggregate of persons exhibiting inadequate performance abilities is the precipitate of genetic segregation between the social classes. All of the factors and constraints previously mentioned contribute to the occurance of a number of people incapable of achieving socio-economic success as defined by the standards of the dominant majority in a given population (Reed, 1966, 13 ff.).

3) Finally, it seems commonly assumed in the literature that the crucial inherited characteristic is mental ability. For the most part, the term *mental ability* could be replaced by the term *intelligence.* However, the broader term is required because a variety of mental illnesses has been suggested to be influenced by genetics and mental illness, *per se,* is not necessarily synonymous with poor intelligence.

In any case, there seems to be common agreement that heredity exerts its greatest impact by predetermining or disposing (take your choice) individuals to inadequate mental functioning. Hence, it must be assumed, in the main, that people become or stay poor because of inadequate mental endowments. Other inherited characteristics such as facial features, motor skills, height, skin color, and so on, are conceived to be of secondary importance, explaining in the aggregate only a minor portion of the variance in the relationship between heredity and poverty. In over simplified terms, mental ability, not race, is the prime hereditary determinant of poverty.

4) There is a final assumption about the role of "welfarism" in the maintenance and propagation of the genetically unfit which is treated incidentally here because it does not seem to be commonly held—or at least not often publicly enunciated—by genetic theorists. In essence, the assumption is that governmental programs which serve to support the survival of those in the lowest socio-economic strata and others with substantial mental impairments actually serve to preserve and propagate future generations of inadequate individuals. Concern is often expressed that these programs will serve to degenerate whole societies because it is held that it is precisely these groups of persons who bear the greatest number of offspring (Shockley, 1970).

We shall have occasion to return to this and other assumptions in the following sections as we review the nature of the evidence in support of or in contradiction to the conclusions derived from them.

The Nature-Nurture Controversy

Nothing encapsulates the dimensions of debate on the causes of human behavior or captures the intensity of the views of opposing advocates quite so well as the nature-nurture controversy. If we must choose the prime determinant of human behavior, which shall it be—heredity or environment?

Recently, advocates of heredity have begun to reassert their views with renewed vigor charging that hereditary explanations have been buried during much of the 20th century in western society by an avalanche of well intentioned social theorists who have sought human equality and in the process ridiculed into virtual silence the motion that there might be inherent limits on the modifiability of individual human performance (Jensen, 1970).

Environmental advocates have countered by cautioning that what we are witnessing is the re-appearance of an elitist philosophy which would have the effect—if adopted—of consigning the poor and unskilled to perpetual poverty (Pearl, 1970). To some, genocide is implied in the reassertion of such views.

Within this cascade of charges and counter-charges, a moderating note has been sounded by a number of genetic theorists and researchers who propose that human behavior is not explainable in either/or terms (Glass, 1967; B. Kaplan, 1954; Lindsley and Riesen, 1968). Following Dobzhansky's lead, they suggest that human behavior is the consequence of a mix of heredity and environmental factors, that in the main, genetics dictates certain broad behavioral parameters but that these parameters take on quite different forms in different environments (Dobzhansky, 1968).

An additional refinement to this view is contributed by the ethologists who suggest that heredity works, especially in early childhood, like a time clock which dictates periods within which a child may be "imprinted" by environmental experiences. If the opportunity is lost at appropriate stages in the child's development, the result may be an irretrievable loss in the child's receptivity and adaptability to subsequent learning experiences (Lorenz, 1952; Tinbergen, 1965).

While these concepts have infiltrated the literature on child development in the U. S. in recent years, little has been done by way of applying them to the explanation of persistent poverty.

In any case, taking the middle ground in this controversy neither diminishes debate (as reflected in the amount of coverage it still receives in the literature) nor sheds much meaningful light upon the amount that each factor contributes to explaining human behavior. Indeed, such a view may have within it a greater potential stifling research than for stimulating it. Taking the middle ground may be the civilized thing for educated men to do, but it may yield—as multicausal "models" most often do—great clouds of circular reasoning and a morass of interwoven relationships ultimately impenetrable by even the most wise and inquiring minds among us.

Methodological Considerations

Is there a way out of the nature-nurture dilemma other than by route of an intellectually mollifying but otherwise useless detente? Is it possible to generate the facts necessary to resolve the issue formed by two compelling explanations of human behavior?

Perhaps, but for those who seek to explore the contribution of heredity to poverty the task is not an easy one. For one thing ethical considerations prohibit the kind of rigorously controlled genetic experimentation with human subjects that is carried out in laboratories with plants and animals (Crow, 1970). For another genetical studies are by their very design longitudinal, often intergenerational. To control properly an experiment from the beginning to end even if ethically approvable—would require the patience of Job and perhaps 25 or 30 years out of one man's career.

Studies of shorter duration could at best yield only partial results. For example, short term studies have been carried out to determine whether certain genetically determined traits have been transmitted from parents to newborn infants; yet, unless such children were followed to adulthood, one could not be certain that heredity made any difference in their development and ultimate achievement (Udry, *et al.,* 1970).

To shortcut the ponderous time requirement while still meeting ethical dictates a variety of research designs have been adopted and carried out by genetic researchers which seek to trace historically personal genetic heritage rather than assess its transmission and consequences on future generations.

The most common designs of this sort are

1) Consanguinity Studies — ranging from the older geneological studies to the newer techniques of taking family medical histories.
2) Twin Studies — studies which seek to compare sets and groups of identical (MZ) and/or fraternal (DZ) twins usually of the same sex (see: Fuller and Thompson, 1960).

Consanguinity studies are open to a variety of methodological objections which generally focus upon the questionable validity of data gathered through records or the recall of subjects. Earlier geneological studies, such as that of the Kallikak family, are now held in disrepute primarily because of the virtual impossibility of verifying the actual behavior of family members dating back to Revolutionary times. To a lesser degree, family medical histories are open to similar objections, namely, that longitudinal medical histories are rarely complete enough to make a valid case. However, more comprehensive medical care, better diagnostic techniques, and better record keeping, will no doubt enhance the effectiveness of this approach in the years ahead (Scheerenberger, 1965).

Twin studies differ in that behavior and other traits are most often measured over periods of time in addition to the gathering of developmental histories. Studies of identical twins at the very least are capable of controlling for two factors which could influence environmental experience and its effects on development, namely, birth order and age (Vandenberg, 1970). A major assumption in such studies is that since identical twins receive the same genetic endowments, they will tend to develop and achieve at similar paces and levels regardless of differing environmental influences, if any. But the extent to which identical twins are subjected to similar or different experiences is hard to determine, thus confounding any simple evaluation of outcomes (Moody, 1967).

Moreover, selection of subjects for such studies is not always as simple as it might seem. Vandenberg has noted that obstetricians and parents alike often make mistakes in identifying types of twins. While blood tests will aid in differentiating fraternal from identical twins, in 1 case in 10 fraternal twins of the same sex will have the same blood factors. Ultimately it is possible to make positive identification by skin-graft techniques (Vandenburg, 1965, 31). The point here, however, is that such facts at least instill some doubt about the accuracy of selection in some twin studies carried out in the distant past and raise doubts about the usefulness of some findings deriving from them.

But that is a minor point. The major point about twin studies is that it has been difficult to truly control environmental effects which could have contributed to similarities or differences noted in twin behavior. The best test of hereditability, as Crow has noted, would be by assessing a large number of half sibs reared in randomized environments, an experimental design patterned after that commonly used by livestock breeders (Crow, 1970, 157).

Clearly, such a design would carry us well beyond the boundaries of proper ethical conduct. Given this, others have suggested large-scale studies of children placed with voluntary adoptive parents (Shockley, 1970). Properly carried out, a child with a known biological inheritance could be placed in a pre-evaluated social environment and the outcome assessed over time.

Studies of this sort have been launched in recent years, and they clearly are a methodological advance toward more precise measurements of environment and genetic contributions to human behavior (for a major example, see: Wender, 1969). In the Wender study, offspring of schizophrenic parents raised in "normal" adoptive homes were followed to determine whether they developed schizophrenic symptoms at better than chance levels. There is some proof that they did. Studies are now under way to test whether schizophrenia can also be environmentally induced. In these studies, children of "normal" parents raised by schizophrenic adoptive parents are being followed (Wender, 1969, 457). The results of these studies have not yet been reported out, but they serve as examples of improvements currently under way in measuring the differential inputs of heredity and environment.

All of these studies still require inferential leaps since, obviously, the direct links between genes and behavior are not observed. A variety of studies seeking to establish links between single genes and specific behaviors have been carried out in laboratory experiments with animals. These single gene experiments have been described by one critic as trivial because the findings have not been capable of transfer in ways which would deepen our understanding of higher psychological behavior (Thiessen, 1971).

Thiessen has countered this view by citing recent work with several strains of laboratory mice relating to conditioning shock avoidance by the onset of a light as a conditioning stimulus. One strain of mice never responded above chance levels and was thus determined cognitively deficient. Further analysis revealed, however that this strain experiences retinal degeneration; hence, the mice probably could not see the light which precedes onset of shock. He concludes that the research is instructive relative to child diagnosis and training at least. The findings should warn against premature "neurologizing" by diagnosticians and too early dismissal of some children as untrainable because tests suggest cognitive inadequacies (Thiessen, 1971).

But whether single gene experiments are trivial or transferable does not seem overly important given the central value of intelligence in the heredity-poverty equation and the current belief that human intelligence is more likely to be polygenetically determined than by a single gene. If human intelligence proves to be polygenetically determined, the transferability of findings from single gene experiments would clearly be more difficult to carry off. At the same time, the genetic influence on behavior through intelligence—or more broadly mental functioning—would be more difficult to trace, assess, and validate. Hence, as theorists move toward a more sophisticated understanding of the role of heredity in human mental performance, they find themselves more restricted than ever in proving their case by existing technological inadequacies and ethical constraints.

The Nature of the Evidence: Does Heredity Lead to Poverty through Mental Ability?

Heredity and Intelligence

In the literature concerned with hereditary effects on human behavior, heavy investment has been lodged in evaluating the impact of biological endowments on mental performance. Socio-economic failure is reasoned —openly or otherwise—to stem primarily from deficiency, incompetence, deviancy, or some combination of these mental aberrations.

Investigators vary in their estimates of the extent to which human intelligence is genetically governed. The lower end of the range is represented by those who estimate that 50 to 60 percent of intelligence is inherited (Vandenberg, 1968; Bajema, 1963). At the upper end Jensen insists the percentage may be as high as 70 to 80 percent (Jensen, 1970). With typical precision, Shockley estimates 75 percent of intelligence is inherited, 21 percent is shaped by environment, and 4 percent is the consequence of accidental factors (Shockley, 1970).

The Modifiability of Intelligence

Such estimates do not go unchallenged. Indeed, Pearl insists that human intelligence may not be measurable at all, at least in terms of the type of culturally biased instruments he suggests are used by Jensen and others in their research (Pearl, 1970). Vandenberg, on the other hand, claims that he has developed unbiased tests of intelligence at least in the areas of performance related to numerical and verbal skills, word fluency, and spacial perception (Vandenberg, 1965, 34-35).

More specifically, Deutsch and Brown, among others, claim to have shown that intelligence levels among "culturally deprived young children" can be modified substantially by the introduction of culturally enriching learning experiences (Deutsch and Brown, 1964). Others have suggested that gains among young children can also be induced by improving mothering techniques (Birren and Hess, 1968).

Jensen responds to this line of reasoning by flatly stating that hereditary evidence is irrefutable:

> The evidence for the major role of hereditary factors in determining individual differences in mental ability is now so consistent and conclusive that it should require little further explication. (Jensen, 1970, 122)

Further, he suggests that the presumed modifiability of intelligence through education derives from naive optimism, not hard fact. At most,

> . . . the environment may influence intelligence in much the same fashion that nutrition affects stature. Beyond the minimum requirements of the essential vitamins, minerals, and proteins, further amounts of these elements or wide variations in diet have negligible effects on stature; hereditary factors then become all-important in determining people's heights. (*Ibid.*, 124)

McCall has recently reported on a piece of well controlled research with white middle class subjects which may help resolve some of the controversy surrounding the issue of intelligence modifiability. He notes that many of the previously cited conclusions are drawn from correlational analyses performed on single-age level genetically related individuals (R. B. McCall, 1970, 644. For similar commentary, see: Burt, 1966). He suggests that such studies do demonstrate the hereditability of a general IQ level, but that they do not demonstrate the hereditability of IQ changes over age.

To test this latter point, McCall compared the similarity of patterns of IQ change over age among siblings and parent-child combinations with patterns observed for unrelated subjects matched for year of birth and parental education levels. Amount of IQ change was determined by subtracting the established general IQ level from IQ levels attained over subsequent periods. Data were available on the general IQ's of parents in the form of test results accumulated on them periodically between the ages of 3 and 12 years during their childhoods. Similar tests (mostly Binet assessments) were administered to children of these parents every 6 months between the ages of 3 to 6 years, and every year thereafter to age 12.

The sample consisted of 18 male pairs of sibs, 28 females sib pairs, and 54 male-female pairs of children. Parent-child matchings were constructed as follows: 13 father-son, 11 mother-daughter, and 11 crossed sex, pair comparisons. The control group was constructed by creating similar numbers of pairings of *unrelated* children and parent-child couplets.

McCall's longitudinal comparisons of IQ's produced the following:

Correlations for parent-child IQ levels were lower than usually found (median r = .29 for 11 comparisons compared to usual r of about .50). This lower correlation may well result because IQ comparisons were between children and the IQ's of their parents *when they were the same age* as their children were at the time of the study (i.e., parent IQ at age 3 and child IQ at age 3).

Higher correlations so often found and used to support the hereditary argument may therefore be spurious because they reflect the relationship between child IQ and parent IQ contemporaneously (for example, child IQ at age 3, parent IQ at age 30). These latter correlations may well reflect a much higher dosage of environmental influence than was previously suspected while McCall's equivalent age comparisons may be a more accurate estimate of hereditary influence on IQ.

Other findings also reflect the substantial influence of environment. For example, parent-child correlations were lower at every age comparison step than those for paired siblings, and parent-child correlations for IQ change (extracting initial general IQ score) did not differ significantly over age changes from those observed for parent-unrelated child comparisons (McCall, 1970, 46).

McCall concludes from this that

> . . . genetic heritage of middle-class normal children partially governs the *general* segment of the total IQ dimension, [but] . . . other factors . . . determine meaningful fluctuations in mental performance over age within that general range. (McCall, 1970, 647)

Of course, such findings do not conclusively resolve the issue of intelligence modifiability. This is so principally because those who argue heredity as the dominant contributor to intelligence are most concerned with how it differentially operates between the races and between classes of individuals grouped according to IQ level. In other words, those who believe that heredity heavily influences the performance of minority races and who believe that persons of low IQ are the chief perpetrators of poverty because they beget low IQ children, might find that results which show the white middle-class to be adaptable quite compatible with their other views. Further investigation is necessary then, on the relationships between heredity and mental deficiency, and race and IQ.

Heredity and Mental Deficiency

There may or may not be useful technical differences in the definitions of the terms *mental deficiency* and *mental retardation.* In any case, both mean mental inadequacy—insufficient intelligence to function at levels considered normal. It is toward this grouping of individuals that geneticists have focused considerable attention and have built many models of genetic transmission. They are often pointed to with concern because they are feared to be a primary source of poverty and its intergenerational perpetration.

Indeed, the mentally retarded constitute a considerable group, 6 million by one recent informed estimate (The President's Committee on Mental Retardation MR, '69 1967, 1), of which about 1.25 million are children (*Ibid.,* 18). Importantly, the highest concentration of mentally retarded persons in the continental U. S. resides in the Southeast—an estimated 303,500. The Southeast also has the unenviable distinction of providing special education for fewer of its retarded citizens than any other section of the country. Over 70 percent are neglected in this regard (*Ibid.*).

The size of this group is a source of concern to those worried about the transmission of sub normal intelligence to the next generation. Yet, only a small percentage of persons labeled mentally retarded appear to be so because of genetic inheritance. Scheerenberger estimates that approximately 15 percent of retardation can be attributed to hereditary factors. (Scheerenberger, 1965, 463). Indeed, in recalling studies done on retardates during this century, Scheerenberger suggests that the percentage of retardation attributed to genetic factors has gradually declined to the present 15 percent level, as illustrated in Table 4-1:

TABLE 4-1.

Trends in Estimated Percentage of Retardation Attributed to Hereditary Factors

Investigator	Year	Estimated Percentage of Hereditary Retardation
Goddard	1914	77.0
Hollingsworth	1920	90.0
Wallin	1922	62.9
Tredgold	1929	80.0
Rosanoff, *et al.*	1937	50.0
Yannet	1945	44.6

Source: R. C. Scheerenberger, "Genetic Aspects of Mental Retardation," *Mental Retardation Abstracts,* II (October-December 1965), 463.

Skeptics, of course, might dismiss such trends as merely reflecting shifts in the biases of investigators toward environmental explanations in recent decades.*

Somewhat better evidence is to be found in the few available longitudinal studies of mental retardates. The now well-known work of Skeels, Dye, and Skodak, with institutionalized retardates in Iowa in the late 30's is to the point. Initially the researchers experimented with 13 children tested in the imbecile range by introducing them to the friendship and care of women inmates in a nearby mental institution. By their own accounts, the intellectual capacities of most children increased remarkably (Skeels, *et al.,* 1938).

Twenty-five years later, two of these same researchers followed up on these 13 children. They found that those who married had produced 28 offspring. When they tested these children, they found they averaged 104 on IQ tests, the range being 85 to 125. All 13 of the original subjects were either self supportive or married to a self supporting individual.

A second follow-up study was then undertaken using as a sample 100 children, comparing the longitudinal outcomes for those who remained in institutions to adulthood to outcomes for those who were adopted. Of those who remained in institutions (N=12) one had died in an institution, 4 were still institutionalized, only 2 ever married, and one was currently divorced, 1 was employed in an institution, and 6 held unskilled jobs.

These 12 children had spent an aggregate of 273 years in institutions at a cost of $138,000 in public funds. In contrast, the adopted children generally rose to self supportive statuses and during the year of 1963 alone, contributed federal income taxes from employment ranging from $38.00 to $848.00 (Asbell, 1967).

In another large-scale longitudinal study, Baller, *et al.,* followed up on three groups of persons who had been initially tested for intelligence during the 30's. Three groups were identified: the "low group" having IQ's below 70, the "middle group" having IQ's between 70 and 80, and the "high group" having average ability. All subjects were 21 years of age at initial point of testing. At follow-up 30 years later, 50 percent of the low group, 72 percent of the middle group, and 60 percent of the higher group, now in their mid-fifties were located.

The findings indicated all three groups did quite well. For example, only 9 of the original 205 persons in the lowest groups were institutionalized at follow-up. Vocationally, 67 percent of the low group were self supporting and about 80 percent were usually employed with half of that number having held the same job for several years. In contrast, only 16 percent were in need of some outside financial aid. Almost the entire number of the two higher groups was found to be self supporting.

While the lowest group did not fare as well, the authors attributed the lower success rate (67 percent *vs.* nearly 100 percent) to early childhood upbringing. Examination of their case histories indicated that the lower group suffered markedly more—and more intense—disadvantages ranging from overly authoritarian to very indifferent parental investments, lack of attention to personal health, lack of instruction in personal appearance, and so on.

Further examination of the successful people in the low group produced the following features. Successful males were found to have

1. acquired a skill early and worked at it continuously thereafter,
2. found a job with a large paternal company rather than holding a series of jobs,
3. stayed in one community rather than drifting around.

Successful females in the low group were characterized by

1. having learned principles of good grooming and health care early,
2. having married well,
3. having worked steadily.

In contrast, unsuccessful females in particular were found to have developed habits of dependence and attachment to their mothers and home early in life (Baller, *et al.,* 1967).

Finally, assumptions about stereotypic personality traits and vocational skills among mental retardates may be as far off the mark as assumptions about inherent limits on their ability to achieve self improvement over the life span. In a recent study of vocational abilities among mental retardates having "borderline" retardation (IQ's above 55) it was found that such abilities are exhibited by retardates in the same range of variability as found among "normals" (Lofquist and Davis, 1970, 93). The researchers concluded that such a wide range of potentials demands the modification of most existing vocational programs for mental retardates well beyond the types of training now being provided.

Taken together, these findings provide little support for the notion that the futures of the great bulk of mental retardates are generally dictated by genetic limitations. At the same time, it is not possible to say that the available longitudinal studies fully refute the genetic argument because a legitimate point can be made that IQ tests may neither be sensitive enough nor comprehensive enough to have adequately classified the individuals studied according to their intelligence levels. Favorable results might derive from failure to detect average or better mental abilities among those considered retarded.

*A counter argument would be that the evidence for hereditary causation of mental retardation is only sound for those falling below IQ 45. If restricted to this group, the evidence is clear on hereditary causes. See: Fuller and Thompson, 1960, 306.

Race and Intelligence

Race, or more commonly, skin color, is an inherited characteristic. Because this is so, it is tempting to researchers to compare the performance of various races to "determine" hereditary differences (Pearl, 1970, 349). Since a great many blacks are poor and intelligence is held central to socio-economic success, the question boils down to whether intelligence levels among blacks are lower than those for whites. If so, the argument goes, poverty is largely explainable according to racially differentiated genetic endowments. It is even possible to argue, as Darlington has, that racial distinctions are preserved genetically as part of the process of natural selection. In other words, the races mate among themselves largely as the consequent of instinctual preference rather than because of social constraints. Hence, the differences between the races will continue (Darlington, 1970).

Jensen has utilized the findings from some of his research to suggest there may be differences in intelligence between the races traceable to genetic sources (Jensen, 1968). Shockley, utilizing data drawn from a variety of sources ranging from "Who's Who" profiles to crime rates concludes that on the average whites currently surpass blacks by the equivalent of 18 IQ points. In another piece of work, the same author compared Armed Forces mental test scores for blacks and whites in 1966 with similar results from tests given some 50 years earlier. He discovered that only 7 percent of the blacks tested exceeded the white median score in 1966 whereas 13 percent of all blacks exceeded the white median 50 years ago. He calculated from these figures that black intelligence has declined by about 5 IQ points over the half century (Shockley, 1970, 142 ff.).

Such a decline, if true, could only be attributed to inferior gene transmission among blacks if blacks were indeed a pure genetic strain and if they continued to mate almost wholly among themselves. Contrary to Darlington's view and the above assumption which underlies the interpretation of Shockley's findings, it now seems pretty well established that the process of racial mixing in the U. S. over the 300 years since black stock was first introduced has been quite substantial. Current estimates are that about 30 percent of the genetic heritage of American blacks stems from the input of white males mating with black females over the centuries (Emery, 1968, 159; B. Glass, 42). Is it possible that the noted decline in black intelligence is traceable to the white contribution made to their genetic heritage?

On the other side of the fence, the point is raised that any detectable relationship between IQ and race is primarily the outcome of differential environmental treatment accorded the races. Hence, as Duncan protests, it is race that is inherited and IQ and poverty are simply the results of how one is treated depending on the skin color he carries into this world (Duncan, 1969). Conclusions of the same order were promulgated in the 50's following a flurry of comparative studies of the IQ's of infant and pre-school aged black and white children. These studies commonly showed no meaningful differences between the races, thus pointing up the role of environment in producing differences in later age groups (Pasamanick, 1946; Gilliland, 1951; Knoblock and Pasamanick, 1953).

However, interpretations of the comparative results of IQ testing controlling for race vary widely. Garrett, in writing the foreword to Shuey's comprehensive compilation of several decades of research on the comparative IQ's of the races concludes that the evidence clearly points to a genetic base for the differences in intelligence levels which have consistently been detected:

> Dr. Shuey finds that at each age level and under a variety of conditions, Negroes regularly score below whites. There is, to be sure, an overlapping of 10-15 percent which means some Negroes achieve high scores. But the mean differences persists and are statistically significant. We are forced to conclude that the regularity and consistency of these results strongly suggest a genetic basis for the differences. (Garret in Shuey, 1966, viii)

Shuey herself concluded that the consistences in the findings "inevitably point to the presence of native differences between Negroes and Whites as determined by intelligence tests" (Shuey, 1966, 521).

Kennedy has pointed out that even Shuey's first edition review of 288 works (170 original investigations) fails to show significant IQ differences between the races among pre-school aged children (Kennedy, 1965, 18 ff.). Consistent differences are only disclosed for older age groups.

Responding to some of the implications of Shuey's conclusions, Kennedy proceeded to do a follow-up study of one fifth of a random sample of 1800 black children residing in the Southeast* whom he originally tested for IQ in 1960. This study, done in 1968, tested the IQ's of 312 (of 360 children drawn for the one fifth sub sample) children, applying to Stanford-Binet L-M instrument.

He found that mean IQ differed little: 78.9 in 1960 and 79.2 in 1965. Importantly, the standard deviation had increased from 12.6 to 14.3, and a noticeable IQ drop associated with chronological age continued to occur (*Ibid.*, 1965, 165 ff.). These latter two facts Kennedy takes as confirmation that IQ is modifiable over time. It is also important to note that no student in the study had up to that time been placed in an integrated school; therefore, school environment influences could be assumed to have undergone no major change over the 5-year period which might conceivably have affected outcomes (*Ibid.*, 6).

For our purposes, it is noteworthy that Kennedy found no major differences in the findings controlling

*Southeast here represents 5 states: Florida, Georgia, Alabama, South Carolina, and Tennessee. The original sample was also weighted to obtain rural, urban, and metropolitan representation and stratified to afford equal numbers controlling for sex and grades 1 through 6.

for rural, urban and metropolitan residence, although decreases in IQ associated with chronological age were more apparent for metropolitan children than for those residing in less populated areas (*Ibid.,* 166). To Kennedy, the most important finding was that there was no clear drop in IQ for the children in the study 5 years after initial testing. The noted association between IQ and chronological age is asserted to be the consequence of sample artifacts: children who were low in 1960 remained so in 1965 lending the impression when data were aggregated that IQ had declined. However, more refined analysis revealed rather stable IQ's over this period (*Ibid.,* 1965, 168).

Kennedy also took to task the instruments commonly used to test intelligence and how they may themselves affect the differences in results obtained between the races. Noting that the revised Stanford-Binet had been "normed" without inclusion of a single minority group member in the normative sample (*Ibid.,* 1965, 1 ff.), he suggests that the black's "cultural deficit" in the Southeast may well yield low scores which do not reflect innate inadequacies. Indeed, he suspects that a considerable portion of the IQ differences found is the consequences of cultured biases in such tests. Hence, it may well be, in Kennedy's words, that "a Negro child, who in spite of facing a cultural deficit scored an IQ of 100, must indeed be a superior—not average child" (*Ibid.,* 2).

He concludes on the basis of findings in several unpublished small studies done in the Southeast, that the IQ of 80 commonly recorded by black children actually reflects normal IQ, and, above that level, intelligence approaches superior levels. Hence, roughly a 20-point IQ difference should be taken into account and adjusted in evaluating true intelligence levels when comparing between the races (*Ibid.,* 1965, 3 ff.).

Another rather unique study of the relationship between race and IQ has reached conclusions similar to those of Kennedy precisely because significant differences were found in the IQ's of comparative groups of 4-years-olds when tested by the abbreviated Stanford-Binet.

Willerman, *et al,* gleaned 186 live births resulting from interracial marriages from records of 42,000 live births in twelve institutions located nationally during a set period of time. Follow-up is to proceed until each child's eighth birthday; however, as of the time of initial testing only 88 children had reached 4 years of age.

Test results indicated that children having white mothers had significantly higher IQ scores than children having black mothers. The conclusion, therefore, was that the mother as primary socializing agent had profound impact on the shaping of the child's pre-school intelligence level. Hence, socialization rather than genetics is the basic influence on child intelligence (Willerman, *et al.,* 1970). One primary limitation in this study which undercuts the strength of such conclusions is that no data was available on parental IQ, the assumption being parental IQ's were roughly equivalent.

There is no way to conclude definitely on this issue, no matter how central it is to the thesis that heredity produces poverty. Studies on both sides seem to have been shamelessly employed by their authors to support their biases, and even if they had not, the fact that most depended upon instruments which measure IQ—given the objections to these instruments previously raised—yields doubts about the overall validity of the data cited throughout the section.

Heredity and Mental Illness / Criminality

Another way that heredity can be reasoned to increase poverty is through its effect on mental competence or the ability or inability to mentally manage one's own life within the broad limits society sets for acceptable socio-economic behavior. As previously noted, inability to manage in these terms is not necessarily synonymous with inadequate general intelligence.

Can mental illness and/or criminal behavior—two contributing factors to poverty—be traced to hereditary sources? As with almost everything else, the answer seems to depend upon which set of results one finds consonant with his own views.

Following from a recent review of the research literature, Roman and Trice have concluded that the evidence is not profound in support of the role heredity plays in inducing mental illness. They suggest that essentially two types of research designs have been implemented which either imply or claim to test the effect of hereditary factors (Roman and Trice, 1967).

One type of design attempts to measure the difference in the rate and persistence of mental illness in various geographic areas grouped according to the general socio-economic level of each area. Genetic factors are drawn in by implication when the authors of such studies attempt to explain differential rates by the concept of social drift. The second type of design openly claims to test genetic factors by assessing the rate of transmission of mental illness between parents and their children or measuring the degree of concordance in manifest mental illness among sibs, most often identical twins. For the sake of convenience, these studies can be referred to as family studies as distinguished from geographic studies.

Data from six major geographic studies were analyzed by Roman and Trice, all of which sought in one way or another to interpret their findings in accord with the notion of social drift. In several studies which followed up on what happened to clinic or discharged mental hospital patients, it was found that a disproportionate number of such persons came to reside in low socio-economic locations in urban areas. This was found to occur regardless of the previous occupational level of the patient or the socio-economic level achieved by his parents. Since such persons apparently sought out such environments, and since they continued to show signs of mental illness even though the duration of their residence was not long enough to logically attribute such behavior to environmental influences, the conclusion often reached was simply that the mentally ill were drawn to reduced socio-economic conditions by personal incapacities.

Roman and Trice point out three methodological inadequacies in all these studies which cast doubt on the validity of such conclusions:

1) In all the studies, subjects were either clinic patients, former mental hospital patients, or both. Hence, they already had exhibited signs of mental disorder at the point the study was undertaken, and it is not possible in such a case to clearly trace causation on follow-up. Moreover, such samples clearly differ from "normal" populations making such findings less than gereralizable.
2) Also, an assumption is made that simply because a person comes to reside in a low rated socio-economic area, he too is doing badly. There is no evidence to support the notion that all people in such areas are either poor or otherwise distinguishable from the population at large.
3) Finally the difficulty in ranking persons or their parents by occupational status in order to trace their socio-economic mobility is well-known, making the drift explanation, which is based on such mechanics, tenuous (Roman and Trice, *Ibid.*).

In short, inferences about the impact of personal inadequacies on poverty status derived from observations of the relationship between rates of mental illness and socio-economic area of residence are open to serious questions.

In the matter of family studies, it remains a wide open question whether mental illness in children is conveyed environmentally or transmitted genetically. While there seems to be general agreement that a better-than-accidental frequency of disturbed children is found to be raised by disturbed parents (Rice, *et al.,* 1971), it cannot be stated generally, or in specific classes of mental illness, that causation is attributable to either genetics or environment(Wender, 1969). Indeed, that bastion of behavior genetics research methodology, the identical twin approach, has been seriously challenged in a series of researches in recent years. These studies have consistently found lower concordance rates among identical twins—some approaching zero—than reported in earlier research (Kringler, 1964; Kringler, 1966; Tienari, 1964). One researcher has hinted that past methodological inadequacies may have accounted for high concordance rates (i.e., if one twin exhibits mental illness, the other will also). His own research has led him to conclude that "the more accurate and careful the samplings, the lower the concordance figures" (Kringler, 1966, 184).

On the other side of the fence, genetic researchers seem just as sure of their position. Roglen, in his review, concludes that present evidence is more favorable to the interpretation that schizophrenia produces family disorganization than the reverse (Rosenthal and Kety, 1968). Wender's as yet incomplete studies of children raised by adoptive parents illustrates the kind of evidence currently utilized in support of this point. As shown in Table 4-2, Wender has found what he considers better than chance rates of appearance of schizoid symptoms in adopted children who had schizophrenic natural parents, comparing to adopted children of "normal" parentage.

Nine percent of the children of schizophrenic parents manifest schizophrenia even when reared in adopted settings, and 30 percent overall exhibit some symptoms compared to 6 percent in the sample of adopted children having non-schizophrenic natural parents. Wender concludes cautiously, that the results at least show that some forms of schizophrenia are genetically transmitted by some schizophrenic parents (Wender, 1969, 499).

Perhaps as good a summary as any of the early research evidence on the relationship between heredity and mental illness is to be found in Fuller and Thompson (1960). They have summarized the evidence for the two major forms of psychosis, schizophrenia and manic-depression, according to the two major types of studies undertaken, family history and twin analyses.

The results on schizophrenia, as the authors find them, are reported in Tables 4-3 and 4-4.

These data present the rates of expectancy throughout the family tree. Of note is the estimate that over two thirds of all children having two schizophrenic parents are expected to fall prey to similar mental illness.

The findings on schizophrenia drawn from a variety of twins studies are reported in Table 4-4.

The results of studies with identical twins, in particular, are quite consistent; and taken together, these data are often used as the backbone of the

TABLE 4-2

Adopted Children Exhibiting Schizoid Symptoms, by Diagnosis of Natural Parents

	Type of Child Symptom			
Parent Diagnosis	**Schizophrenic**	**Borderline**	**Other**	**Total N**
Schizophrenic	8 (9%)	18 (21%)	60	86
Non-Schizophrenic	0	6 (6%)	91	97

Source: Paul H. Wender, "The Role of Genetics in the Etiology of the Schizophrenias," *American Journal of Orthopsychiatry*, XXXIX (April 3, 1969).

TABLE 4-3

Expectancy of Schizophrenia in Relations of Proband Cases*

Relationship to Proband	Percent Expectancy
Step-Sibs	1.8
Half-Sibs	7.0- 7.6**
Full Sibs	11.5-14.3
Children	
One parent affected	16.4
Both parents affected	68.1
Parents	9.3-10.3
Grandparents	3.9
Grandchildren	4.3
Nephews and Nieces	3.9

*The term *proband* represents the technique of random case selection from a population having known psychiatric impairment.

**Ranges are shown where different studies produced different rates. All findings summarize H. Kallman's work in 1942 and 1946.

Source: J. L. Fuller and W. R. Thompson, *Behavior Genetics*. 1960, 274, Table 9-1.

genetic argument for the transmission of at least certain types of schizophrenia.

Fuller and Thompson also present data summarizing much of the earlier research on the genetic transmission of manic depression, drawn from both family and twin studies, as shown in Table 4-5.

High expectancy rates are again consistently noticeable in the data on identical twins. Taken together, these data lend the impression that a variety of mental disorders may—at least in some cases—be traced to genetic sources.

Finally, Fuller and Thompson provide an important service in summarizing a variety of twin studies which have attempted to assess the link between heredity and criminality. Such a link has often been asserted and just as often dismissed as nonsense during the last century or so. The cumulative evidence, while hardly definitive, presents the interesting fact that as genetic differences increase between sets of twins (from identical to fraternal like sex, to fraternal unlike sex) so do discordance rates, as shown in Table 4-6.

The relationship between IQ and criminality has also been assessed, controlling for race, in Shuey's recent work. In regard to delinquency, Shuey's analysis of 28 studies reveals that the average IQ of 3480 blacks in 22 researches was 74.44, that in 15 studies of comparable whites, 80.64. The average IQ of white delinquents was also pegged at about 20.0 points below that of white non-delinquents (Shuey, 1966, 432-33).

Her summarization of various studies of black and white criminals shows similar results. Aggregating the results discloses that the average IQ of 1670 black criminals was 81.26, that of 2407 comparable whites 91.84. Hence, black IQ was consistently shown to be lower than white IQ among delinquents and criminals, and, generally, the average IQ of the criminal and delinquent was shown to be clearly below that of the average non criminal and non delinquent (*Ibid.*, 451).

Noting the common assertions of a link between IQ and heredity it is but a short jump from such findings to a conclusion that deviant behavior of the delinquent and criminal varieties, stems in part from hereditary sources.

But the evidence is hardly unequivocal. Fuller and Thompson express reservations about the extent to which mental illness and deviant behavior are transmitted genetically in noting that if this were perfectly so, then it would be expected that 100 percent of all

TABLE 4-4

Expectancy Rates in MZ and DZ Cotwins of Schizophrenics

Investigator	DZ (Fraternal) N	DZ (Fraternal) % Expectancy	MZ (Identical) N	MZ (Identical) % Expectancy
Lupenberger (1928, 1930)	60*	3.3	21	66.6
Rosanoff, *et al.* (1934)	101	14.9	41	68.3
Essen-Moller (1941)	24	16.7	7	71.4
Slater (1951)	115	14.0	41	76.0
Kallman (1938-1953)	685	14.0	286	86.2

*Includes 23 cases of twins whose zygosity was definitely determined.

Source: Fuller and Thompson, 1960, 276, Table 9-3.

TABLE 4-5

Expectancy Rates for Manic-Depression
Among Relatives and Cotwins of Probands
(in percents)

Relatives of Manic-Depressive Probands

Investigator	General Population	Parents	Children	Sibs	DZ Cotwins	MZ Cotwins
Lupenberger (1927-36)	0.4	10.6—24.4	30.6—38.7	12.7		75.0
Banze (1929)		11.8		18.1		
Shulz, Rudin (1931-51)	0.4	15.7		13.3 29.1		
Slater (1938-51)	0.5-0.8	10.2—15.5	12.8 22.2	11.7	23.3	66.7
Tomasson (1941)		2.0		7.1		
Stromgren (1948)	0.2-0.4	7.0		4.0		
Sjorgren (1948)	0.6-0.8	7.4		4.1		
Pollack, *et al.* (1939)		3.7		4.2		
Kallman (1950)		23.4		23.0	23.6	92.6
Rosanoff, *et al.* (1935)				1.5	16.4	69.6

Source: Fuller and Thompson, 1960, 285, Table 9-7.

children of 2 schizophrenic parents, and 25 percent of all siblings of schizophrenics would manifest similar symptoms (Fuller and Thompson, 1960, 281). The probabilities would be the same for the manifestation of deviant and criminal behavior. The data reviewed, and more recent data cited earlier, however, do not reflect such rates—either in terms of mental illness or criminality. Certainly we are in no position at this point in time to declare that we have isolated the hereditary effects on occurrance of mental illness and/or deviant behavior. On the other hand, the advocate of environmental effects rejects these findings at his own peril.

SES and IQ

Ultimately, it comes down to this: if heredity is a major determinant of mental functioning and mental functioning is found highly and positively related to socio-economic status, then heredity has a substantial role to play in the creation and maintenance of poverty.

More than a few believe that the data presented here are sufficient to make the case. Jensen, for example, suggests:

> Since SES is closely linked to occupational and educational levels, the criteria for successful performance in this realm act as a crude screening device for abilities. This fact, along with the possibilities for social mobility and assortive mating, results in some degree of genetic segregation among the social classes. (Jensen, 1970, 126)

Eckland tempers this generalization a bit by suggesting that heredity is probably a stronger factor in white poverty than black poverty. This conclusion follows from the assumption that poverty is less correlated with intellectual ability among blacks than whites because blacks are subjected to opportunity barriers more often (Eckland, 1967). This, of course, suggests we should be able to find a higher proportion of the more intelligent persons among the black poor than the white poor.

If social screening works in these ways, then it follows according to some that poverty will be self perpetuating. Crow, for example, asserts that we know enough about genetics to predict that when two low IQ persons mate, they will produce offspring of even lesser intelligence, and vice versa (Crow, 1970). Vandenberg provides a counter point to this view by suggesting that heredity is still primarily the result of random factors, that such assertions (of the type made by Crow) are imprecise. He suggests that

TABLE 4-6
Summary of Researches Done on Hereditary
Factors in the Determination of Crime and Delinquency
(In Numbers of Twin Pairs)

Condition Studied	Investigator Country	MZ Concordant	MZ Discordant	DZ Like Sex Concordant	DZ Like Sex Discordant	MZ Unlike Sex Concordant	MZ Unlike Sex Discordant
Adult Crime	Lang (1929) Germany	10	3	3	15	—	—
Adult Crime	Stumpfl (1936) Germany	11	7	7	12	2	26
Adult Crime	Kranz Germany	20	11	23	20	7	43
Adult Crime	Borgstorm (1939) Finland	3	1	2	3	2	8
Adult Crime	Rosanoff, *et al.* (1934) U.S.A.	25	12	5	23	1	31
Juvenile Delinquency	Rosanoff, *et al.* (1934) U.S.A.	39	3	20	5	8	32
Behavior Disorder	Rosanoff, *et al.* (1934) U.S.A.	41	6	20	34	8	21
Juvenile Personality Disorder	Kranz (1937) Germany	7	4	0	3	2	6
Child Maladjustment	Kent (1949) U.S.A.	7	0	4	2	2	1
Hysteria	Stumpfl (1937) Germany	3	6	0	9	—	—
Psychopathology Neurosis	Slater (1953) England	2	6	4	25	1	13
	TOTALS	168	59	94	161	33	181

Source: Fuller and Thompson, 1960, 300, Table 9-13.

> high ability may be due to a particular constellation of genes which can be produced *just as often* by the combination of genes of two low ability parents as of high ability parents. (Vandenberg, 1970, 166, emphasis mine)

This statement would seem to come as close as any to denying the entire genetic rationale upon which predictions of intergenerational transmission of behavior are predicated.

But such a comment, even from a person of Vandenberg's stature, would hardly dissuade those who believe hereditary contributions to socio-economic status to be clearly traceable, nor should it. Udry, *et al.*, have recently reported on a rather unique study proporting to show that the biologically fit are also the socio-economically fit.

These researchers set out to study whether poverty in childhood among American Negro women increases the likelihood of a woman's giving birth to low birth weight infants. Data were gathered on 1404 middle class black women who had live born babies in the District of Columbia between July 1, 1965 and June 30, 1966. They found that rates of premature birth did not differ significantly between mothers of the two social classes, nor did they differ significantly controlling for class status as derived from husband's occupation.

What they did find, however, was that women moving out of the lower class having significantly lower prematurity rates than women moving down out of the middle class (as measured by whether a woman's husband was of higher or lower occupational classification than that of her father). They concluded that "we do not believe that any environmental explanation of the genesis of class differences in prematurity rates fits our data" (Udry, *et al.,* 1970, 194).

The explanation they find most plausible, "assumes that the basis of selection for mobility is genetically related to the probability of prematurity" (*Ibid.*).

The implications of these findings are fascinating because insofar as prematurity and low birth rates are linked to subsequent difficulties in child development (see: Clara Johnson, 1971), to that extent support is lent to the proposition that factors contributing to poverty are transmitted genetically. Further, the upward mobility of the more biologically fit, and vice versa, suggested in the Udry data, provides another slant on how social classes may become, in Jensen's view, genetically segregated over time.

There is no way to tell how genetically segregated the social classes may be; however, Vandenberg cites a study done in Belgium which purports to show that high intelligence is more broadly distributed across the social classes than would be likely if genetic segregation were operating to a high degree. In this study 1514 children were tested for intelligence and grouped according to where they fit within a 5-part breakdown for socio-economic status.

Findings did show a link between being in the top SES group (N=91) and high intelligence, with the opposite occurring in the lower two SES groups. However, Vandenberg's evaluation of these data disclosed that 85 percent of the top scorers on the IQ test actually came from the 4 lower SES groups. He takes this as evidence that the lower SES groups contain a goodly enough number of high intelligence persons to prevent such classes from slipping toward lower intellectual capacities over time (Vandenberg, 1970).

It should be noted however, that while only 15 percent of the top scores came from the top SES group, the top SES group represented only 6 percent of the total sample (91 of 1514 subjects). Taking this into account suggests that high intelligence, at least, is over represented in the top SES group.

The Larger Picture: Are We Propagating the Unfit?

The foregoing has attempted—however inadequately—to summarize what is known or claimed about the role of heredity in predisposing individuals to a life of inadequate mental functioning and perhaps poverty. There is another level of analysis which centers around estimating the effects of the interaction of social and hereditary factors upon the destinies of large sub groups or indeed, whole societies.

Most concern seems to be expressed over three conditions which may have an effect on increasing the proportion and/or absolute number of mentally inadequate individuals in a collectivity.

1) Some concern is expressed over the combined effect of social and geographical isolation in the creation of a gene pool among a sub group (tribe, extended family, remote village, etc.) through inbreeding capable of transmitting recessive genes with greater frequency than expected in a less isolated population.
2) A more prominent concern relates to whether we are creating an ever increasing stock of mentally inadequate people by maintaining the mentally deficient to reproductive ages.
3) Finally, substantial interest is focused on whether or not higher birth rates among the lower socio-economic and/or lower IQ groups are leading to a generally less capable—less intelligent—population.

Shot through much of the debate on these concerns is the thinly veiled Social Darwinist view point that social welfare programing—such as better health care and income supports—simply serves to preserve the unfit and enable them to propogate in sufficient members to eventually undercut the viability of society. Shockley, for example, has reasoned from his data convincing him that Negro intelligence is declining, that this decline is directly attributable to the invention of welfare programs which have encouraged the least effective elements in the U.S. population to have large families (Tallahassee *Democrat,* 1969, 24; and K. Davis, 1966, 189). Much of the theory and research that has been done in recent years, on the other hand, seems to have been launched with the aim of undermining such assumptions.

The Effect of Socio-Geographical Isolation

A variety of conventions, socializing patterns, and constraints can, in Kingsley Davis' words, "alter the biological capacities and traits of the human organism by artificial selection" (K. Davis, 1966, 174). Emery has suggested similarly that when geographic, social, religious, and other factors prohibit outside mating, then

> the increase in homozygosity which results from inbreeding is reflected in the number of severe recessive conditions which are often found in these (isolated) communities. (Emery, 1968, 156)

Many examples of the consequences of such inbreeding have been cited in the literature such as the abnormal blood-group frequencies among some North American Indian tribes and the Dunkers, a small religious group of isolates in Pennsylvania (*Ibid.,* 158). Reed illustrates the process by citing the fact that albinism occurs only about once in 20,000 births in Caucasian populations whereas it occurs at the rate of 1 in 200 births in certain isolated Indian tribes in central America and the South Western U. S. (Reed, 1966, 12).

Such isolation may stimulate the rate of transmission of recessive genes by way of increasing the likelihood of mating within blood lines (Scheerenberger, 1965, 473); but more commonly in small populations the rate may be simply the product of "genetic drift," the process by which "a gene can get a foothold as a result of random sampling in numerically small populations" (Reed, 1966, 13).

Unless the isolated population is penetrated from outside, this process over time may yield the fixation of a recessive gene, that is, the irreversible transmission of traits influenced by such a gene (or genes), as illustrated in Figure 4-1.

The available data do document that such a process appears to occur in small groups isolated by geography and/or social preference. As yet there seems to be little interest in extrapolating such findings to a more general explanation of the mental dispositions and social behaviors of such groups.

Moreover, it becomes increasingly difficult to apply

FIGURE 4-1

Genetic Fixation-Extinction in a Small Population

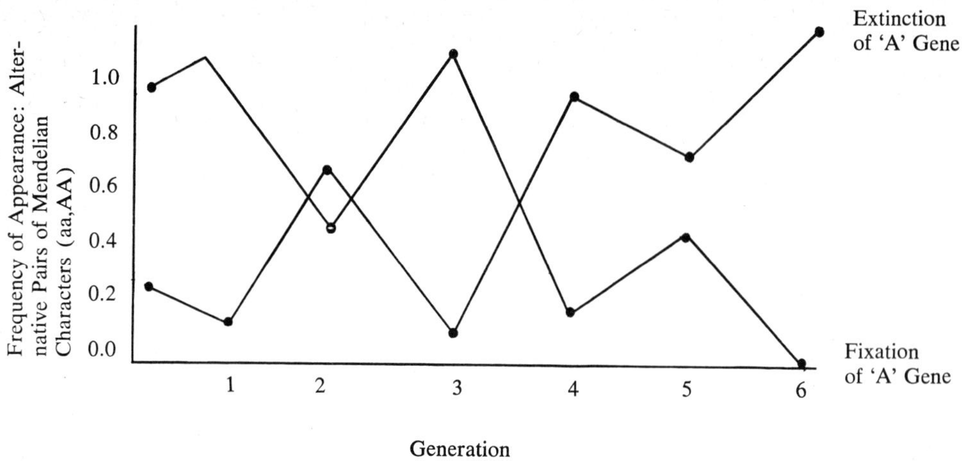

Source: A. E. H. Emery, *Heredity, Disease, and Man,* 1968, Figure 37.

the theory to the consequences for other population groups of larger size, those experiencing exchange of population through migration and/or those exhibiting fewer or less intense social prohibitions against mixing. All these factors lessen the likelihood that recessive genes will concentrate in a given locality and/or population grouping.

Indeed, social prohibitions against mixing may not themselves be indicative of the actual extent to which it occurs. Laws and conventions preventing the marriage of blacks and whites over the centuries in the U.S., for example, have not prevented the races from mating in fairly large numbers. As previously noted, geneticists commonly estimate that about 30 percent of the gene pool of U.S. blacks today is of Caucasian origin, the flow being almost exclusively from Caucasion to Negro since the introduction of pure stock some 300 years ago (Emery 1968, 159; Glass, 1966, 41). Glass has estimated that if the flow continues at the rate of 2.5 to 3.0 percent per generation, complete equilibrium would be reached in 75 generations, or about 2,000 years (Glass, 1966, 42). Shockley's position that Negro intelligence is declining seems to depend in part on an assumption of intense racial inbreeding, but these estimates would cast some doubt on the extent to which the races are genetically isolated today.

It may also be argued that migration may not increase the genetic variability in small populations. This would not occur if migration is as selective as many demographers believe it to be. For example, it is often suggested in demographic research that the more vigorous, adaptable, motivated, youthful, and educated migrate from rural areas, this being so in the poverty areas of the South as elsewhere. If this is the case, an argument could be advanced that the remaining people may represent a residual gene pool heavily loaded with recessive genes. Over time, the remaining people might bear an ever higher proportion of offspring incapable of adequate mental functioning and socio-economic performance.

Shuey's review of the research done to date on the attributes of Southern migrants to the urban North provides little support for assuming important effects of this sort as deriving from selective migration.

She notes that black children born in the urban North commonly test 3 or 4 IQ points higher than black children in the same schools who had been born in the South. Such findings do not disprove the notion of selective migration; rather, they reduce its importance in her view. Summing up, she suggests that

> our single best estimate was that approximately seven points separate the average IQ of Southern colored children from Northern children of their race. If this is correct, then about half or possibly a little more than half (3 to 4 IQ points) of this difference may be accounted for by environmental factors and the remainder by selective migration. (Shuey, 1966, 490)

It is Lee's contention that an even larger proportion of IQ differences between rural and urban blacks can be traced to educational and environmental differences than Shuey's review suggests (Lee, 1951).

While the evidence is incomplete, the available data cast considerable doubt on the notion that selective migration from isolated rural areas implies a continuing drain of the genetically well endowed. Yet hard and fast conclusions on this matter would certainly be premature. The best conclusion at this point seems to be that the issues surrounding selective migration and other issues raised in this section deserve much greater attention than they have received to date. Until more serious study is undertaken, it will remain highly problematical as to the role played by genetics—if any—in sustaining isolated and remote "pockets of poverty."

The Effect of Preserving the Mentally Deficient to Reproductive Age

> Our ethics promote mercy and our machines and surgery preserve to the reproductive age numerous genetic types that in a more ruthless society and a more rigorous age would never have had children. (B. Glass, 1966, 43)

There is little doubt that scientific advances have preserved some "genetic types" to reproductive age that would not have otherwise lived so long. Scheerenberger's review of the literature on mongolism, for example, revealed that life expectancy of those so afflicted is increasing. In 1929, the ratio of live mongoloids among 10-year-old children was 1:4000; in 1949, the ratio was 1:1000 (Scheerenberger, 1965, 486).

This does not mean, however, that if increasing numbers are reaching reproductive age, they actually reproduce. In fact the evidence is quite the opposite. Reed's findings are consistent with Skeel's and Skodak's work, which showed on follow-up that only 2 of 12 children institutionalized until adulthood ever married. Reed followed up 289 kinships and subsequent descendents from a random sample of persons institutionalized as mentally retarded in Minnesota in 1911 (Reed, 1966).

He found, in common with others (see: Penrose, 1950, 425), that higher IQ persons had smaller families than lower IQ institutional cohorts. But more detailed examination revealed that 42 percent of those who never married were mentally retarded while only 4 percent of those with IQ below 70 ever married. The average IQ of those who married was above 100 while that of the never married was about 80 (Reed, 1966, 17 ff.). People below IQ 70 who ever married averaged 2.09 children while people above IQ 131 averaged 2.98 children (*Ibid.,* 19).

Bajema reports similar findings in a follow up study of 1114 persons born between 1916-1917 who were tested for IQ while in 6th grade in Kalamazoo, Michigain. He found that the proportion of individuals who left no offspring declined linearly as IQ declined, ranging from 13.4 percent for those of 120 IQ or above to 30.0 percent for those in the 69-78 range (Bajema, 1963, 182).

Apparently the mentally disorganized follow a pattern similar to that of the mentally deficient. Fuller and Thompson reviewed the literature on marriage and fertility rates among schizophrenics and manic depressives finding that rates in both categories fall below those evidenced for "normals" as illustrated in Table 4-7 and Figure 4-2.

In another early but larger study, Penrose measured the relationship between IQ and fertility among 1214 fathers and 1251 mothers in England. His results, as shown in Table 4-8, indicated that fertility was higher among women of lower IQ than among men at similar levels. He attributed this to the likelihood that lower IQ women would mate more often than lower IQ men. In any case, fertility is low among very low IQ individuals.

TABLE 4-7

Marriage and Birth Rates in Normal and Schizophrenic Populations

	%Marriage Rate	% Birth Rate
General Population (U.S.)	71	3.3
Schizophrenics		
Nuclear Group	39.1	1.4
Peripheral Group	70.1	3.1
All Schizophrenics	50.3	1.9

Source: Fuller and Thompson, 1960, Table 9-2.

TABLE 4-8

IQ and Fertility Rates among a Sample of Mothers and Fathers

	Fathers (N 12143)		Mothers (N 1251)	
IQ	%	Fertility*	%	Fertility
122	0.7	0.50	0.2	0.13
100	83.0	1.04	72.0	0.93
78	12.3	1.27	16.2	1.38
56	3.9	0.64	11.4	2.04
34	0.1	0.04	0.2	0.09
12	0.0	0.00	0.0	0.00

*Fertility=relative fertility (% parents/% children in each IQ class; % children not shown).

Source: L. S. Penrose, "Propagation of the Unfit," *The Lancet,* CCLIX (September 30, 1950), 426.

Further analysis showed greater variability in IQ among off-spring than among parents as reflected in standard deviations from group mean IQ scores for the two age groups of 13.71 and 17.64 respectively (Penrose, 1950, 426). From these data Penrose concluded that

> the population is being replenished from the middle of the range. If hereditary factors which contribute to the variation are mainly additive, the central part of the distribution must be, on the whole, heterozygous for the genes concerned, whereas the extremes are homozygous. Thus, the population is being bred chiefly by heterozygotes. (*Ibid.*)

FIGURE 4-2

Marriage and Birth Rate in Normal and Manic-Depressive Populations

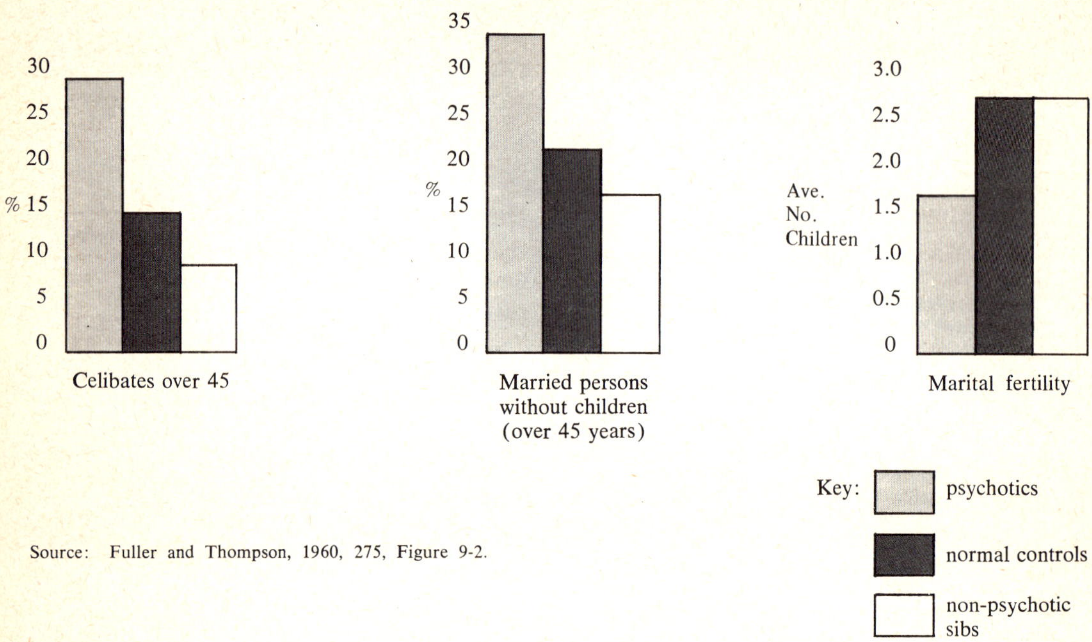

Source: Fuller and Thompson, 1960, 275, Figure 9-2.

Rather than propagating the unfit,* the population seems to be holding its own, with low fertility rates at both ends of the IQ continuum cancelling each other out (Penrose, 1948; Penrose, 1950; Burt, 1963).

Preserving the mentally deficient and disoriented to reproductive age, therefore, appears to constitute no basic threat to the intelligence levels of large populations and societies.

The Effect of Higher Birth Rates in the Lower Socio-Economic Strata

While it is an uncontestable fact that those in the lower SES classifications have higher birth rates, it does not necessarily follow that this is contributing to a decline in the general intelligence of our population as some would contend. Nor does it follow that welfare programs which support such large families are actually contributing to the degeneration of our society by underwriting the permanence and growth of a poverty class having with every passing generation greater numbers with less mental capacity to lift themselves above their status at birth (Shockley, 1970).

*Unfitness here and throughout means biological unfitness. Biological unfitness and net fertility are considered synonymous; hence, the unfit are those unable to propagate efficiently (see: Penrose, 1950, 425).

Given the present state of our knowledge, the issue between high birth rates and lessening of mental capacities is itself not scientifically resolvable. The data on IQ simply do not show a high correlation consistently between IQ level and SES (Anastasi, 1956). The evidence often used to prove this case has been drawn from studies which have shown a substantial correlation between IQ and family size, which somehow carries over into the relationship between family size and SES (Anastasi, 1956; Scott and Nisbet, 1955). This finding is hardly useful in making the kinds of dire predictions Shockley and others advance, however, since it has been found that those from large families having low IQ's generally have small families themselves (Higgens, *et al.*, 1962). Even if the relationship were highly significant between IQ and family size (and between family size and SES), the reproductive rate of such people hardly indicates that they are compounding societal problems by repeating the performances of their parents.

These findings, coupled with previous findings suggesting that the population replenishes itself from the middle of the IQ range, cast the major assumptions about the consequences of high birth rates in the lower socio-economic groups in an unfavorable light. To conclude that high birth rates among such groups are leading society down hill requires the assumptions that at least a high proportion of such persons have low IQ's and that an equally high proportion are reproducing in large numbers. Neither assumption is strongly supported by the evidence. Hence the further contention that the statistical relationship between the two portends a decline in civilization—or at least the proliferation of poverty—appears, at present, quite unfounded in fact.

Summary Points: Implications for Poverty in the Nonmetropolitan South

Little of the work reviewed in this chapter has been either carried out in the South or applied specifically to an understanding of poverty in the nonmetropolitan South. Thus, any conclusions—however hesitant—to be drawn about the role of heredity in creating poverty in the nonmetropolitan South must be arrived at by inferring the generalizability of the findings to this region of the country.

Such inferential leaps are not wholly unwarranted since the proven results of genetic research may be considered to have wide validity. Vandenberg's views on the applicability of findings resulting from his studies in Louisville are illustrative of this point. He considers such findings to have wide validity,

> inasmuch as a characteristic that can be inherited in Kentucky presumably can be inherited anywhere else. However, the way the characteristic is expressed, if at all, may depend in large part upon the environment. (Vandenberg, 1965, 33)

His second point is also instructive in that the environment of the nonmetropolitan South in particular may be such as to encourage the development and expression of maladaptive behavior, the potential for which may have been hereditarily transmitted.

But the role of environment in calling out hereditary potential is not the only reason why it is important to apply the data on the Genetic Thesis to the issue of nonmetropolitan Southern poverty. In conjunction with the characteristics of the nonmetropolitan Southern environment—relatively more isolated and socio-economically deprived—it is important to recall that the majority of the poor in this region are black and that, as a group, they exhibit substantially higher than average fertility rates.

Given these facts, if all the assumptions and contentions in this chapter about the role of heredity in shaping human behavior proved true, it would be hard to escape the conclusion that heredity constitutes a significant—if not the dominant—cause of poverty at least in certain areas of the more rural South.

The number of "if's" which would have to be proven true to arrive at this conclusion include the following:

——If the poor in the rural South could be shown to live in small enclaves which exhibit low in/out migration and strong socio-religious constraints against mixing with strangers and others who are different.

——If inadequate mental functioning could be consistently and on a large scale traced to groups of people in isolated-deprived environments, regardless of race.

——If IQ, or more broadly, mental functioning could be shown to be the *central* determinant of socio-economic success in present day society.

——If intelligence were to be proven essentially unmodifiable.

——If those in the lowest socio-economic strata could be proven generally to have the lowest IQ's.

——If those of low IQ could be demonstrated to generally have low IQ children, and to be reproducing at rates in excess of averages for other IQ groups.

——If the intelligence levels of blacks, and all other races, could be proven traceable to hereditary causes.

These "if's" are convertible into priority items for research. Such research would be needed to test more throughly the Genetic Thesis. Current evidence does not support the broad applicability of the thesis to poverty in the rural South, let alone the broader area of the nonmetropolitan South.

Our review suggests that the rural South has experienced substantial migration and inter-racial mating over the last several generations at least. On the other hand, there may be reason to believe that genetics plays a larger role than might be suspected in the plight of small groups of people who continue to live in very isolated rural localities.

There is good reason to believe that level of mental functioning is *not* the central determinant of socio-economic success in current society, especially for the poor rural black.

The contention that the social classes are becoming more genetically segregated has very little in the way of fact to support it. The substantial mixing of the races, the questionable data purporting to show the relationship between IQ and socio-economic level, and the shaky assumption that assortive mating based on similarities in cultural, educational, and other factors, actually reflects assortive mating on an intelligence factor, create large doubts about the extent of genetic segregation between the social classes.

Contrary to the contentions of some social investigators, the evidence seems to be relatively sound in support of the conclusion that the mentally deficient and disorganized actually reproduce at far lower rates than "normals."

The contention that intelligence is essentially unmodifiable has been challenged as being based on spurious correlations deriving from associating parent-child IQ's at a given point in time. Data comparing the IQ's of parents when they were the same age as their children—when the children were studied—do not yield high correlations. Moreover, data exist to show that IQ may well change (increase or decrease) among children as their ages increase. At the very least the findings are inconsistent on the modifiability of intelligence.

Finally, comparative studies of the IQ's of black and white pre-school age children consistently reveal no significant differences. Such findings raise questions about the importance of heredity in shaping differences in IQ among older white and black children.

It would be foolhardy in the extreme to expect a scientific resolution of these contentions in the near future, even though genetic researchers recognize the needs which must be met if more definite data are to be gathered. Among these are

1. improved detection of carrier individuals of abnormal gentic material in live born and fetal populations,

2. intensification of mass genetic screening to obtain sound incidence and prevalence data,

3. evaluation of the importance and implications of genetic screening as a diagnostic tool. (Borgaonkar and Shak, 1970, 348)

Supposing that such research were carried out on a scale which would beyond question pinpoint the role of genetics in governing human mental and social performance, how likely would it be that such information could be converted into programs to control heredity in ways that would, among other things, contribute to the reduction of poverty in the nonmetropolitan South? No one knows the answer to such a question. But this much could be anticipated: an intensely hostile reaction from the poor to any public sponsored program which would openly seek to improve their socio-economic condition by in any way altering their genetic inheritance.

In short, the required research would be very costly and regardless of its results, may not be capable of implementation. Insofar as such research might be publicly sponsored in the hope of finding some answers to why people are poor or remain poor, the investment might be of highly questionable value, to the poor or to the nation.

Chapter 5

ASSESSING THE CULTURE OF POVERTY THESIS

Defining The Term

Anthropologists have a way of approaching the term *culture* as though it were their own personal property. When examining how professionals in other disciplines use the word, they can sometimes be found to exhibit all the resentment of children objecting to the use of their toys by others (Valentine, 1968, Ch. 1). One of the more usual objections is that the term has been reduced to its here and now social interaction components. There is no doubt that culture implies a considerably richer content than conveyed by such a definition; however, for our purposes a parsimonious definition built upon the concept of social interaction —both horizontal and longitudinal dimensions—proves to be both more useful and meaningful.

Rainwater comes close to setting the dimensions of culture in these terms, by defining it as follows:

> Culture is social heredity, transmitted by one generation, learned by another, and shared in the particular collectivity that possesses it. More conceptually, culture is a system of symbols that orders experience and guides behavior (Rainwater, 1969, 240).

Poverty, then, is induced by the culture an individual experiences:

> If an individual lives in a highly deprived environment, he will be taught practices and have expectations that will allow him to adapt to deprivation. Generally, in learning how to *live* in an environment, the individual doesn't learn how to *escape from* it." (H. M. Miller, no date, 3-4)

Intergenerational transmission of poverty is conceived to be the logical end result of this process:

> Incompetence and poverty are interrelated. As a characteristic of individual persons, incompetence results in poverty. And, the poverty of one generation becomes, by virtue of the circumstances which hamper the development of abilities and motives, a basis for the incompetence of the next generation. (J. M. Hunt, 1969, vii)

These views suggest three basic dimensions of a culture of poverty, as follows:

1) Distinct attitudinal-behavioral patterns exhibited at least fairly commonly and consistently in a collectivity which differ from the patterns of the dominant majority in a geographically defined area.
2) Distinct socializing mechanisms in direct social relationships (peer and family) which logically can be tied to the production of behaviors and attitudes noted in item 1.
3) Persistence and preservation of such mechanisms over time to a degree sufficient to guarantee the transmission of poverty predisposing attitudes and behaviors to the next generation of offspring.

Arriving at a working definition this quickly cannot possibly do justice to the virtually limitless academic debate which surrounds the culture of poverty. While it would be worth little to enter this arena, it does seem appropriate to mention, in setting the stage, some of the more enduring conflicts over how the term should be defined and applied.

Common Culture or Isolated Culture

Roach and Gursslin in their evaluation of the concept culture of poverty conclude that it is most descriptive of poverty in isolated groups:

> It would seem, then, that the Culture of Poverty theses would be most relevant for subgroups of the long term poor such as the residents of regional enclaves (e.g. the Appalachian poor) or those living in ethnic and racial enclaves. (Roach and Gursslin, 1967, 389-390)

Oscar Lewis, on the other hand, sees in the concept a culture common to all poor people:

> The culture of poverty transcends regional, rural-urban, and national differences and shows remarkable cross-national similarities in family structure, interpersonal relations, time presentation, value systems, and spending patterns. . . . They are common adaptations to common problems. (O. Lewis, 1969, 187)

> Little seems to be gained from this type of debate, but it is worth noting that this kind of issue absorbs a fair amount of energy in some intellectual circles.

Sub-Culture or Counter-Culture

Another bone of contention is whether the culture of the poor is a spin-off of the dominant culture or a unique culture developed in response to conflict with the dominant culture.

As Valentine has pointed out, the sub-cultural theorists usually conceive the sub-culture to be a negative derivative of the dominant culture; that is, the sub-culture reflects all those features of deviancy defined by the dominant culture (Valentine, 1968, Ch. 6). In any case, sub-cultural theorists view the two cultures as forming a functional unity, having considerable interdependence, each requiring the other to enable continued existence (Yinger, 1960).

Yinger has advanced the concept of counter culture to typify a group whenever its normative system contains

> a theme of conflict with the values of the total society, where personality variables are directly involved in the development and maintenance of the group's values and wherever its norms can be understood only by reference to the relationships of the group to the surrounding dominant culture. (*Ibid.*, 629)

A counter culture would have an integrity of its own, the conflict upon which it is based serving to help the normative system separate from that of the dominant culture and preserve it from modifying influences from the outside.

But whether the culture of poverty is simply the negative side of the dominant culture, or a distinct and separate entity, is of importance only insofar as each view assumes a different process or mechanism as being at the root of poverty. Neither side seems to assert such a distinction. Whether the culture of the poor is determined by the dominant culture and imposed upon them or developed by the poor in resistence to the dominant culture, the socialization processes hypothesized in the literature seem to be quite similar. For our purposes then, this debate has more academic than practical import.

Situation or Culture

There is one challenge to the notion of a culture of poverty which is more compelling, namely, that poverty is situationally rather than culturally induced. The first order assumption required of this point of view is that the poor are more like the non poor than they are different (Yancey, 1965, 1-3). This assumption, in effect, rejects the notion of sub-culture or counter-culture and asserts that all people in a given society hold to the dominant normative system governing behavior (Kriesberg, 1963). Poverty is simply the consequence of the inability to perform as one would like because of situational constraints (Cazden, 1970; Guttentag, 1970a).

Situational hypotheses derive at least in part from observations of the wide variety of persons of differing age, race, sex, and other characteristics who are poor. They appear so heterogeneous in make-up as to defy identifying them as commonly the product of a single type of culture (Mahoney, *et al.*, 1969, 1). Another contribution to the hypothesis derives from laboratory research which has found a variety of behaviors—from mothering techniques to developing relationships with researchers—to be more governed by situational factors than personality factors (J. M. Hunt, 1965; Radin and Glasser, 1965; Van Es and Wilkening, 1970). Yancey has advanced the view that the poor and the middle class do differ behaviorally, the former being more prone to "action seeking," the latter to "routine seeking." Even so, these behavioral differences can be accounted for, he believes, by the differences in environmental situations the two groups encounter. Only a small group of the poor are seen as being so because of cultural influences (Yancey, 1965, 14).

Whether this is so or not, the general conclusion of the view that poverty is situationally caused is that behavior may be immediately modified by modifying the environment—at least for most of the poor. One recent and prominent document on poverty puts it this way:

> The social and psychological problems specifically related to poverty (relationships yet to be proved) would eventually cease to exist if the conditions of poverty were eliminated." (The President's Commission on Income Maintenance Programs, *Background Papers,* 1970, 107)

This conclusion is countered by the theorist of sub-culture, one of whom asserts:

> For the sub-cultures of the very poor, changes in the situation alone are not enough. The values, goods, attitudes, and behavioral styles of many of the lower-lower class individuals appear to interact with the poverty situation in such a way as to make it difficult for them to escape from poverty, even when opportunities for this escape are opened. (Chilman, 1966, 22)

And so it goes. It is impossible to say who is right; and to suggest, as Gans has, that the truth probably lies somewhere in between provides little comfort (Gans, 1969, 206). However these issues are resolved, there is little likelihood that the outcomes will have a major, direct impact upon poverty itself. It seems more prudent to avoid the pitfalls of lengthy debate on such matters and to proceed at once to stipulate what seems to be the major assumption underlying the Culture of Poverty Thesis. Available evidence can then be marshalled to evaluate these assumptions and assess the usefulness of the concept.

Assumptions in the Culture of Poverty Thesis

1. A basic assumption is that poverty is the consequence of socialization through primary (peer and family) social relationships.
2. Secondly, motivation, not intelligence, is conceived to be a basic factor inhibiting socioeconomic success. Contrary to the genetic view, intelligence is not held to be fixed. With proper intervention, both intelligence and motivation are upwardly modifiable.
3. Thirdly, removing opportunity barriers will have little effect, since socialization to a poverty life style would prevent perception and utiliza-

tion of opportunities. Changing environments and providing above poverty level income subsidies would not guarantee that the next generation would think and behave differently than the present generation of the poor.

4. Finally, the root causes of poverty lie within the socialized individual. The elimination of poverty depends upon converting the individual to new ways of thinking, rearing children, and engaging in institutions approved by the dominant culture (e.g. education and vocational training).

What Are the Common Characteristics of the Poor?

What Class Are We Talking About?

Before an attempt can be made to draw out of the literature what are thought to be the common characteristics of the poor, a problem must be contended with about which group of the poor are to be described (Blum and Rossi, 1969, 350 ff.). The so-called customary attitudes and behaviors of the poor may be found to differ radically from expectations depending on which type of group and level of poorness is examined (W. B. Miller, 1959).

Many models differentiating the social classes according to a variety of variables have been constructed following from the early work of Lloyd Warner and his associates. As previously noted, Yancey differentiates according to "action seeking" and "routine seeking" behavior patterns in the lower and middle classes respectively. In recent years, greater emphasis has been placed upon differentiating between strata in the lower class itself. The so-called lower-lower class (Gans, 1969; Rainwater, 1970) has become the designated repository of the very poor, those really in poverty. Distinctions have also been made between the working class poor and those beneath this group who collectively comprise the majority of those with whom poverty theorists are concerned (Keller, 1968; Komarovsky, 1964).

Using class (economic) and status (cultural) variables, Miller has constructed one of the few actual models of lower class strata, as shown in figure 5-1.

Cell 1 represents the regularly employed, low skilled, stable family. Miller interestingly groups most of the rural population in this cell and asserts the children in these families will probably be upwardly mobile. Cell 2 represents the *transitional poor* who have economic security but family instability. Cell 3 includes the copers, a group which increases as a function of unemployment. Here we expect to find large numbers of blacks and the downwardly mobile. Cell 4 represents the *hard core poor,* the physically handicapped and aged, the intergenerational poor white family, and the rural-urban migrant (Miller, 1964).

FIGURE 5-1

Typology of the Lower Class

	Familial Stability	Familial Instability
Economic Security	+ + (1)	+ — (2)
Economic Insecurity	— + (3)	— — (4)

Source: S. M. Miller, "The American Lower Class: A Typological Approach," *Social Research,* XXXI (Spring 1964).

It is possible to fit Miller's typology roughly to the writings of other theorists by suggesting that Cell 1 is basically representative of the working class poor while the other three cells are in varying degrees the more central concerns of poverty theorists and researchers.

While a real service has been done by those who have sought to differentiate socio-economic strata among the poor, similar rigor is not as consistently noticed in the writings of many poverty researchers and theorists. It is often hard to tell whether the attributes being described are those of the working class poor or the hard core poor. Hence, we cannot in all fairness pretend in the discussion to follow to be presenting exclusively the hypothesized attributes of the very poor, the lower-lower class. With that caveat, we can proceed to summarize what the poor are presumed to have and be in common.

Common Attitudes, Values, Beliefs

A variety of terms such as the above are used to categorize the psychological orientations of the poor. Others include ideology and opinions. Following Berelson and Steiner (1964), we prefer to arrange such expressions of psychological states on a continuum ranging from opinions to beliefs. Opinions are transitory, situation and time specific, subject to change with modifications of situation and over time. Beliefs, on the other hand are more durable, deeply seated, and generalizable, that is, consistent over situations. It appears that it is the latter which is of most concern to the Culture of Poverty Thesis since the thesis itself hinges in part on the assumption of constancy in psychological orientations. Indeed, it is possible to visualize a culture of poverty theorist rejecting the evidence on which the situational causal argument rests as being data primarily on the opinions of the poor. Since opinions change with situations, it is quite possible to be led to the false conclusion that the poor are more psychologically flexible and adaptive than they really are.

Rainwater suggests that the enduring and distinctive aspects of the orientations of the poor are now well established:

> About the distinctiveness of the existential perspective of lower class people there is relatively little disagreement. All investigators who have studied lower class groups seem to come up with comparable findings to the general effect that the

lower class world view involves conceptions of the world as a hostile and relatively chaotic place in which one must be careful about trusting others, in which the reward for effort expended is always problematic, in which good intentions net very little. (Rainwater, 1970, 141)

The laundry list of specific attributes within this "general effect" is substantial. Many writers suggest the lower class to be generally characterised by fatalism, belief in luck, apathy, passivity, hopelessness, powerlessness, resignation, present orientedness, defeatism, magical thinking, lack of long range goal commitment, impulse gratification, lack of logical reasoning, poor ego integration, distrust of strangers, new experiences, and helping agency personnel, and projection of blame for failure on others (Herzog, 1966; Gladwin, 1961; E. Gordon, 1970; Chilman, 1966; Thomas and Carter, 1967; Roach and Gursslin, 1967).

Miller adds an unusual list of "six focal concerns," to wit: trouble, toughness, smartness, excitement, fate, and autonomy (W. B. Miller, 1966). And Banfield sums up much of this in concluding that lower class problems stem from a single base:

> . . . the existence of an outlook and style of life which is radically present-oriented and which therefore attaches no value to work, sacrifice, self-improvement, or service to family, friends, or community. (Banfield, 1970, 27)

Behavioral Practices

A variety of distinctive behaviors are held to be consistent with these psychological attributes among the poor. Among the major common behavioral practices are the following:

In the area of sex behavior, the poor are held to date indiscriminately, to enter marriage after brief dating, to be initiated to sex at early ages, to engage heavily in pre-marital and extra-marital sex, to be promiscuous, to enter into free unions frequently, and to have less negative orientations toward illegitimacy (Herzog, 1966; Thomas and Carter, 1967; O. Lewis, 1969).

In marital relations the poor experience higher rates of desertion and separation, and men particularly enter frequently into extra-marital sex and excessive drinking (Thomas and Carter, 1967).

In social relations, the poor are held to be inexperienced in the subtleties of interpersonal relations, unpracticed in middle class role requirements, and as having few friends beyond nuclear and extended family ties, although, somewhat curiously, Oscar Lewis also describes them as somewhat gregarious (Chilman, 1966; O. Lewis, 1966).

In the broader context, the poor are viewed as alienated in that they do not utilize helping agency services to a high degree and exhibit low participation in voluntary agencies and political organizations (Blum and Rossi, 1969; Roach and Gursslin, 1965).

Finally, the poor do not plan or save as family units for the future (Herzog, 1966).

Family Structure and Roles

Taking note of the fact that one fourth of all poor families are fatherless and one third of all children of the poor are being raised in such families (Orshansky, 1965a), it is often stated that the female headed household is a common — if not the most common — family form in the lower class (Thomas and Carter, 1967; Herzog, 1966; O. Lewis, 1969; Chilman, 1966).

Within the lower class, even if the male is present, family decision making rests largely on the shoulders of the woman. Masculine-feminine worlds are rigidly separated, and sex relationships are viewed as being exploitative by women in the lower class (Chilman, 1966). Families engage in very little discussion of problems and the role of the male, when present, is punitive in nature. Considerable distrust between partners is believed to exist, and the free-wheeling behavior of males results in high levels of family disorganization, female self-reliance and hostility towards males (Roach and Gursslin, 1965). These characteristics are commonly exhibited but tend to appear with even greater intensity than expected in the lower class because of the fact that there is a high proportion of teenage marriages which tend to produce or exacerbate these stresses.

Child Rearing Patterns

In general, according to Keller,

> the lower class family, in its current form typically cannot educate its children, cure their ills, provide them with jobs, or effectively control their behavior. The reasons for this are due not only to economic privations suffered by lower class families, but also to the personal and cultural adaptations to these developed over several generations. (Keller, 1968, 5)

The poor are also theorized to short change their children in other ways. For example, Lewis suggests that in lower class life there is no real childhood, that the exigencies of making a living—or indeed surviving—cause the child to move into adult activity at an early age, thus depriving him of an extended and play filled maturation period (O. Lewis, 1969).

Additionally, the children of the poor are seen as being reared in authoritarian ways in a mother-centered environment. Discipline is often harsh, inconsistent, and physical. The child is judged for what he does and rarely are the reasons for what he does examined. Ridicule is often used to silence and control children; yet poor parents view these methods as basically ineffective and experience feelings of impotence over handling their children's behavior. The main objective of parent to child instruction appears to be to "stay out of trouble" (Chilman, 1966; Thomas and Carter, 1967; Keller, 1968; O. Lewis, 1969).

One common end result of this process is higher rates of child neglect and/or abuse among the poor (Thomas and Carter, 1967); and, in Keller's view, an increased probability that children reared in this way will themselves be consigned to a life of poverty.

These then seem to be the major beliefs, behavioral practices, family structures, and child rearing practices held in common by the poor which mutually reinforce one another and comprise the basic components of the so-called lower class life style. Adding the dimension of the intergenerational passage of these beliefs, forms, and practices creates the essence of the culture of poverty.

We are now in a position to review research findings in order to assess whether the culture of poverty exists, how commonly it prevails, and how well it explains the perpetuation of poverty in the rural South.

The Perfunctory Evidence: SES and Behavior

Much of the evidence used—when evidence is used at all—to support the Culture of Poverty Thesis derives from surveys which attempt to measure some facet of psychological or social behavior while controlling for the socio-economic level of those interviewed. As Blum and Rossi note, the poor themselves have not often been the independent subject of such studies, most of the available data being that which is collected on the lowest SES group in the process of studying differences between several socio-economic strata (Blum and Rossi, 1969, 344). Nonetheless, such data have frequently been aggregated in an attempt to present a composite picture of the functioning of the poor.

In the matter of the mental functioning of the poor, several good reviews of the literature are available (Blum and Rossi, 1969; Petras and Curtis, 1968). Blum and Rossi's review shows that the "lower-lowers" tend consistently to demonstrate lower self esteem and lower aspirations than persons in higher socio-economic groups. Lower-lower blacks consistently fall below lower-lower whites in such findings also. Importantly, most of the large-scale studies have been carried out in northern urban areas (Blum and Rossi, 1969, 380-386).

The lowest SES group has also frequently been determined to experience higher rates of serious mental illness (Hollingshead and Redlich, 1958; Turner and Wagenfield, 1967), lower ego integration and tolerance for formal modes of learning (F. Riessman, *et al.*, 1964), and higher rates of mental deficiency or retardation (Hurley, 1969). Occasionally, many of these observations are drawn together as a base for the conclusion that psychiatric and social therapies, not money, are the first order service priorities for the poor (Hutchinson, 1967).

Health, utilization of health services, and health practices has been another area of considerable investigation among the lower-lower socio-economic group. Data on differences in health between various socio-economic strata have been brought together recently by Lerner. His review shows that the poor are consistently worse off in all measures of health from infant mortality to dental morbidity (Lerner, 1969, 69-102).

Rosenstock's review of studies on preventative health practices (e.g. tooth brushing) and utilization of health services also shows small but nonetheless consistent differences in practices and rates between the various socio-economic strata. Again, the poor do consistently—if slightly—less well in these matters (Rosenstock, 1969, 168-190).

Pratt interviewed 401 mothers with children aged 9 to 13, living with their husbands in a northern New Jersey city to determine differences in health practices, controlling for SES. While she did not find significant differences in overall health or health practices between the various socio-economic groups, she did find that the poor differed significantly in taking less exercise, having poorer nutrition, and having poorer dental hygiene (Pratt, 1971, 381-291).

Other studies and reviews of the literature tend to suggest that differences in health matters may at least in part be traceable to the poor somatizing their psychological states. Blum and Rossi, for example, conclude from the available evidence that the lower class tends to be more conscious and fearful of physical disorders (Blum and Rossi, 1969). Pomeroy's recent study of health practices among welfare clients in New York City led him to conclude that high levels of anxiety over social, economic, and family problems, may also be converted to or represented as physical problems more often by the poor. They may perform in this manner in an effort to locate an objective source for their vague and nameless worries (Pomeroy, 1969, 96-97; David, 1964, 255).

Finally a wealth of studies have been produced which tend to show that the lower socio-economic group differs from those above it in such matters as high illiteracy rates, low levels of social organization, more consensual marriages, greater feelings of inferiority, and a greater propensity toward authoritarianism (U.S.D.H.E.W., P.H.S., N.I.C.H.H.D., 1968, 192).

Aggregating these kinds of data to support the Culture of Poverty Thesis and conclusions about the kinds of remedies needed is faulty on at least two important counts. First, as Blum and Rossi note, to do so lends the impression that all the poor are commonly afflicted with all the shortcomings found in various studies. Such an impression is unfortunate since little or no work has been done to test the interrelationships between these various characteristics within a large and scientifically representative sample of poor people. Until such studies are done—and presuming they will confirm the assumption of strong inter-relationships—the method of constructing composite pictures of the poor from disparate findings remains a highly questionable practice (Blum and Rossi, 1969, 353).

Secondly, almost all such studies are one-shot or cross sectional surveys. Few of these studies employ designs that allow for longitudinal analysis of the continuity of the relationship between SES and certain behaviors. Without longitudinal tests of the continuity of such behaviors among the poor, even valid cross-sectional data showing strong interrelationships among several behaviors would be inadequate to the testing of the Culture of Poverty Thesis:

> What makes the culture of poverty unique is not simply the concentration of these characteristics among the poor, but in addition and perhaps more importantly, the fact that these behavior patterns are rational responses to the condition of deprivation, are part of their life style, and are handed down through generations. The degradation, continuity, and segregation of the poor serve to identify them as a separate culture (U.S.D.H.E.W., P.H.S., N.I.C.H.H.D., 1968, 192)

At the very least "cultural poverty" must imply that "many features of lower-lower life are passed on generation to generation forming a 'culture' (or subculture) of poverty" (Blum and Rossi, 1969, 353).

Kriesberg, recognizing some of these inadequacies in the present literature on the culture of poverty, has attempted to draw together data from several studies done over a span of years in a way which would test time trends—or levels of consistency—in the behavior and views of the poor (Kriesberg, 1963). He gathered data from studies on voting behavior, educational preferences, and medical and dental—or health—practices, which have controlled for SES level. Comparing findings from studies done on similar subject matter but at different times, Kriesberg concluded that for the most part the behaviors and views of the poor have changed over the last several decades as situations changed. Only in the matter of educational preferences has there been a measure of consistency over time and this consistency Kriesberg takes as partial evidence that cultural influences are operating in the formation of views toward education.

But the studies he utilizes to produce these conclusions are themselves of highly questionable value. For example, he suggests that political party affiliation is well known to be associated with SES level: the rich are Republicans, the poor Democrats. Also, it is "well known" that party affiliation, being highly visable to others, is subject to being influenced by those one associates with socially and in the type of work he does. Hence, the upwardly mobile poor person can be expected to change his politics as his socio-economic position improves (Kriesberg, 1963, 339 ff.).

The evidence here is shaky and Kriesberg's generalizations about the poor are open to question. He might have profited from Verba's well documented analysis of the effects of family socialization on political behavior. For example, Verba shows that in France at least, families which have a Communist orientation prove to have a very strong and continuing influence on the political preferences of their children well into adulthood (Verba, 1961). Nothing in the Kriesberg data, in short, disproves the possibility that the upwardly mobile (or downwardly mobile) poor changed their politics. It is possible to conceive that the type of family socialization which produces upward mobility also inculcates certain types of political beliefs simultaneously.

Similar arguments can be marshalled in interpreting the studies of trends in medical-dental practices and utilization. The studies utilized by Kriesberg all control by income level and show over time that, as opportunities for health care have increased, practices have improved (Kriesberg, 1963, 345 ff.). Such findings do not refute cultural influences. It is possible to reason that the poor were acculturated toward better health care and that increased opportunities simply allowed them to exercise their preferences.

On the other hand, Kriesberg's data show that even though opportunities for higher education have increased radically over the last several years, the poor have not increased percentage-wise in their preferences for higher education as reflected in the preferences of high school aged children of the poor (Kriesberg, 1963, 344).

Because of the plausibility of alternate explanations, Kriesberg's general conclusion that much of the behavior of the poor is situationally rather than culturally induced cannot be taken seriously. A more important objection to such conclusions can be made on methodological grounds. Much of the data Kriesberg uses is opinion data, data on preferences. As previously suggested, it is precisely opinion data which is most likely to show fluctuations in response to situational changes. Hence, to conclude that such time trends actually show fundamental changes in the views and behaviors of the poor is questionable at best.

But Kriesberg is to be applauded for at least making a beginning at longitudinal tests of the Culture of Poverty Thesis. To some extent his work escapes the general criticism of the literature on the relationship between SES and various behaviors, as stated by Blum and Rossi:

> Most of the writers have been so impressed with the finding that socio-economic position (no matter how measured) is associated with a variety of dependent variables that they generally have not taken the further steps of assessing the strength or degrees of relationship in attempting to explain why such relationships are found. Furthermore, . . . most social scientists typically regard such findings as ultimate explanations requiring little further exploration. (Blum and Rossi, 1969, 348)

It is tempting to let the force of this presentation carry over into a ringing conclusion that studies of the relationship between SES and various behaviors are of no use as a test of the Culture of Poverty Thesis. This would be an over simplification. It is perhaps better to consider this material as a starting point, prefunctory evidence, upon which more definitive analyses can build. Generalizations built on aggregating data from SES studies at best are premature; at worst they represent just plain sloppy reasoning.

The Nature of the Evidence: Aspiration of the Poor and Southern Poor

The psychological orientations of the poor most crucial to the Culture of Poverty Thesis are those which might logically contribute directly to the degree of desire for upward mobility the poor exhibit. Drawing upon Allen's review of the literature on the personality correlates of poverty, it seems that the evidence we are after relates to the aspiration levels of the poor and how they are affected by or related to their time orientations (immediacy of need gratification) and their estimates of how much they believe they can do personally to fulfill their aspirations (fate control-self esteem). A lot of ten dollar words are used to label these orientations, but the basic questions have to do with whether the poor have long-range lofty goals; whether they are willing to delay gratification, and whether they believe their own efforts will make a meaningful contribution to long-term goal fulfillment or not (V. L. Allen, 1970a).

The Culture of Poverty Thesis would predict the poor to demonstrate low aspirations, impulse gratification and fatalism. Further it would predict intergenerational passage of these orientations and/or their continuation even if environment were to be radically altered as in the case of the migration of the rural poor to the cities. What is the evidence favoring these predictions?

Achievement Orientations

Although achievement orientation is widely discussed as a basic factor in the poor remaining poor, few studies are available which have actually attempted to measure the relationship between SES and achievement motivation (Blum and Rossi, 1969, 374). More frequently, level of achievement motivation—or need achievement and similar terms—is inferred from findings on educational and occupational preferences, controlling for SES level.

Hyman, for example, uses evidence from a 1947 NORC opinion survey on values toward higher education and a 1945 Roper study on parents' desires for their children's educations to demonstrate that educational aspirational levels differ between the various social classes (Hyman, 1953; also see: Roach and Gursslin, 1965). On the other hand clinical observations have been used as a base for concluding that aspiration levels between the poor and nonpoor do not differ, at least in terms of their broad perspectives (Gottlieb, 1967).

Delayed Gratifications and Fate Control

The data often used to infer that the poor are much more impulsive and defeatist also merit some attention (W. B. Miller, 1966). Loosely controlling for SES levels, some authors take the fact that the poor save less and exhibit more "impulsive" buying habits as evidence of impulse gratification (Schneider and Lysgaard, 1953). Others, leaning more heavily again on the relationship between SES level and educational aspirations, school drop-out rates, and so on, come to similar conclusions (Trahan, 1958; M. A. Straus, 1962; Le Shan, 1952).

In the matter of fate control—or sense of independence and self command—a variety of studies have sought to document the defeatism level of the poor by administering various tests or questions to children representing hypothetical situations to which the children are supposed to respond. The level of initiative represented in the responses tends to consistently show lower class children to express less feeling of mastery over their own environs (Battle and Rotter, 1963; Crandell, *et al.*, 1965; Goodman, in Irelan, 1966).

Race and Aspirations

When race is controlled for, as it has been in several of the studies with children regarding fate control, blacks generally are interpreted as doing less well than whites (Mingione, 1965). By utilizing the by now familiar test of SES and educational preferences, it has been found that blacks also differ among themselves in aspirations depending on whether they are at middle or lower income levels. Gittell's study in New York City disclosed that 43 percent of low income blacks had low aspirations compared to 27 percent in the middle income group, as reflected in their educational expectations for their children (1965).

Others argue that race is not really a factor in the noted differences in aspiration levels between the races. Schneiderman argues, on the basis of a study of 35 public welfare families in Minnesota who were almost white, that these welfare clients show the same low aspiration patterns as low income persons of other races, as measured by the Kluchholm value scales.

In noting that 28 of the 35 parents had been themselves raised in homes supported by public welfare, Schneiderman suggests that a culture of poverty actually exists, chief components of which are low aspirations, impulse gratification, and defeatism, regardless of race (Schneiderman, 1964). Henderson takes a somewhat different tact in suggesting that the mass media have had a leveling effect in recent years on the aspirations of differing races and social classes (G. Henderson, 1966). Finally, Garza attempts to explain aspiration differences between the races in terms of differences in perceived opportunity. Some blacks, perceiving that opportunities are simply not open to them, revise and perhaps scale down their aspirations accordingly (Garza, 1969).

Recognizing that the conclusions on aspirations by class and race are basically inferred rather than derived from actual tests, Rosen undertook two studies in the middle 50's to get to the heart of the matter. In both studies he controlled for SES by utilizing the Hollingshead Index (three factors in the New Haven Study, 2 factors in the Northeastern Study) and tested orientations by utilizing the form of the Thematic Apperception Test (TAT) developed by McClelland to test achievement motivations. Additionally, he utilized a variant of the Kluckholm scales to measure delayed gratification (time orientation) and fate control (individualism).

In the first study Rosen arranged the entire male populations of two New Haven high schools into SES groupings and then took random samples of the 5 groups thus derived (N=120). Analysis of the findings disclosed that the upper SES boys (Classes I and II) were higher on the values of delayed gratification and individualism than lower SES boys. Seventy-seven percent of the higher SES's scored high on these values compared to 33 percent in Class IV and 17 percent in Class V (30 boys in each collapsed comparison group). He also found that grades were associated with achievement motivation: 79 percent of the "B or above" group were high in achievement motivation while only 18 percent of the "C or below" group placed in this bracket. Importantly, Rosen found very little relationship between achievement motivation and preference for college education: 51 percent of those high in achievement motivation wanted to go to college compared to 46 percent of those low in achievement motivation (Rosen, 1956a). This finding clearly calls into question much of the past work which infers motivation from the observed relationship between SES and preferences for higher education.

Rosen's second study applied similar methodology to 427 pairs of mothers having sons between the age of 8 and 14 who resided in 62 urban areas of 4 Northeastern states. Additionally, he categorized subjects by racial/ethnic origins. He found what he considered to be important (by chi square tests of significance) differences in achievement motivation and other values between the various ethnic/racial groupings. In the two tables that follow, higher mean scores reflect higher achievement motivation and greater activity (future time and individualism) orientations respectively.

Rosen observes that the data demonstrate relatively consistent differences between ethnic groups across social classes and a general decline in means across all ethnic groups as SES drops. On this basis he concludes that the evidence is firm that ethnic-social class factors combine to form differing cultural milieus which produce children of distinctly different achievement and broader value orientations (Rosen, 1956b).

While this seems to be rather substantial evidence in support of some aspects of the Culture of Poverty Thesis, it should be noted in closing that the debate has not subsided. More recently, Morgan, *et al.,* have concluded that achievement motivation is highly correlated with family income level (1962, 92), while Barnett, utilizing Rosen's scales for achievement motivation found such motivation levels unrelated to income level in his sample (1970).

In sum, then, the "evidence" on the aspiration levels of the poor is more inferential than direct. The best of the lot, Rosen's work, remains open to question since a partial replication did not fully confirm his findings.

TABLE 5-1

Mean Achievement Motivation Scores, by Ethnicity and Social Class

Ethnicity	Social Class I-II	III	IV	V	N
French-Canadian	10.0*	10.6	8.8	7.6	62
Italian	8.9	12.8	7.5	10.2	74
Greek	9.2	12.1	10.4	8.8	47
Jew	10.1	10.4	10.9	11.2	57
Negro	11.4	9.0	8.2	6.7	65
White Protestant	11.7	10.9	9.4	7.3	122

*Means have been rounded for clarity of presentation in both tables.

Source: B. C. Rosen, "Race, Ethnicity, and the Achievement Syndrome," *American Sociological Review* XXI (1956b), 219, Table 2.

TABLE 5-2

Summed Mean Value Scores (Activity-Future Time Individualism), by Ethnicity and Social Class

Ethnicity	Social Class I-II	III	IV	V	N
French-Canadian	4.0	4.2	4.6	2.5	62
Italian	5.9	4.0	4.0	3.4	74
Greek	6.3	5.5	4.8	3.3	47
Jew	5.4	5.5	5.4	4.8	57
Negro	6.0	5.0	4.9	4.7	65
White Protestant	5.9	5.5	5.0	3.5	122

Source: B. C. Rosen, 1956b; 223, Table 3.

Aspirations of the Rural Southern Poor

In concert with Blum and Rossi's previous observation, Slocum has concluded from his review of the research literature that few studies of the relationship between SES and aspirations have been done with rural people (1967). One that was done in rural Wisconsin found no significant differences in occupational aspirations of farm-nonfarm males or females. Differences were slight for males on educational aspirations but not farm-nonfarm females. The poor were not, however, specifically studied in this piece of research (Haller and Sewell, 1957).

One of the more important lines of study on the rural poor is that which has sought to assess how rural life styles contribute to the perpetuation of poverty. In recent years, for example, a series of participant observation reports have discussed how holding to learned farming methods among the rural poor inhibits their acceptance of technological advances which would enable them to move from subsistence to commercial farming (Ford, 1965; Metzler, 1959; Ramsey, *et al.,* 1959).

Ayers has also concluded that the values the rural poor learn as they grow up inhibit their chances of accepting the changes in their personal lives necessary to successful vocational rehabilitation. Among other tests, he administered parts of the MMPI to a random sample of 300 rural poor drawn from a rural area population of 62,000. The results indicated that the rural poor reflected high levels of depression and "high covert preference for matriarchy," but were not as fatalistic as expected. Nonetheless, he concludes that the only plausible solution is to remove bodily the rural poor from their environments long enough to break their neurotic expectation patterns (Ayers, 1967).

Bryan and Bertrand, in their study of several hundred rural families in the Mississippi Delta, on the other hand, conclude that inability to accept innovation and personal change is a selective, rather general characteristic of the rural Southern poor. Their findings suggest to them that ability to accept change required for upward mobility is highest among blacks, small families, and those who are younger and better educated (Byran and Bertrand, 1970).

Two specific features of the rural person's psychological orientations have come in for more than passing comment: their treasured values about independence and individualism, and their religious orientations.

On the matter of values about individualism, most commentary has been directed toward the Appalachian poor white, although similar belief patterns are reputed to exist among other socially isolated rural populations, such as farmers in Wyoming and the Latter Day Saints in Utah (C. L. Anderson, 1965). The conclusion of these observers is generally that those rural poor who staunchly believe in individualism are contributing in real ways to the perpetuation of their own poverty. This is so because such beliefs dictate that when one needs help, he relies only on familiar others—friends and kin. They will likely be the least able to help since they also will likely be poor and poorly educated (Thomas and Carter, 1967; Dunkelberger, 1965; Kentucky Department of Education, Bureau of Rehabilitation Services, 1969).

Fundamentalist religious beliefs also may contribute to the perpetuation of poverty by reducing the rural person's level of aspiration for the acquisition of "worldly goods" (B. H. Kaplan, 1965).

Hofley's analysis of data gathered by the North Carolina Fund shows that among rural Southern residents, those with below $4,000 in income and less than 9th-grade educations tend to be high in fatalism and fundamentalist religious beliefs (Hofley, 1969).

Another way to infer the aspiration levels of the rural Southern poor is by examining and interpreting migration data. Rubin's follow up analysis of migration patterns among 114 rural poor blacks who originated in northern Mississippi moved him to conclude that respondents generally relocate in an attempt to fulfill their aspirations for a better way of life (Rubin, 1960).

Others would argue that such a general conclusion is unwarranted because migration itself is selective. For one thing, it seems that the longer a person resides in a given locality and the older he is, the less likely he is to move regardless of his other predispositions (Morrison, 1967). For another, only the more vigorous and capable seem to migrate. Marckwardt's analysis of a 1/1000 sample from the 1960 census of population indicated that migrants were generally younger, better educated, and of higher occupational status and income than nonmigrants (1968).

Further support for the thesis of selective migration and another dimension of the process bearing on the Culture of Poverty Thesis is added by the continuing studies of migration patterns among people originating in rural eastern Kentucky by Schwarzweller and his associates.

In an earlier study which followed up 20 years later on the migration patterns of people who resided in rural eastern Kentucky in 1942, the authors found that a powerful factor in such patterns were kin and friends who had moved to new locations. The researchers concluded that what often occurs is the development of "branch families" in new localities to assist immigrant kin in adjusting to the new environment upon arrival (Brown, *et al.,* 1963). This finding, if generalizable, is quite interesting because it proves the possibility that the rural poor are carrying their culture with them to the cities and developing socially viable structures to at least temporarily preserve it.

A further analysis of virtually the same data some years later allows for more refined conclusions. In this study the authors controlled for SES level among the outmigrant group and discovered that those in the higher SES group moved out earlier, settled away more permanantly (i.e., fewer ever returned even to temporarily relocate in their areas of origin), and most were found to have moved to small towns. In contrast, the lower SES group was found to be the group which most followed the pattern of forming branch families. They most often moved to the larger cities of Cincinnati and Dayton and formed "little Kentuckys" in sections of these cities (Schwarzweller and Brown, 1967). These results even more clearly suggest that some groups of the rural Southern poor—in this case whites—transport their culture with them when they migrate. Such findings also warn against any general conclusion that migration is a simple indicator of the existence of high aspirations among the rural Southern poor.

Another source of data on the aspirations of rural people exists in studies which have undertaken to assess the occupational and educational preferences of rural youth, and their parents' preferences for them.

Earlier studies of the psychological orientations of rural youth were often more concerned with personality measurement than they were achievement motivations. Very often such studies revealed no significant differences between urban and rural youth. Typical of this genre is Smith's evaluation of 150 11th- and 12th-grade urban and rural black youths in North Carolina in 1957. He concludes on the basis of results from the Test of Personality that the groups do not differ on the important dimensions of "sense of personal freedom," but that both groups fall below the established norms for this part of the test (P. M. Smith, 1961).

Nelsen and Storey applied the Mooney Check List to 245 9th-grade boys in two adjacent Kentucky counties in 1968 to further measure rural-urban differences. The sample was roughly 20 percent rural, 13 percent town, and 67 percent urban in residence. Their results indicate vaguely that rural boys experience considerably more personality maladjustment and that this may be traced to the poverty such youth experience as they grow up (Nelsen and Storey, 1969).

More to the point, Haller and Ellis undertook to assess the relationship between SES and aspiration levels among 442 17-year-old boys from farm, rural non-farm, village, and small urban locations in Michigan in 1957. The researchers administered the Cattel 16 Personality-Factor Test, Culture Free IQ test, and California Test of Personality in addition to work belief and occupational aspirations scales. The findings indicated farm boys score lowest in occupational and educational aspirations and tend to believe man has little control over events (fatalism). In contrast, urban boys scored highest in aspirations and demonstrated a strong belief in man's ability to control events—fate control (Haller and Ellis, 1962). Some similar findings have also been reported by Burchinal (1961) and others (Middleton and Grigg, 1959).

These are "classic" findings quite consistent with the expectations of the Culture of Poverty thesis. Since they seem to consistently show up more among rural than urban youth, the very tentative conclusion would be that the thesis may have more explanatory power for rural than urban poverty.

Yet, to say the least, such a conclusion would be premature. The effects in this case may be as selective as migration effects. The previous findings, for example, tend to show that rural youth have lower aspirations than urban youth, that this is most pronounced among farm boys and blacks.

Consistent with these observations are the findings that farmers have lower aspirations for their children than men in other professions, for their daughters (Burchinal, 1960), as well as their sons (David, *et al.,* 1961). Moreover, Schwarzweller has found that mothers—particularly those who do not work out of the home (and this might include many farm families)—exercise a disproportionate influence on the aspirations of rural youth. Differences in urban youths' aspirations may at least in part stem from greater freedom from parental influence and the actuality of more concrete career alternatives (Schwarzweller, 1959).

In any case, when one shifts away from a preoccupation with farm youth toward a broader evaluation of rural youth in general, the closeness of the aspirational ties between parents and youth seems to evaporate: results of several investigations tend to show that lower-class youths in rural areas are unwilling to enter the same occupations as their fathers (Emprey, 1956; Folkman and Cowhig, 1963); and Mole's data, cited in Chapter 6, indicate that as many as 50 to 70 percent of rural males—black and white—actually succeed in occupationally surpassing their fathers (Moles, 1970).

Sustaining Family and Social Structure: The Poor and the Rural Southern Poor

The Culture of Poverty Thesis holds that the psychological orientations of the poor—their low aspirations, high impulse gratification, and high dependency—are the enduring and inevitable outcomes of unique family and social structures which nourish and sustain them. The poor do not conform to any neat stereotype in these matters and neither do theorists who attempt to link poverty with family functioning. Some try to identify the debilitating factors in family and social functioning unique and seemingly common to all the poor, others concentrate on the one-parent family, and still others focus specifically on the one-parent black family. All nonetheless seek to evaluate the relationship between family and social structure and functioning and the perpetuation of poverty.

The two-parent poor family is viewed typically as a rather bleak and sterile construct. Relationships between partners are conceived to lack meaningful interaction, to be comprised of rigidly defined sex and parental roles which tend to be exploitative in nature. The parental role models from which the children of the poor learn thus tend to be one-sided or distorted. The father is portrayed as an impersonal and arbitrarily punitive authoritarian, the mother as hostile and wily in her relations with her spouse and domineering in her dictatorial control of her children (Chilman, 1966; Bresner, 1965).

Importantly, these writers and others see such consequences in marriage as the result of socialization patterns which produce many early marriages among immature people following casual, impersonal, brief and "fatalistic" courting (Handel and Rainwater, 1961, 18ff.; Rainwater, 1960, 61-63). The "poverty cycle" is completed, according to Aldous and Hill, when the adolescent coming out of such an environment is thrown into adult roles for which he or she has had inadequate preparation. They conclude that

> it is probably at this point in the family cycle that parental poverty patterns are most likely to be transmitted to the next generation. (Aldous and Hill, 1969, 9-10).

Among the poor, peer pressures are reasoned to contribute as much or more than lack of parental guidance to the inadequate preparation of adolescents for adult marital and parental roles. Group cohesiveness fostered by ethnic and racial identification factors—particularly among the non-mobile poor—is conceived to be a powerful socializing instrument, powerful enough to often override the characteristics of nuclear family units (Guttentag, 1970a).

The influence of peer associations on the socialization of adolescents in poverty is conceived to be more pervasive and enduring than is the case for adolescents in better off families. The lower class family is seen as losing its children at an earlier stage to the socializing influences of peer groups (H. Lewis, 1966), and it has been observed that the poor continue to maintain such associations even after marriage and well into adulthood (Besner, 1965; Cohen and Hodges, 1963).

Some of the reasons why peer group associations take on such importance in the socialization of the poor have been suggested to relate to their absence of participation in formally organized social activities and organizations (Dotson, 1951) and their minimal social associations even among themselves at the community level (Wright and Hyman, 1958), stemming at least in part from their reluctance to engage in relationships beyond the limits of their own environs and nuclear family (L. Reissman, 1954).

All of this works to thrust the adolescent into the company of his own age group depriving him of contact with adult role models and preventing him from maturing beyond the values and concerns of adolescence. Intense concerns with sexual identity and verility, toughness, smartness, and avoidance of intense social relationships which would threaten encroachment on personal freedom are thereby carried into marriage and adulthood. Thus, even if parental role models are conceived to be adequate, they are viewed as being incapable of competing with the attractions of peer group associations.

Again, the counterargument can be raised that what has been described here either doesn't apply commonly to poor families or that they may be expectable reactions to low incomes rather than the outcomes of cultural factors.

Hylan Lewis' more-or-less case analysis approach to 39 low-income families in Washington, D. C., for example, led him to conclude that there is a wide variety of life style adaptations to poverty as reflected in marital relations, child rearing, and aspiration levels in his sample. Among the many problems in this study which weaken its value, however, are the vague definition of a low-income family (a working man's budget for a family of 4) and the failure to identify the families studied as two-parent, one-parent, or a percentage mix in structure (H. Lewis, 1963). In this case, the evidence against a Culture of Poverty is as weak as the evidence favoring it.

Stone and Schlamp, attempting to study psychosocial factors linked to family poverty in a group of about 1,000 families on public welfare in California, came to the stunning conclusion that it is often impossible to tell whether long-term assistance cases behave as they do because of lack of money or because of past socialization (Stone and Schlamp, 1965). Such indeterminate findings often characterize the conclusions of available studies focusing on the public assistance family. In their present state such studies shed little light on factors contributing to public assistance status.

The One-Parent Family

In recent years considerable interest has emerged in one-parent poor families. Many writers have taken the time to analyse the separation, divorce, desertion, and unmarried mother rates among lower income households (Blau and Duncan, 1967, 331; Goode, 1951 and 1962; Epstein, 1961; Chilman and Sussman, 1964; Jones, *et al.,* 1962, 224-230; Herzog and Sudia, 1968). From these data it is frequently implied that the one-parent family is the model type among the very poor, and that the one-parent family is the principle carrier of the culture of poverty. Such inferences have been made often enough to stimulate at least a little research on the matter.

Duncan and Duncan, for example, found to their satisfaction that men who grew up in broken families were no more likely to be living apart from their families or to be unmarried than those who did not (Duncan and Duncan, 1969). Broken families do not breed broken families according to these findings.

On the other hand, a study aimed at identifying family competence compared the school performance of children in 65 families — 40 one-parent AFDC and 25 two-parent moderate income families. Children from two-parent families clearly outdistanced AFDC children in aspirations and performance. The report concludes:

> The most competent families in the school project tended to be intact families with good relations between parents, reasonably good communication among family members, a sense of family solidarity, and a real investment of the parents in the children's development. (Community Service Society of New York, 1969, 28)

It further observed on the basis of a review of parental histories that level of mothers' affection was a key variable, and that the model environment could be described as

> a home free of gross pathology in which basic adult roles were at least moderately well defined and appropriate, and responsibilities of the children were suited to their age. [Such factors provide] an opportunity for role learning and for the acquisition of practical and interpersonal skills. (*Ibid.*)

Kriesberg's is perhaps the most thorough-going research on the one-parent poor family yet reported in the literature. His review of the literature on the one-parent family reveals how varied in structure, roles, behavioral practices, and aspiration levels the one-parent family is. His analysis of a group of such families in a northern urban area further indicated to him that the level of mothers' affection for their children was not diminished by the absence of the father and that many of the behavioral manifestations attributed to one-parent structures may be more attributable to other economic and social factors than inadequate family role performance (Kriesberg, 1970). Elsewhere, Kriesberg has reported that unmarried mothers in his studies actually expressed more concern with educational achievement than those who were married. Again, he cites behavioral deviance from these verbal expressions of aspirations as being situationally induced (Kriesberg, 1967).

The general evidence on the one-parent family as the principal carrier of the culture of poverty is sketchy at best. More is revealed about such families by examining the extensive literature on the one-parent poor black family. In doing so, however, it is well to keep in mind that the one-parent variable is being compounded by the introduction of the racial variable.

The One-Parent Black Family

Statistical reports on the rates of divorce, separation, desertion, and unmarried mothers among blacks are as common as other reports previously cited which generally linked such outcomes with poverty. Typically, such reports show that blacks exceed whites on all these measures (Monahan, 1960; Dreger and Miller, 1960). On the other hand, several writers have interpreted similar statistical tabulations as reflecting more of an income than a racial factor in rates of marital breakdown (Jones, *et al.*, 1962; Lefcowitz, 1965).

Whether the black family—one- or two-parent—is matriarchal or mother-centered, has long been a controversial topic (Pettigrew, 1964). Frazier's earlier work traces matriarchy back to the black's history of slavery in the U. S. (Frazier, 1950; Frazier, 1966). Hylan Lewis has insisted that even if such accounts were accurate, changes in black families in recent times have altered the degree and nature of the black mother's importance (H. Lewis, 1960).

In the last few years the controversy over matriarchy in black families has taken on new impetus. Moynihan sounded an ominous note by asserting that his data on the relationship between black male unemployment and broken families indicated that the phenomenon of broken families seemed to be taking on a life of its own—that, in short, broken families seemed to be transmitted intergenerationally independent of rises or falls in male employment (Moynihan, 1965). Criticism of Moynihan's analysis was almost immediate (Rainwater and Yancey, 1967). One tact taken was to marshall data which tended to show that degree of matriarchy tended to be more a consequence of class than racial factors. The sex of the parent who rules the family roost is contended to be more a function of parental, occupational, educational, and other background features than a function of racially related historical factors (Herzog, 1967; Mack, 1971).

Billingsley's studies of lower-class black families in urban areas tend toward a similar line of reasoning. In one study of 40 white and 40 black low income female headed families, he found that 38 percent of the whites and only 13 percent of the black mothers "abused" their children. In another, he reports that among 316 low income two-parent black families, 48 percent of the couples said they shared in major decisions. Both studies suggest to Billingsley that the black mother is less domineering than matriarchal concepts would indicate (Billingsley, 1969).

Wasserman's study compared interview data on 55 two-parent and 62 father-absent black families. He found that the personal histories of the mothers in the two groups showed no startling differences nor did the school performance of boys in the families. The women differed on only one point, perhaps a significant one: women who had been raised in two-parent homes were more likely to have a husband present. In spite of this, Wasserman concludes that there is no evidence that fatherless black families are inherently unstable (Wasserman, 1968).

Shulz carried his investigation of fatherless low income black families a step further by analyzing in depth 10 families through the participant observation method. He found that such families have a high degree of contact with adult males, who, depending on their relationship with the mothers, function in father-like roles. Although his sample is small, he develops an interesting typology of male relationships in low income families, as shown in Figure 5-2.

The interesting possibility here is that, according to Shulz, the male's authority in child rearing and other matters increases as a function of his role involvement or investment, not simply as a function of legal status and/or economic support as is often believed (Shulz, 1968). If this typology proves a reflection of reality, the concept of matriarchy is in for substantial revision.

Willie in a sense sums up the evidence against black family matriarchy by citing the fact that over 90 percent of adult black men in the labor force are working to support families, 70 percent of all black families have two parents, and 60 percent of all black children grow up in two-parent homes (Willie, 1970).

Yet, what Willie clearly intends here is to show simply that it would be inaccurate to apply the concept of matriarchy generally to most or all black families. His own data deriving from a study of 92 problem and stable black families in a Syracuse housing project attempts to isolate the characteristics of families which might and might not properly be defined as matriarchal and/or unstable. It was found that 20 percent of the problem family heads had multiple marriages, 39 percent had been married before the age of 19, 10 to 15 percent had illegitimate children, and, generally, problem families averaged 3.9 children compared to 2.7 in stable families. While Willie rejects the argument that the low income single-parent black family differs because it is heavily matriarchal, he does conclude that unstable or problem families in his sample differ so much from stable families that the difference may constitute "one of kind rather than one of degree" (Willie and Weinandy, 1963, 443).

Opinions differ on how matriarchal the one-parent —or two-parent—black family is. Indeed, a series of small studies suggest that—married or not—the black

Figure 5-2

A Typology of Male Relationships in Low Income Families

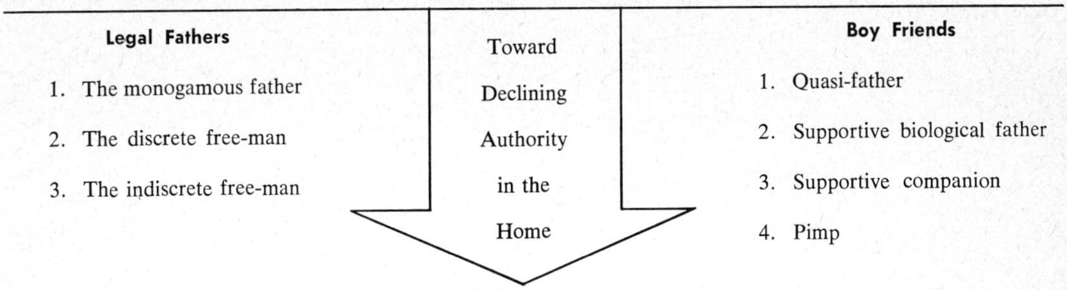

Source: D. A. Shulz, "Variations in Complete and Incomplete Families of the Negro Lower Class," Doctoral Dissertation, Washington University of St. Louis, 1968.

male may play a larger role than is often suggested. Finally, conclusions in many of these same studies vary on whether one-parent families are necessarily harmful to the socialization of children raised in them, the claim that negative socialization consequences commonly derive from being raised in one-parent matriarchal homes notwithstanding.

It would be nice to have a rigorously designed large-scale study of the poor black family which would be capable of clearing the air. Sadly, none seems to be available:

> A study of the structure and function of the Negro family in the U. S., to the best of our knowledge, has not been published (Blum and Rossi, 1969, 348-49).

The Rural Southern Poor Family

The rural South* has its share of female headed households, according to the 1960 census. These data indicate that the rural South had a larger proportion of such families at that time living in poverty regardless of race than the nation as a whole. For the nation as a whole, about 57 percent of all white female headed families were poor compared to 81 percent of non white female headed families, while about 75 percent of all female headed white families were in poverty** in the rural South compared to over 90 percent of none-white families of the same type (U.S.D.C., B. of C., Census of Population, Volume 8, 18, Table 1).

These figures do not, of course, indicate the proportion of "broken families" in the rural South, but the relatively high percentage of such families who are poor, particularly among non whites, gives some indication that many such families face severe problems. Moreover, if we recall data from Chapter 2 showing that state illegitimacy rates in the region are keeping pace with the national average, we can fairly arrive at a conclusion that a goodly number of such households fall into the "broken family" category. More recent data gathered in the state of Georgia give substance to the suspicion that the proportion of such families has not been declining in recent years. Early child-bearing is considered a major factor in subsequent broken marriages, and in Georgia in 1969, almost 21,000 babies were born to teenage mothers, a fifth of whom were illegitimate (C. L. Johnson, 1971, 8).

Parenthetically, Goode some years ago advanced a theory claiming to show why rural rates of illegitimacy should be higher than urban rates. In the U. S. he drew attention to such rates among blacks in the rural South. His view was that cultural breakdown in rural areas deriving from the western world's march toward urbanization is a prime contributer to illegitimacy. When he observed in his data, however, that illegitimacy rates among urban and rural blacks in the South were roughly equivalent in 1957, he neatly concluded that this was so because the black in the U. S. does not become culturally integrated in urban areas as one would expect, because of racial segregation (Goode, 1961).

About the most that can be said from these skimpy and ancient data is that the rural South embodies a large number of female headed households, a goodly number who are poor; that illegitimacy and early childbirth may be of significance to both the number of female headed households and the proportion in poverty; and that incidence rates in all these matters are more pronounced for blacks.

But whether the one-parent family is the principle carrier of the culture of poverty seems no more answerable from the existing evidence for the rural Southern family than those in the urban North. If we turn to the wider social environs in search of socializing influences which may contribute to poverty, we can detect what researchers commonly find to be distinct fea-

*Comprised of 16 Southern states.

**"Poor" is defined here as family income below $3,000 per year in 1959 dollars.

tures of rural life. Blum and Rossi's review of 750 works on the correlates of social class touches on many of the studies which have noted the importance of family to the rural resident, regardless of income level (Blum and Rossi, 1969).

Additionally, Chamberlain's study of 471 people in a rural county in Missouri indicated that the farther removed one's residence from a major metropolitan center, the greater the homogeneity of one's social contacts. While distance did not seem to affect level of participation in voluntary organizations, civic activity, and the like, it was strongly correlated with the number of interests respondents had in common with those they identified as friends (Chamberlain, 1969).

This high level of homogeneity has been noted by one writer to perhaps contribute to curtailing the search for marriage partners to a small group of social intimates in rural areas (Polansky, 1970). On the other hand, Miller's observations of a rural county in Georgia suggested to him that such intense contacts enable the accomplishment of many tasks through mutual help activities which residents would otherwise not be able to afford (H. M. Miller, no date, 6 ff.). Miller also noted that leisure time activities tended to be individualistic (e.g. fishing) rather than group oriented, an observation which would be consistent with the rural person's reputed value on personal independence.

Smith's work, cited elsewhere, is also to the point here. His efforts, aimed at measuring the social class structure in the rural South, have yielded at least the tentative conclusion that much of the agricultural South is basically a single class, primarily a lower class, structurally (T. L. Smith, 1969). A single class structure of low income people certainly could be conceived to enhance the social insularity of people who prefer homogeneity in interpersonal relationships and above all personal independence from group ties beyond family. This picture, if at all accurate, would differ considerably from the content and intensity of social influences—as well as the social preferences—commonly asserted to be descriptive of the environs and orientations of the urban poor.

But whether such summarization represents meaningful differences between the rural Southern poor and those who are urban and/or better off cannot be said with any certainty. As Blum and Rossi have concluded,

> The available studies lead us to suspect the existence of appreciable regional and ethnic differences in class-related behavior, but these sub-group variations have yet to be systematically documented (Blum and Rossi, 1969, 347).

There is another dimension of family and wider social patterns held to distinguish the rural resident —particularly the rural poor—which has been much discussed and which bears on the culture of poverty argument. It is the dimension of the degree of durability of the so-called rural life style following the rural person's relocation to a more urban environment. Even if we cannot answer definitely how much—and whether—differences in rural social patterns contribute to poverty, we can ask whether such patterns persist in similar enough form following a radical change in environment to warrant calling them "culturally" indoctrinated.

One of the more frequently investigated phenomena in this regard is that of the durability of close family ties following relocation (Burchinal, 1963; Schwarzweller, 1964). An early study of Southern Appalachian migrants to Cincinnati revealed that they had marked disadvantages in finding employment but that during the initial period of job seeking, those looking for work were socially buoyed up by others who had precedented them into the urban area (Leyburn, 1937). A usual pattern is to send for one's family after work has been found, but here again, the in-migrant family tends to locate in the midst of similar others, a fact which is considered to be central in the family's efforts to retain their past life style in the new setting (Frumkin, 1961). Frumkin found this pattern in his follow up study of the migration of 26 rural families in Colorado, the finding being quite similar to that noted for Appalachian migrants by Leyburn and others (Sharp and Peterson, 1967).

Some other studies would take issue with the implied durability of the rural poor in-migrant's life style. Bultena's observations of the web of family relationships among a group of rural aged persons in Wisconsin, for example, indicated that the old folks appear to have no greater frequency or intensity of contact with their children than do the urban aged. He suggests that when the young leave the rural areas, their orientation toward family ties change toward greater similarity with the more impersonal orientations of urban dwellers (Bultena, 1969).

Jerome, in another study in Wisconsin, addressed the issue from the standpoint of food habits among 63 black households in Milwaukee, all having in common that they were of rural Southern origin. He found that dietary changes incorporating food consumption patterns common to the upper midwest were related to the degree of acculturation a given household had experienced (as measured, in part, by their length of residence). Diets in any case were considered to be generally quite adequate. While Jerome's study would suggest that the food habits of the rural Southerner do change over time following migration, it should be noted that the study was not exclusively of low income blacks (Jerome, 1967). Hence, it cannot be stated with certainty that the results reveal a high level of cultural penetrability on the part of the rural in-migrant poor.

The evidence on the matter of cultural durability is neither comprehensive nor particularly convincing. It should be clear, however, that these studies do illustrate at least some of the ways that fuller and better data could be gathered to assess the issue. Both the relationship between distinctive rural family/social patterns and poverty, and the degree to which such patterns endure in new, more urban environments warrant much more investigation. Both are crucial tests of the applicability of the Culture of Poverty Thesis to rural Southern poverty.

The Development of Children in Poverty

The Culture of Poverty Thesis relies heavily on the family as a major component in the development, continuation, and intergenerational transmission of poverty. While it has been previously noted that the poor may lose their children to wider sources of social influences at an earlier age—such as peer groups—there are many who suggest that the destinies of the children of the poor have already been largely formed by what they experience during the first few years of life.

Indeed, some view early childhood development in poverty to be so damaging as to be irreversible if not dealt with before the child reaches school age. The irreversibility of the effects of such experiences would thus consign the child to a life of poverty regardless of subsequent remedial intervention. Hunt has summed up the irreversibility argument in the following comments:

> The plasticity of infancy diminishes rapidly as children grow older. Thus, the longer children live under the stultifying conditions of poverty, the harder it must inevitably be to overcome the deficit resulting [p. 196]. It becomes clear that the inertia increases with age because more and more of the individual's abilities, attitudes, motives, and values must be changed. It appears that the longer a developing organism lives under any given set of circumstances, the harder it is to alter their influence on both developing behavior and body. (J. H. Hunt, 1969, 151).

There are two basic kinds of early childhood effects related to poverty which have most often been dealt with in the literature, the physical and the social. On the physical side, major emphasis has been placed upon the long-term effects of early childhood malnutrition,* while on the social, greatest emphasis has been placed on the effects of certain patterns of child rearing associated with the poor.

Malnutrition and Child Development

The relationship between malnutrition and poverty has recently been rather forcefully brought to the public's attention through the presentation of early findings of a national study which reported out findings from initial work done in Louisiana and Texas. Interviews were obtained from 965 families, of whom 60.8 percent in Texas and 46.4 percent in Louisiana fell below the poverty line. A total of 13,373 persons were represented: 7,351 black, 2,247 white, and 3,775 Spanish speaking (U.S. Congress, Senate, Select Committee on Nutrition and Human Needs, 1970).

The findings do not present an unequivocal picture of the relationship between poverty and malnutrition. The poor seem to be selectively malnourished. The poor were markedly deficient in iron intake (except for the aged) but levels of vitamin A and Thiamine were found unrelated to income. While a slight relationship was detected between riboflavin deficiency and low income, vitamin C deficiency actually was found more strongly associated with above poverty income in Louisiana (*Ibid.,* 770 ff.).

Only when the extremes of the income distribution were compared did a clear relationship with malnutrition appear:

> Persons living in households with a poverty income of less than ½ the poverty line had a rate (16.3 percent) of 3 or more unacceptably low biochemical levels more than 5 times greater than the rate (2.8 percent) of persons from households having incomes twice the size of the poverty line or larger. (*Ibid.,* 770)

Even so, writers drawing upon these findings have asserted that malnutrition is damning for the poor, that remedial food programs may come too late—"too late, because some of the by-products of poverty, and chronic malnutrition, are irreversible" (R. C. Allen, 1970, 72).

Others have completed the cycle by suggesting that malnutrition creates poverty by inhibiting the development of central nerve system functions, specifically brain development (Scrimshaw, 1969; Stock and Smythe, 1963).

Some following this line of reasoning, attribute much of mental retardation (Culley, 1965), and/or school failure, to the effects of early childhood malnutrition (Birch and Gussow, 1970).

In the rural South food consumption habits are changing according to a recent evaluation, and these changes bode badly for the nutrition of residents of these areas (Clark, 1970). Utilizing data to form trends, the report shows, for example, that farm families in rural Georgia and Mississippi produced 60-70 percent of the food they consumed in 1935-36. This declined to 40 percent by 1955 and stood at 25 percent in 1965 (*Ibid.,* 8).

Certain basic foods have been most affected within these broader trends. While 60 percent of farm families produced their own milk in 1955, the figure had dropped to 30 percent by 1965. The number of families using home ground corn meal fell from 20 percent to 4 percent, and the number producing their own eggs declined from 75 to 50 percent during the same period. Generally, meat, fish, and poultry production did not decline over this decade (*Ibid.,* 9 ff.).

The effects on the rural poor in the South were most critical. Residents of these areas who fell into the lowest third of the income distribution consumed on the average 1 pound less of meat, fish, and poultry

*I am not unmindful here of a growing literature which is beginning to focus on the long-term effects of prematurity and early motherhood on the subsequent mental and social development of children (see: C. L. Johnson, 1971, for a thorough review of this literature). The rate of "reproductive error" and "developmental defect," for example, has been reasoned to be greatest among that portion of the population which, among other things, is least well nourished (E. Gordon, 1970, 6).

per week in 1965 than they did in 1955. Trends indicate, particularly for the poor, that the diets of rural residents are rapidly deteriorating. In 1950 rural diets were held to be superior to urban diets; by 1955 they were considered equivalent; by 1965 rural diets were considered slightly less adequate than urban diets (*Ibid.,* 10).

In sum, it was estimated that 40 percent of Southern poor families had inadequate diets in 1965, the situation being worse in rural than urban areas of the South. Part of this conclusion derives from a 1965 USDA Survey which showed that fewer than 20 percent of the poor in the rural South ate green-yellow vegetables and only 25 percent had citrus fruit during an average day, i.e., the day of the survey (*Ibid.,* 20 ff.). Moreover, nutrition for the rural Southern poor can be expected to continue to decline, if trends remain unaltered, since home food production is on a downward slide while the cost of commercially marketed food continues to rise (*Ibid.,* 24).

Efforts to stem these trends in the South have not yet met with overpowering success. One such effort, the school lunch program, is reaching only about half of the children in poverty in three of the states in the region, and fewer in other states according to the best available data, as shown in Table 5-3.

in its infancy. As Osofsky has noted, many of the conclusions to date have been drawn from a handful of studies done on animals carried out in laboratories (1969). He notes also the methodological difficulties a researcher faces in trying to isolate the effects of malnutrition when doing work on the subject with a human sample. In sum, to date, we simply do not have the data to make anything like definitive conclusions:

> Studies [on malnutrition] have often been too broad in nature—and, as a result, poorly controlled. Surprisingly, in light of available physiologic knowledge concerning brain development before and shortly after birth, almost no work has been done in this critical area. One has to draw upon later infancy and childhood studies and attempt to draw analogies. The possible effects of cumulative influences of malnutrition across generations has received no attention. Yet, where available, human data do confirm the association between malnutrition and subsequent developmental problems. (*Ibid.,* 1158)

Child Rearing Practice and Child Development

We are never more equal, writes Bronfenbrenner, than we are at birth (1970, 214). This being so,

TABLE 5-3

Number and Percent of Poor Children Receiving Free School Lunches, by States (1969)

	*Number of Children Receiving Free School Lunches	Estimated Number of Poor Children Eligible for Free Lunches	Percent Reached
Alabama	112,000	310,000	36.1
Florida	105,000	310,000	33.8
Georgia	NR**	350,000	—
Kentucky	NR	350,000	—
Mississippi	67,000	150,000	44.6
N. Carolina	311,000	574,000	54.1
S. Carolina	NR	207,000	—
Tennessee	112,000	228,000	49.1

*Numbers rounded for clarity of presentation

**Data not reported

Source: U. S. Congress, Senate, Select Committee on Nutrition and Human Needs, *Nutrition and Human Needs*

If nutrition is critical to the long-term development of the children of the poor, the data presented here do not reflect a very rosy future for the children of poverty in the rural South.

Yet, conclusions on the long-term effects of malnutrition cannot be accepted as glibly as they are advanced. Research into the relationship is literally

how we are raised makes the critical difference in how we turn out, and the first years of life are critical in this.

Spitz (1946), Bowlby (1951), and Bronfenbrenner (1967), have discussed the outcome in infants of severe maternal deprivation, or in other terms, the lack of mothering and physical contact with a caring mother. In extreme cases, such children simply become autistic, unable or unwilling to respond to others with any meaningful gesture or verbal sign. In recent years theorists have turned toward a broader group of children who are less extremely impaired, namely, the pre-school aged child who shows marked deficits in a variety of skills. Blank, in summarizing the assumptions underlying pre-school intervention programs, lists the major deficits of concern. Broadly, these children are portrayed as coming from experientially deprived home environments and as exhibiting deficiencies in cognitive-perceptual orientations and limitations in language and manual skills (Blank, 1970). Typically, children from low income homes are viewed as more impaired in these matters than children coming from high income homes (F. Riessman, 1962; Grotberg, 1965; E. W. Gordon, 1965).

As noted previously, many believe that the way the poor raise their children stunts their emotional development as in the case of blunting their occupational/educational motivations. Interestingly enough, Reissman rejects this notion, asserting that low income parents instill high aspirations as often as do parents in other social classes. Instead, he chooses to focus upon the cognitive deficits stemming from being brought up in a poor home. What the child of poverty lacks—or is deprived of—are those cognitive and manual skills he needs to get off to a good start in his schooling. Lacking these, he will—barring intervention—remain a step behind others in his age group throughout life (F. Reissman, 1964).

Presumably then, it is in the cognitive rather than the affective side of life that the child of poverty is short changed. However, Strodtbeck's work with a sample of 20 teenagers, 10 of whom had superior I.Q.'s (120+) and 10 of normal I.Q. (110-120) tends to suggest that the affective and cognitive go hand in hand. His tentative conclusions are that families with higher overall I.Q. level have greater problem solving abilities and that they also are found to have the most open and warm parent-child relationships which both foster and enhance the intelligent solution of family problems (Strodtbeck, 1965). While this was not a study of low income families, the conclusion might be that it is unlikely that a family could do a good job in child development in one component without also enhancing the other, and vice versa.

In simple terms, if low income parents raise their children by using arbitrary punitive discipline as often suggested (Kohn, 1964), such measures could hardly be conceived to be "warm" and contributory to the affective development of the child. At the same time, such disciplinary measures can be reasoned to be rarely accompanied by patience, discussion, and explanation of the actions taken. Thus, the child's cognitive powers may also be stunted in the process.

Indeed, on the affective side of things, the better off seem to be more successful in inculcating their own values in their children than the poor, according to Rosen's work (Rosen, 1964). He attributes this higher rate of parent-child value similarity to the findings that mothers in the middle class and above train their children for independence at an earlier age and utilize more affectionate modes of discipline. These factors appear to spur higher identification with parental socialization preference among their children

Rosen's findings and those of others run contrary to Davis and Havighurst's early research which attributed differences in child behavior between the social classes to the higher degree of permissiveness exhibited by the poor in raising their children (Davis and Havighurst, 1946). Bronfenbrenner has attempted to reconcile such findings by suggesting that in recent decades there has been a trend toward more permissiveness in middle class child rearing (Bronfenbrenner, 1958).

Be that as it may, it is important to note that in recent years a clear shift toward greater emphasis on the cognitive components of child development has occurred as reflected in the literature on the subject. Value assimilation and aspiration levels are not conceived to be as crucial to a child's learning progress as are his levels of language, perceptual, and manual skills. The question, then, is what do we know about how the child rearing practices of the poor affect the learning skills of their children?

First it might be said that parents who are younger and/or lower in emotional maturity often make poor teachers for their young children. The poor may well have higher proportions of both types of parents and, of course, both attributes could quite obviously appear in a single poor family. Aldous and Hill, for example, suggest that early marriage is contributory to long-term poverty because of the incapability of many young people to shoulder other stresses of married life coincidentally with raising children (Aldous and Hill, 1969). One might add that in such circumstances young people, emotionally fatigued and lacking in experience, may not qualify often as the best role models for small children.

In a somewhat similar vein, Polansky laments that white families in poverty in Appalachia may simply lack the emotional and intellectual maturity necessary to stimulate their children to better performance than that of which they themselves are capable. How, he asks, is it possible to expect parents who are themselves childlike to raise children with any hopes that they will become mature adults (Polansky, 1970; see also: Aquizap and Vargas, 1970).

Rosen's work makes a contribution here also in the sense that he found value similarity between mothers and children to be higher as the age of the mother increased, regardless of family size, social class standing, or other factors (Rosen, 1964). Perhaps there is something reflected in the age of the parent which leads a child to accept more of what he is taught by the parent in addition to the likelihood that the older parent would have more substance to impart.

Hess and others (cf. R. R. Bell, 1965), have noted that the disparity between the verbal expressions of high aspirations for their children by low income mothers and their children's actual school performance may clothe hidden attitudes. He suggests that a mother's attitudes are better predictors of a child's subsequent social development than either the mother's or the child's measured I.Q. His observations lead him to believe that the crucial factors governing child development in poor families are the mother's feelings of powerlessness to convey their own values to their children, their underlying rarely verbalized belief that their children really won't do well in life anyway, and the fact that they rarely introduce their children to stimulating activities in or out of the home (Hess, 1964).

In another study, Franks studied the school progress of 56 11- and 12-year-old black children from poverty level homes who had at least 5 years schooling in the same urban school system. Her analysis yielded the finding that there was a high correlation between a child's school success and the educational level achieved by its mother: the more educated the mother, the more successful the child (Franks, 1967).

Obviously, most of this work has drawn upon observations and data collected in urban areas. Even less is available on the poor child in the rural South. One study of 1500 school children begun in 1961 has been partially reported on the literature (Baughman and Dahlstrom, 1965). The researchers applied forms of the MMPI and the California Picture Test (a form of the TAT) to various age and racial groups throughout a wide area of rural North Carolina.

Their impressionistic findings suggest to them high levels of learning skills inadequacies especially in the youngest children, and most pronouncedly among blacks. Children from low income homes consistently demonstrated fewer learning skills when they first arrived for schooling. Such simple skills as using a pencil seemed commonly absent, some children never having used one before coming to school. Unfortunately, though the study is large in size, it has limited utility because little data were gathered on the child rearing practices of the children's parents.

It would seem, in sum, that those mothers who are somewhat older, more experienced generally in life, more emotionally mature, and/or better educated, do the better job of preparing their children cognitively to compete in subsequent learning experiences. This seems to be true regardless of present socio-economic location of the families investigated.

The relationship between mothers and children has been given much attention in the literature. While our knowledge of how the mother contributes to the learning skills of her child is limited to say the least, next to nothing is known about the father's role in such matters. Two kinds of conclusions appear and reappear in the literature on lower class life: either the father is determined to have little or no role in child rearing (Kohn and Carroll, 1960), or he is portrayed as an impersonal authoritarian (Elder, 1962).

Others have held, in observing the father-absent home, that the presence or absence of the father seems to make little difference in the socialization of the child (Herzog and Lewis, 1970, 381); at least, no adverse effects can be attributed to his absence.

A differing point of view is advanced by Yancey, who suggests that in father-absent families, the mother often conjures up a negative male role image in the process of raising her young. Hence children of such families frequently are taught that their fathers, and perhaps men generally are "worthless bums" (Yancey, 1965, 17). In any case, none of this sheds much light on how the father contributes to or impedes the learning progress of his children, either by virtue of his presence or absence. One of the most obscure facets of low income family functioning is that of the role of the father in the development of his children.

On the basis of the available evidence very little can be concluded about the extent to which the child rearing practices of the poor contribute to the poverty of their offspring. This is unfortunate, considering the central importance of the hypothesized impact of parental child rearing patterns in the socialization of the child to the Culture of Poverty Thesis. Unless it can be established that parents play a major role in inculcating learning habits (or "dishabits") which predispose the child to poor performance and ultimately poverty in adulthood, the case for the Culture of Poverty Thesis cannot be seriously entertained. To date, the literature on child development simply does not seem capable of yielding the required proof.

There is another whole issue which some think invalidates even the few seemingly clear findings between child rearing and child learning abilities discussed in this section. That issue has to do with the measurement of child learning abilities itself, particularly as such measurement is related to assessing lower class children. The point is a well worn one but nonetheless worth repeating, to wit:

> Accumulated evidence indicates the difficulty of interpreting the results of standardized tests with populations for which they were not designed and against which they have not been normal. Doubts have been raised concerning the applicability of many presently used psychometric procedures with particular sub-populations of children. (Peters, 1970, 122)

Peters adds the further objection to past research to the effect that even if measurements were valid, most studies have been concerned only with tapping short term changes in learning following from the introduction of an experimental technique. Hence it is currently not possible to say anything about the long term effects of learning disabilities and/or learning improvements following intervention among children whatever their level of socio-economic origin (*Ibid.,* 103).

How Much Intergenerational Family Poverty Is There?

For some, the fact that a certain proportion of the nation's population continues in poverty decade after decade is sufficient evidence to conclude that there is a "vicious cycle of poverty," repeated over and over again by succeeding waves of offspring of the poor.

For others, the observation that many blacks are poor because of oppressive social conditions is sufficient proof to predict the intergenerational transmission of poverty among blacks unless social conditions radically change (M. David, 1964, 258 ff.).

Both types of concerns over the continuation of poverty may be legitimate, but both interpretations are misplaced to the extent that such evidence is taken as directly indicative of the degree of intergenerational family poverty. The real questions, unanswered in such analyses, are which families and how many, and which black families and how many?

Direct evidence bearing on these questions is inadequate and hard to come by, doubly so for the poor in the rural South. There seem to be three conventional approaches employed in the research which has dealt with the overall issue of intergenerational family poverty:

1. First is the approach of analyzing the type of family experiencing intergenerational receipt of some form of public assistance funds.
2. A second approach attempts to assess the extent of upward occupational mobility of the sons of poor families.
3. A third approach is a mixed bag which attempts to predict future poverty from knowledge of the present attributes of poor people or to infer certain positive characteristics about the prior background of poor people who subsequently attain some measure of occupational or educational success.

Intergenerational Receipt of Public Assistance Support

One of the more common figures cited in the literature on poverty is that about 40 percent of current public assistance grantees were themselves raised in homes that received some form of public assistance (Seligman, 1968, 39; Burgess and Price, 1963). This figure derives from a major study of AFDC families carried out during the 1960-62 period.

The study itself produced interview data on 3,658 white and 1,740 black AFDC families distributed throughout the United States. Forty percent of the 4,156 families on whom background data were gathered were found to have had parents who also received some form of public assistance; hence, 40 percent of the total represented third generation public assistance recipients. As reported by Burgess, the third generation families also were found to have proportionately more "socially unacceptable" types as grantees, such as a disproportionate number of mothers of illegitimate children (Burgess, 1964).

Only one other major study of the intergenerational dimension of the receipt of public assistance was uncovered. Levinson researched children of AFDC families in an unidentified city. Children were drawn from the total school system enrollment of 16,000 (in the 8 to 12 grade range) who had, according to records, demonstrated one or more school behavior problems ranging from dropping out, premarital pregnancy, and low attendance, to discipline problems, low school achievement, and low aptitude. Comparisons were made by grouping the children variously by SES and welfare-nonwelfare status.

Levinson found that children of AFDC recipients exceeded children of non-recipients on all measures of school behavior problems, regardless of sex or race. But for our purposes, it is more important to note that children in third generation AFDC families did not meaningfully in rates of school behavior problems from children in first and second generations AFDC families, again regardless of race or sex (Levinson, 1969).

While Levinson cautions against generalizing findings deriving from the study of a population in a single locality, broader conclusions will no doubt be tempting to some of the reading public. What, after all, are we to think of the fact that children in AFDC families experience far more serious school behavior problems than those from non-AFDC families? Everything that we hear is that girls who have illegitimate babies and boys who drop out of school are prime candidates for a life of poverty. In short, substantial intergenerational poverty in a range similar to that revealed in the earlier study is implied (based on the fact that rates of incidence in the various school behavior categories ranged for the most part roughly between 40-60 percent).

Finally, poor school behavior rates for first and second generation AFDC families (grouped together) do not vary much from rates for third generation children. While this observation goes essentially unanalyzed in the study, it is possible to raise the question whether there is something about AFDC families which keeps the intergenerational rate of appearance of problematic childhood behaviors at roughly similar levels. Is there something behind all these data which would lead us to expect approximately 40 percent intergenerational transmission of welfare status among all those who become public assistance recipients? From the data at hand, there seems to be no way to definitely respond to this question.

Family Role in Vocational Rehabilitation

While studies of AFDC recipients indicate a rather substantial level of intergenerational receipt of public assistance, one recent study attempted to show that the employability of AFDC mothers is on the rise, as measured by the increasing educational levels and growing job experience histories of 7,062 AFDC women residing in 35 selected counties. By combining education levels with employment histories, Levinson created a "mobility potential" index which was then used to estimate trends between the years 1961 and 1968, as shown in table 5-4.

TABLE 5-4

Mobility Potential Trends Among AFDC Mothers for Selected Years

(in Percents of Total)

Mobility Potential	1961	1967	1968
Low	74.6	67.4	55.5
High	25.3	32.6	44.5

Source: P. Levinson, "How Employable are AFDC Women?" *Welfare in Review*, VIII (July-August, 1970), 12.

In concert with this note of optimism are the findings from the 5 year Wood County Rehabilitation project which reported that county relief roles were lowered by almost one half, from 115 cases at the beginning to 59 by the end of the project (Dunn, 1970, 30).

If employment potential is on the rise and vocational rehabilitation really works, then the intergenerational transmission of poverty can be at least slowed, perhaps halted. But the factors which make for successful rehabilitation are not well known. From the culture of poverty standpoint, the question posed is to what extent do family and wider social influences foster or inhibit rehabilitation?

The data are skimpy but suggest that family and other social contracts may play a larger role than professional supportive services. Sneden, for example, found that upward mobility among the people of poverty is more closely tied to the number and intensity of contacts a poor person has with middle class "referents" than to his level of knowledge about opportunities or the number of supportive services and facilities open to him (Sneden, 1968).

In a follow-up evaluation of 1,062 trainees in an MDTA sponsored program in Atlanta, Georgia, Trooboff found that 84 percent who completed training found jobs compared to 67 percent who dropped out. Seventy-nine percent of those who finished improved their earnings compared to only 29 percent who dropped out, and improved earnings were most marked for females and blacks. Most importantly for our purposes, those post trainees who experienced the most sustained and marked improvement were found to be those who had more stable marital relationships, regardless of sex or race (Trooboff, 1968).

On the other hand, the Arkansas Rehabilitation Service employed an experimental design to evaluate the effect of professional supportive services in keeping post trainees employed. Intense services including supportive counseling, further training, clothing, transportation, limited medical care, and other assistance were provided the randomly selected experimental group (N=99) while only normal follow-up was extended to a group of controls (N=93). Follow-up of the employment patterns of both groups over a three-year period produced no significant differences, leading the researchers to conclude that

> provision of intense follow up services . . . does not contribute substantially to their [experimentals] continued employment. (Arkansas Rehabilitation Service, 1970, 37)

Such findings taken together suggest that the web of family and wider social relationships may play a significant role in the degree of success vocational rehabilitation programs experience in intervening the progress of poverty in families. Turning things around, it may be as likely that some types of families contribute heavily to the perpetuation of their own poverty, and the failure of vocational rehabilitation services.

Intergenerational Occupational Mobility

A rush of commentary on the rate of upward mobility among the poor has appeared in the literature in recent years ranging from Banfield's unsupported claims that "there is no direct evidence of there ever having been any upward mobility from the lower classes" (1970, 212), to Moles' rather optimistic conclusion that better than two thirds of the sons of the poor have surpassed the accomplishments of their fathers in this generation (1970). Moles flatly rejects the Culture of Poverty Thesis on the basis of his findings.*

Drawing on the same data later used by Moles, Morgan, *et al.*, conclude to the contrary that "it appears that a number of the heads of poor families have moved into less skilled jobs than their fathers had" (1962, 210).

Rushing's investigation of the intergenerational inheritance of tenant farmer status among 1,023 persons so employed in the state of Washington in 1967 indicated that over half were repeating the type of work done by their fathers. Forty-six percent said their fathers were also tenant farm workers and another 9 percent said the fathers were un-skilled laborers (Rushing, 1968, 274 ff.). The relationship between limited or insular social relations and immobility is seen to some extent in these findings as well: fully 66 percent of the tenant farmers said their best friends were also tenant farmers (*Ibid.*, 277).

Fried, in citing Thernstrom's compilation of 10 different studies of occupational changes from father to son covering periods between 1860 to 1956, turned up consistently similar estimated percentages of immobility among the poor. He concludes that

> approximately 50 to 60 percent (ranging from 48 to 71 percent) of the sons of unskilled laborers were themselves either unskilled or semi-skilled laborers. (M. Fried, 1969, 140)

These consistencies in percentage estimates in the 40 to 60 range, are difficult to dismiss as common if undetected artifacts of the methodology of various studies. Such a charge would, in fact, be better placed on studies such as Moles' which found a much higher

* See Chapter 6 for a thorough analysis of the Moles' study.

percentage of upward mobility than is found elsewhere in the literature. The major artifact which may lend to overly optimistic conclusions relates to the ranking of occupational titles itself. Ballas has shown through regression analysis on a sample of persons having below $3,000 yearly incomes according to the 1960 U.S. Census, that the principle route upward generationally for the very poor, particularly the farmer, is through blue collar occupations (1968). But it remains an open question, for example, whether a move (often forced rather than by choice) from farm work to one of several semi-skilled blue collar types of jobs constitutes upward mobility. Moreover, farm work no doubt had higher status and respect in past generations. Hence, comparing intergenerationally, it is quite problematic whether a semi-skilled laborer son has actually surpassed the achievement level of his farmer father. In part, Moles' conclusions are based on rather superficial assumptions about the measurement of upward mobility by occupational categories.

A final methodological point has to be considered from the standpoint of what rates of upward mobility mean about the validity of the Culture of Poverty Thesis. It has to do with the comparative progress of siblings in families of the poor. In simple terms, if the culture of poverty is a major force in the intergenerational transmission of family poverty, then it could be expected that most—if not all—children raised in such an environment should wind up in poverty.

Upward mobility studies overlook this issue with singular regularity. All such studies which have come to our attention seek to measure the intergenerational mobility of a son comparing to his father. In the aggregate, such data represent what is generally known about the upward mobility of the poor. Present methods of measuring the upward mobility of the poor are also inadequate in that they provide precious little data on the upward mobility of females. Over all, the available data prove to be of little use as a test of the Culture of Poverty Thesis.

Inferring Intergenerational Poverty from Educational Levels

The line between poverty and education has often been noted. Advocates of the Culture of Poverty Thesis suggest that cultural influences embedded in poor families hamper the educational progress of the children of the poor (Ribich, 1968). The implication is clear: without adequate education another generation of poor people is created.

The evidence on whether the poor transmit low educational attainment to their children is limited, however, and not entirely unequivocal in nature. Morgan, *et al.,* for example, contribute support to the above line of reasoning in noting that in their study of 2,800 families about 60 percent of all current family heads exceeded the educational levels of their fathers whereas only 40 percent of the current heads of poor families had (1962, 208).

But such a finding could represent substantial downward mobility as well as intergenerational transmission of inadequate educational attainment. Indeed, the authors later suggest that failure to achieve educationally may be traced to individual or personal factors rather than parental influences:

> The low educational attainments of heads of poor families result from a failure to improve attainments relative to the previous generation at the same rate as the remaining population. The data offer little support to the hypothesis that a majority of the poor failed to obtain education because of inadequate education on the parts of their fathers. It is quite possible that other children of these same parents may have attained more education and are in good economic positions. (*Ibid.,* 208)

Finally, Dailey's study of the relationship between male students' family income, rates of college attendance, and level of student intelligence (as measured by the Projective Talent Test on an unspecified sample size) indicates that all of the top 2 percent in intelligence in families having less than $3,000 in family income reached college within 1 year after high school graduation. Indeed, 76 percent of low income students in the top 25 percent intellectually were found to be attending college the year following graduation (Dailey, 1964).

While education and poverty prove in the broadest way to be strongly linked statistically, the limited available data do not necessarily support the conclusion that educational attainment levels are passed intergenerationally among the poor. Anything stronger than this comment is obviously not warranted, given the present level of knowledge on the matter.

Summary Points

This chapter has taken a long look at the Culture of Poverty Thesis from a variety of perspectives. In almost every case, assertions about the potency of this causal explanation evaporate into hollow claims when the available evidence is examined. On the other hand, those who equally glibly dismiss family and interpersonal socializing influences as causative factors in poverty (as many opportunity and maldistribution advocates do) would do well to examine how often such factors are found related to specific aspects of poverty throughout this chapter.

Problems in defining the concept let alone measuring its impact abound. The data on the intergenerational transmission of beliefs, socializing mechanisms (e.g. peer and family role structures), and ultimately poverty among poor families is especially weak, the more so because it is so crucial to an adequate test of the thesis.

Finally, of all the causal explanations of poverty covered in this work, the culture of poverty explanation suffers most from being "over ghettoized." What data there is derives almost entirely from studies done in the ghettoes of the urban North. The suspicion that rural family life and socialization patterns may differ substantially from those exhibited in urban areas, particularly among the Southern poor is little more than just that.

Whereas the comments of knowledgeable persons have been cited throughout this chapter to the effect that isolated, ethnically unified localities in the rural South might be more likely to be carriers of culturally induced poverty than other localities, there is little evidence in the literature that any major attention has ever been paid to testing this notion through research.

It is both ironical and understandable—given the nature of the beast—that more seems to have been written about this causal explanation and yet it remains more difficult to define and assess than any of the others.

Chapter 6

ASSESSING THE OPPORTUNITY THESIS

Two types of evidential proofs are required to establish the validity of the Opportunity Thesis as a general causal explanation of poverty. First, it must be shown that poverty prone people are, in the main, rational, pragmatic decision-makers. Secondly, it must be shown that people in poverty remain there largely as a consequence of unjust social policies and practices.

Here, as in other chapters, we are interested in the generalizability of research findings as a test of the comprehensiveness of this particular causal thesis. If the evidence seems to fall short of a general defense of the thesis, we will be interested in identifying the subgroup or groups of people within the poverty population for whom this causal explanation has greatest meaning and applicability.

Are the Poor Rational Pragmatic Decision-Makers?

Are Their Values Deviant?

Those who contend that the poor are rational, pragmatic decision-makers must assume the correctness of one or more of the following propositions:

1. The values and goals of the poor are essentially in line with those of the dominant better-off majority.
2. The expectancies of the poor (their perceived probabilities of success in obtaining personal goals) are shaped by realistic assessments of alternatives available to them.
3. Lack of information—or ignorance—rather than distorted values is what governs assessment of alternatives and choice.
4. The poor are socially and politically unorganized or disorganized, but are, nonetheless organizable.

The weight of the evidence in the preceding chapter on the Culture of Poverty Thesis raises substantial doubts about the generalizability of that explanation to the totality of poverty. Some observers, such as Ireland and Bresner, who find the Culture of Poverty Thesis attractive, are willing to concede that the poor may not start out as apathetic but rather only become that way as a consequence of prolonged exposure to the value environment surrounding a life of poverty.

Counterpointing this view, Rodman, who rejects the culture of poverty explanation, conceives of a "lower-class value stretch" or a wider range of values than is present in any other social class from which the poor pick and choose in adapting to deprived circumstances. Because this value selection process operates to support coping behavior which constantly requires modification across situations, Rodman suggests the lower class is really characterized by little permanent commitment to any given set of values (Rodman, 1963).

Neither view is attractive to opportunity theorists who reject notions of the poor as either succumbing to a deviant value system or remaining uncommitted to any system of values. Rather they would hold that the value system and level of commitment to it of the poor closely approximates that found among better-off segments of society.

Evidence for this contention derives from a variety of sources. For example, based on an extensive review of the literature on the relationship between personality and physical disability, Yuker, *et al.,* were able to conclude that there is no established evidence that major physical disability results in prolonged personality modifications, depreciation of self-respect, lowered reasoning powers, or similar negative consequences, whether linked to poverty or not (1967). Whether a similar conclusion could be reached about the nondisabled in poverty, or not, is problematic, but certainly not out of the question.*

Billingsley's previously cited works on urban AFDC families are also to the point. He found that such families with husbands present reflect a relatively democratic decision-making process—a sharing between partners rather than matriarchal dominance. Even when fathers were absent, family decision-making by the mother reflected the same concerns for family welfare and advancement of her children's opportunities and well being most often associated with the better-off majority (Billingsley, 1969).

In a somewhat similar vein, Morgan, *et al.,* in their well known study of family spending patterns suggest that spending decisions among poor families do not deviate much from those among their better-off counterparts (J. N. Morgan, *et al.,* 1962). What seem to be deviant decisions are best understood in terms of outcomes necessitated by a lack of resources. For example, the fact that the poor do not put "something away for a rainy day," may be more a consequence of a lack of sufficient income to set aside than it is the result of a value orientation which depreciates savings.

---

*For one study which shows some attitude-self perception similarities between disabled and welfare clients in rehabilitation programs see: Walls and Miller, 1970,793-4.

Specific to the rural South, Glasgow and Taylor interviewed 1,074 employed household heads in rural areas of 8 states in 1961* most of whom were in blue collar and farm types of employment. They found that the interviewees had relatively modest aspirations for themselves based on their assessments of their own educational, experiential and health backgrounds. At the same time, they expressed high aspirations for their children, aspirations very much in line with those presumably held by the better-off majority (Taylor and Glasgow, 1963).

While this study tended to find the value orientations of low income rural Southerners to be in concert with those thought to prevail in society generally, there is reason to believe that there are indeed differences in value orientations among low income Southerners influenced by ethnic, racial, and age factors, within this general frame of reference.

Harmeling's in depth study of 51 low income white Appalachian families in eastern Kentucky, for example, illustrated how Appalachian whites' high regard for personal initiative, self reliance, and general independence enhanced their ability to assimilate upon migrating to urban settings. While these values enhance assimilation, it was also clear from the findings that successful assimilation depended upon obtaining employment to enable expression of these values (Harmeling, 1969). Apparently, at least, assimilation was not impeded among this group of people by differing or deviant value orientations.

Another study of several hundred black and white low income adults in six rural north Florida counties done in 1962 found that these respondents reflected similar beliefs in the values of hard work and education as the means to upward mobility. One possible qualitative difference between the value orientations of these respondents and Appalachian whites might lie in their identification with and the importance they place upon extended family ties in their immediate environs (Youmans, *et al.*, 1969). Both blacks and whites in this sample expressed strong beliefs in the lasting importance of extended kinship ties and remaining geographically tied into this network. This may be indicative of greater dependence on family and perhaps partly explains the previously established fact that Appalachian whites exhibited a much higher migration rate in recent years than that of residents of the rural "deep South" in general.

This same study also proceeded to interview 411 black and white children, a group comprising all children currently in 12th grade in 11 different high schools within the families being studied. Something of a generation gap was disclosed in that these children, on the brink of entering the labor market, tended to be less committed to the constraints inherent in family ties than their elders. They generally expressed a desire to be free of such constraints.

Moreover, differences along racial lines were noted regarding values toward hard work, individual initative, and ability, with black adolescents expressing much stronger cynicism about such values than white age cohorts. Importantly, both races tended to be less uncertain and more overtly demanding about control over their future destinies than their parents. These findings led the authors to specifically conclude about black youth that they are

> by virtue of their value orientation, ideally equipped to identify with the aims of the Negro movement in urban areas [where the majority hoped to go]. (Youmans' *et al.*, 1969, 311)

A final study which recently compared the value orientations of 685 sixth-grade children in rural and urban settings in Tennessee found value orientations—and differences along racial lines—similar to those in the Youmans and Grigsby work. Data obtained by administering the Tennessee Self Concept Scale and the MMPI disclosed that black children tended to appraise their environments more realistically than whites and displayed more cynicism (Wendlend, 1968). It bears re-emphasizing here that cynicism is some distance from apathy, just as in the previous study rejection of the "hard work ethic" did not mean youth holding this view felt any high degree of "anomie" or lack of direction.

Wendlend's study tends to suggest that the value orientation of rural adolescents are a long time in the process of development, not just an adolescent reaction to a need for a feeling of self direction and independence.

Her study also showed that rural children generally had a more positive view of the world, higher self esteem, and less feeling of being isolated from the world than their urban counterparts. She attempts to explain this finding by theorizing that rural children encounter fewer personally devaluating situations and relationships in the process of growing up than do urban children.

Collectively, these data establish the likelihood that a goodly number of low-income rural adults and children hold to value orientations presumed common to the dominant majority in varying degrees and with varying emphases. It may be that black rural residents of the deep South displace their own ambitions pressing more for success within their children than do say, Appalachian whites. It may also be that such displacements create pressures upon youth which show up as rejection of many parental values in concert with greater emphasis upon self-direction and control. In any case, the findings do not reflect the widespread existence of a value orientation expressive of apathy, isolation, and desperation among low income people in the rural South.

Are Their Expectancies Realistic?

How realistic are the nonmetropolitan Southern poor about their chances for future improvement? This deceptively simple and extremely important question cannot be answered with any precision given

*The states were Alabama, Florida, Kentucky, Louisiana, Mississippi, North Carolina, Tennessee, and Texas.

the present lack of data. Some of the previous findings would suggest that the rural Southern poor may not be characterized by apathy (W. L. Slocum, 1967), but this tells us little or nothing about whether their expectations are above, below, or even with their capabilities to operationalize their values (Bender *et. al.*, 1967).

Put more simply, do the nonmetropolitan Southern poor set their goals lower than need be in order to increase the likelihood of successful accomplishment while coincidently lowering the likelihood that success will yield an end to their poverty?* Is it possible for example, that the rural poor translate the values of hard work and self-reliance into terms reflective of persistence and dependability (e.g., pride in working long hours, working with one's hands, never missing work, staying at a job, etc.), blinding themselves in the process to alternative meanings for these values centered on self improvement and advancement (e.g., flexibility in changing jobs, obtaining more training, requesting salary increases, etc.)?**

There really is no way to tell. Gurin and Gurin have recently attempted to review and summarize the research which has been done over the last 20 years or so on the concept of expectancy, especially as it sheds light on the orientations of people in poverty. They have concluded with good reason that very little of the research is directly applicable to assessing the expectancies of poor people simply because very few studies have gone beyond the use of middle class subjects, particularly white college sophomores (Gurin and Gurin, 1970).

From the handful of studies that have been done with low income subjects, they conclude that there is no evidence to support an assumption that low expectancies are necessarily associated with poverty level incomes. Available data do suggest that low income people are capable of changing their expectancies about their future prospects upward, but there is no systematically gathered information as to whether present or changed expectancies are realistic or whether—and to what extent—such expectancies influence actual performance and behavior (*Ibid.*, 90).

Thus, discussion of the nature of personal expectancies among nonmetropolitan Southern poor people ends abruptly without shedding much light. Lack of evidence on this matter limits our testing of the contention that the poor are rational, pragmatic decision-makers, and points up one of the glaring inadequacies of the overall Opportunity Thesis.

Does Lack of Information Influence Choice and Behavior?

There is a temptation to dismiss this question since choices must be made and behavior negotiated almost always within the context of imperfect information. But the contention here is somewhat more specific, namely, that the poor have inadequate access to existing information which is presumed available to them through government agency, school, mass media, and other established informational outlets.

Scattered evidence does suggest that people in poverty often lack necessary information and that, as a consequence, uninformed choices are made leading to self defeating behavior.

Briar's study of 46 urban AFDC-UP couples (N=92), for example, indicated that these welfare clients had imprecise information as to their civil rights. Responses to several questions showed that a large minority didn't believe that some constitutional guarantees applied to them so long as they held the status of welfare clients. He concludes that such clients may submit to intrusive and harrassing tactics by welfare agencies at least in part because they are unaware of their rights (Briar, 1966).

He also hints at what others state more boldly (see: Keith-Lucas, 1957, and Gouldner, 1963), namely, that welfare agencies may control the client's access to information as one means of maintaining control over his behavior.

Dunmore, in a recent study of 173 mothers in a Northern poverty ghetto, tested specifically whether the rate of non-use of a neighborhood educational program aimed at their children resulted from a culture of poverty value orientation or a lack of information about the program. She found that over 60 percent of the mothers had migrated from the rural South to improve their life chances, that in general they did not express fatalism, and that non-use did not significantly relate to their own level of education. Further examination led her to conconclude that non-use was most directly attributable to poor information, lack of information, or distorted information (e.g., rumor) about the program, which program personnel did not attempt to correct by use of public information outlets (Dunmore, 1969).

Specific to low income people in the rural South, Bryan interviewed a randomized 1 percent sample (N=1300) from rural parts of a four-state area (Arkansas, Missouri, Mississippi, and Louisiana) in 1967. He was particularly interested in assessing what factors seem to inhibit low income people in this region from pursuing a course of action which might improve their lives. He found that younger aged groups, married couples, heads of small families, blacks, and those with higher education were most predisposed toward change. Importantly, measures of fatalism did not show a strong relationship with low propensity for change. Moreover, the lack of action toward change among those highly predisposed to change was strongly linked to a lack of information about available opportunity in the region (Bryan, 1968).

These studies suggest that lack of information may contribute heavily to the apparent sluggish or resigned behavior among people in nonmetropolitan poverty. They also suggest that a major factor in the

*This is part of the circular reasoning Hines suggests as being characteristic of the "culturally deprived black." See: R. H. Hines, 1964, 136-142.

**Rushing's work has informational value here. See: Rushing, 1968.

matter is the inadequacy of responsible agencies in providing needed information to the poor.

In the absence of organized informational programs, Park has suggested that the main information mechanism relied upon by the rural poor is the extended family network. He recently located and interviewed 166 of a total 500 white males who claimed unemployment compensation in the summer of 1956, in 6 rural Tennessee counties. He was interested in knowing how these unemployed males had obtained non-local job information a decade or so ago and what had happened to them. He found 90 percent of those who had migrated did so to places where kin or friends had already located, and that over 60 percent of that number had received job information from this source prior to moving.

Importantly, less than 1 percent received job information from local employment services, and the inadequacy of the family-friend information system is shown in the finding that job information from that source only proved useful when unskilled jobs were in fact plentiful in the area of relocation anyway (Park, 1968). In short, public agencies provided practically no helpful information, and success in obtaining work following migration depended more on the random availability of appropriate work than upon precise information and the spotting of opportunities provided by family or friends .

What all of these studies show is that those in poverty lack information which would be of specific usefulness to them in gaining employment, education, and other opportunities. Kunce, *et al.,* have commented on this in their St. Louis rehabilitation studies discussed elsewhere. They note that while the poor have most of the needed devices for receipt of information (e.g., newspapers, TV, telephone, etc.), government agencies rarely use these resources to inform the poor of job, educational, and other available opportunities (Kunce, *et al.,* 1969).

Kunce's comments at least in part explain the curious facts disclosed in an in depth study of 50 rural poor white families in central Wisconsin carried out in 1966. In this study, it was found that rural poor people were highly informed about national and world events but quite uninformed about local government and issues. Moreover, although every family had used at least one social welfare agency in the county in the preceding 20 years, there was almost a total absence of information on the type, location, and nature of services currently available within the county.

Most of the respondents were *not* isolated in the sense that 60 percent characterized themselves as regular attenders of church, PTA, and allied activities; a majority shopped weekly in the central city located in the county; and almost all were well informed on major events, as previously noted. What is important about all this is that, while they did not feel isolated, almost without exception they expressed a sense of powerlessness to do anything specific to improve their own lives or the quality of life in their rural area (O'Reilly, 1968).

The key issue here is their pattern of information, knowledge about major events but ignorance of local happenings and programs. We can only wonder whether these rural poor people were truly expressing feelings of powerlessness or whether they were well motivated toward self improvement and simply ignorant of ways to go about it.

All of these studies undermine any complacency we might have about our being the "best informed nation on earth." Little satisfaction should be taken in studies which show the poor in rural areas to be "plugged in" because a high proportion now possess such devices affording access to communication as autos, TV's, telephones, and so on. Rather, it would seem that the poor do lack essential information necessary to identifying specific opportunities and gaining available government benefits and that such information, for a variety of reasons, simply is not communicated well to those in poverty.

Are the Poor Organizable?

Finally, if those in poverty are really rational, pragmatic decision-makers, it would seem reasonable to assume that, given proper information and perhaps some outside assistance, they should be capable of organized group action to improve their lot collectively.

Systematically developed and rigorously examined data supportive of this contention are as scarce as the proverbial hen's teeth.* Firebrand rhetoric on the other hand is in abundant supply. There is a virtual glut of visable personages claiming to be representative of the organized interests of the poor. Saul Alinsky, Richard Cloward, George Wiley, and an army of less prominent "indigenous" leaders in CAP programs immediately come to mind.

But almost as quickly questions arise. For example, how successfully did Alinsky's earlier efforts, such as TWO and the "Back of the Yards" movements in Chicago, engage the truly poverty stricken? Why has he decided in recent years that there is greater impact in organizing the middle-class "silent majority"? Is Wiley's continued visability actually reflective of a viable organization, or is he simply lobbying for a label? What is NWRO's record of achievement, and how well has it generally built in participation of current welfare clients into leadership roles?

In this matter, we cannot overlook the rather pessimistic conclusion about the activities of welfare rights groups that participation may be of short duration for many persons. It has been observed that substantial numbers of welfare clients tend to drop out of such movements as soon as their immediate and concrete objectives are realized or assuaged (Cloward and Piven, 1968).

What is the experience of organized labor? Are we right in accusing organized labor of publicly supporting the notion that the very poor are unorganizable, as Graham has implied (1970), simply because

*For one minor exception see: Brager, 1965.

such efforts, even if successful, prove unprofitable? Did the trash collectors in Memphis win concessions as a result of their collective efforts, or were concessions extended as a consequence of an outpouring of public sentiment stemming from the association of that conflict with Martin Luther King's assassination?

In what manner are the poor participating in the so-called New Militant movements being carried out by some of the nation's youth. One of the few thorough looks we have had at a non-revolutionary movement of this type is Keniston's report on the Viet Nam Summer (1968). But he reports the participants were almost exclusively white youth from middle to upper income family backgrounds. What evidence is there from the black side of the fence that Eldredge Cleaver, Rap Brown, Stokely Carmichael, and others, have relied upon low income blacks for ideas, decisions, leadership, or anything other than mass participation. How much leadership and direction in Abernathy's and SCLC's struggle to end poverty and hunger is actually exerted by low income blacks?

In the area of violent mass or crowd events, it is not absurd to raise the question of the extent, nature, and duration of participation by very low income residents of the urban ghetto areas where riots have occurred in recent years. Were very low income persons leaders or followers in these events? Did they carry out the lion's share of the arson and sacking, or simply move in and pick up what remained after the fact?

Evaluations of the Watts riot indicate most activities were carried out by the young, with older residents acting as an audience providing tacit approval (Cohen and Murphy, 1966). Does this mean that older low income people could not be stirred to action under even the most volatile circumstances. Or does it mean that their values, in concert with those of the dominant society, held their inclinations in check?

What about the participation of persons in poverty in "War on Poverty" programs, particularly CAP projects? No battery of programs has ever more closely followed from the Opportunity Thesis as Moynihan so clearly documents in his recent book (1969b). No program or set of programs, therefore, has ever—presumably—provided a better test of whether the poor were or are organizable. Yet, how well the poor responded to the opportunities seemingly shot through these programs cannot be determined. Marris and Rein observed, in their penetrating analysis of major CAP projects and their precursors (e.g., Mobilization for Youth and HARYOU), that the truly poor participated very little because

> the formal organizational structure through which the projects authorized their decisions inevitably precluded effective participation or unsophisticated people. . . . The project boards do not, in fact, seem to have included a single poor man or woman. (Marris and Rein, 1969, 167-68)

It is in fact difficult to tell from all this whether the poor are organizable or not. True tests and/or sound evaluations simply have not been made on the whole. In addition, almost all of the opinions of theorists, actual programs evaluations, and observations of the activities of low income persons relating to their social-political behavior center on the metropolitan ghetto poor.

Little or none of this may be applicable in responding to the question whether the nonmetropolitan poor in the South are organizable. Equally as important, we do not even know whether nonmetropolitan low income migrants in urban ghettoes participate in the kinds of programs and activities discussed. We do know from the Kerner Report (Report of the National Advisory Commission on Civil Disorders, 1968, 127 ff.) that the great majority of persons arrested during various recent urban riots were native born or long time residents of those cities. Does this mean that recent nonmetropolitan in-migrants are less responsive, less action prone, less organizable than natives? Paul Good suggests not (see: Paul Good, 1969). Certainly we cannot tell from one piece of minor evidence, but knowledge about the organizability of recent nonmetropolitan low income migrants would be well worth having.

One recent study of the organizability of black female domestic workers, almost all rural in-migrants to a growing Southern city, was done in direct response to Tolan's assertion that such low-income workers were not organizable (Tobin, 1966). The study compared the orientations of 41 household domestics with those of 24 women doing equivalent work in a variety of business and government oragnizations.

One thing immediately apparent from the findings was that young women are choosing work in organizations. These women were somewhat predisposed to organized activity—through unionization if possible—to obtain greater job benefits and so on. Household domestics, on the other hand, not only were on the average much older (between 45 and 65 years), they also were quite openly resistant to organized activity aimed at improving their conditions which were, generally, much worse than those of workers in organizations. The primary reason for this resistance was the fear of loss of a prized relationship with their white employers, a very paternalistic relationship, which they felt would be damaged even if pay and other benefits were extracted through impersonal collective action (Thomas, 1971).

This is, of course, another urban study. But it does deal with rural, black, low income in-migrants, and does, as much of the previous material did, raise the apparent importance of the age factor in the organizability of the poor.

Of the poverty areas of the rural South, little can really be said. If materials presented here cast doubt on the organizability of the urban poor, particularly those other than youth, then the additional burdens of sparse population and geographical distance lead to more gloomy prospects in the rural South. But the fact is, so little is known that such speculation may be wholly unwarranted.

There may be, counterbalancing the issue, some

bright spots, particularly in regard to self-help community enterprise projects in rural areas of the South currently being sponsored by OEO (see: *Athens Banner-Herald and The Daily News,* (1971). These projects remain question marks because of a dearth of sound reporting and evaluation of data. Yet we do know that it is in precisely the rural areas of the South with high concentrations of poverty that the population is growing younger (increasing proportions of young people). If it is the young among the poor who are prone to organized action, and if increased numbers are a necessary ingredient, then some optimism may be warranted about the potential for action among the rural Southern poor. A major question, of course, is whether youth will remain in the rural South to shoulder such responsibility.

How much improvement organized efforts in rural areas would yield is in itself problematic. Smith's analysis of class structure in farm areas of the rural South suggests a very tiny elite of wealthy land owners often absent from their holdings (T. L. Smith, 1969). This, coupled with the potent role sheriffs exercise in controlling Southern nonmetropolitan county governments (Margolis, 1970), raises serious questions about the degree of responsiveness to organized demands inherent in current local "power structures" (U. S. Advisory Commission on Intergovernmental Relations, 1968).

Researchable questions arise at almost every juncture in this section. Insofar as they cannot be satisfied on the basis of current knowledge—and most cannot—the question of the organizability of the nonmetropolitan poor remains unanswerable. The extent to which the Opportunity Thesis applies as an explanation of nonmetropolitan Southern poverty is more difficult to assess as a result.

Are the poor rational, pragmatic decision-makers? In sum, we can say that there is evidence that many of the poor in the rural South seem "tuned in" to the values of the dominant society, and that a lack of information does play a role in their decisions which may lead ultimately to untimely, inappropriate, or inadequate behavior. We really do not know if their expectancies for themselves and their children are realistically based on assessments of their environments and personal competencies, and, with some possible exceptions relating to the young, it is really not possible to declare whether the poor generally are capable of sustaining organized activity and producing indigenous leadership for collective action.

The Impact of Inequality in Social Practices, Programs, and Policies

The first part of this chapter attempted to assess whether people in poverty have the capacity to rise above it, if given the chance. This part takes up the issue of how and to what extent the poor remain poor because of denial of access to and arbitrary exclusion from opportunities, goods, and servcies.

Everything associated with such an issue cannot, of course, be encompassed in a part of one chapter. Since opportunity theorists lay heaviest emphasis upon the factors of education, employment, and the role of government in these matters insofar as they all relate to income, we have decided to limit ourselves to this arena and attempt a close inspection of the effects of inequality in these areas.

Are the Poor Utilizing Existing Opportunity?

As a first order of business we might ask whether people in poverty are utilizing the existing opportunities available to them. This is not, after all, a country totally devoid of opportunity for those in poverty. If it cannot be reasoned—and better yet shown—that the poverty population is utilizing present opportunities, however limited, then doubt increases about how effective large scale equal opportunity programs would be in reducing or eliminating poverty.

Some data exist which provide hopeful signs. For example, the level of formal education completed by blacks, particularly at lower and middle income levels is fast closing toward parity with that being achieved by whites (Deuterman, 1970). This would suggest that low income blacks are increasingly utilizing available educational opportunities. If so, then this means we can proceed to raise questions directly related to discrimination in education such as, is the quality of education of equivalent nature? and/or do equivalent levels of educational achievement yield similar employment and income opportunities for both races?

Similarly, in the matter of occupational mobility, it would be questionable to contend that there is absolutely no opportunity for upward movement by those in poverty.

The avenues upward may be narrow and limited to the lower rungs of the occupational ladder, but it cannot be reasoned *prima facie* that no opportunity exists at all. The specific question then is, have the poor advantaged themselves of existing, available opportunities?

Based on a recent study of 883 men whose fathers held low income occupations, Moles responds with a resounding yes: about 73 percent of the sons of laborers and service workers (N=577) and 66 percent of the sons of farmers and farm laborers (N=306) were found to be employed in higher manual or nonmanual jobs than their fathers ever achieved (Moles, 1970, 9). Pronounced improvements were noted for black as well as white men in the study, although blacks did show somewhat less occupational progress.* Moles utilizes these findings to assert that

> a strong majority of those whose families were poor had been able to move up to better economic circumstance. It provides little support to the proponents of the 'cycle of poverty' theory, who say

*Eighty percent of white laborers' sons and 68 percent of white farmers' sons showed advancement over their fathers whereas about 50 percent of black sons showed advancement in both occupational categories (Moles, 1970, 13).

that being poor is passed on from generation to generation. (*Ibid.*)

This assertion should be leavened with a grain or two of salt. First, it should be noted that he utilized essentially the same data originally collected by Morgan, *et al.,* for their 1962 study, a study which found sufficient warrant in examining these data to conclude that there is, indeed, substantial intergenerational poverty (Morgan, *et al.,* 1962, 210).

Secondly, some reordering of Moles' data shows that 40 percent of the sons of laborers who started at the same level as their fathers (55 percent of this occupational category) never rose above that level, and 48 percent of sons of farmers who started in the same occupation as their fathers (60 percent of this occupational category) never rose either. Thus, a substantial minority of sons never really moved beyond their fathers' achievements. Moreover, *downward mobility* is hidden in Moles' presentation: roughly 45 percent of laborers' sons started working at a higher occupational level than their fathers ever achieved, but of this group, 24.6 percent are now employed at levels below their initial level. For farmers' sons, 40 percent started out better than their fathers, but 21.2 percent of that group experienced downward occupational mobility to their current job levels. Correcting for downward mobility, however, still results in slightly over 60 percent of all sons currently being in a superior occupational position to that ever achieved by their fathers.*

Several other reservations should be noted. The great majority of upwardly mobile sons had reached, at the time of the study, only one level above their fathers' achievements (i.e., employment in skilled manual labor).** Kelly's previously cited flow analysis which assessed upward-downward mobility over a two-year span, also suggests that the generational type of study discussed here may be insensitive to substantial short term fluctuations in the life conditions of these men, resulting in overly sanguine long range interpretations. Finally, we have little knowledge about the upward mobility of women from poverty, although Polansky hints in recent work with 65 low-income families in rural North Carolina that women of this background in this area cannot be expected to marry into higher status very often. The reasons for this are the lack of achieving males from which to choose and the values and other orientations of these women which lead them to poor mate selection (Polansky, 1970).

Given all of this, the Moles findings still show that some men have advanced out of poverty, even if we were to suppose a very limited opportunity structure.* A similar observation is applicable to a somewhat lesser degree to blacks and men of rural origin. These observations at least allow the possibility that increased opportunity might yield further reductions in poverty. Some people in poverty appear capable of achieving under less than optimum conditions. This adds some weight to the notion that people in poverty are rational, pragmatic decision-makers, but it does not necessarily support generalizing this contention to the full poverty population.

How Serious Is the Impact of Inequality in Employment Related Social Policies and Other Employment Practices?

Social policies play a vital role in defining the employment opportunity structure for low-skilled, low-income citizens, in two important ways. First, employed currently or not—policy reflects the level of regard government holds for such persons *vis a vis* other groups of workers in such matters as job income protection programs. Do current policies afford these people adequate protection for maintaining a decent standard of living during periods of employment and unemployment, or not?

How well the states in the region are doing in protecting the income of low skilled workers is partly reflected in the data presented in Table 6-1.

From Table 6-1 it is possible to conclude that the states in the region express very little concern with minimum wage protection independent of federal requirements. For the already unemployed, the picture is even more bleak. No state in the region has yet adopted the AFDC-UP program to provide income protection for unemployed male family heads, and clearly only a small proportion of unemployed persons obtain temporary relief from General Assistance programs: the region's General Assistance case load comprises slightly more than 3.5 percent of all such cases nationally.

In addition, the vast majority of the unemployed in the region are not eligible for Unemployment Compensation Benefits (UCB), and for those who are insured, benefits are not progressive: each state pays a flat percentage of the computed average weekly earnings (up to a maximum) regardless of level of earnings. The percentage of weekly earnings protected in all states is low in comparison to the protection afforded in many states outside the region, and does not exceed 50 percent in any state.

Finally, while benefits under Workman's Compensation in all states are progressive (higher percent-

---

*This 60-40 percentage split is almost exactly reversed in the original data presented by Morgan, *et al.,* 1962, 210. Of 698 current heads of poor families, 62 percent had not gone beyond the occupational accomplishments of their fathers.

**Moles' data are also problematic from the standpoint that some fathers with better-than-poverty-level jobs were probably included as having low income occupations. For example, foremen were included in the labor-service worker category, and farm managers were included in the farmer category. Controlling for these occupations might well have shown a larger number of sons who had *not* surpassed their fathers' achievements.

*A Similar type of father-son occupational mobility design was utilized by Galloway on data also aggregated in 1962, with a similar finding: there is substantial intergenerational upward mobility. See: Lowell E. Galloway, 1966.

TABLE 6-1

Income Protection for Employable, Low-Skilled Persons, by States

	(1) Has State Minimum Wage Law	(2) Has AFDC-UP Program	(3) Number of General Assistance Cases (Nov. 1970)	(4) % Unemployed Also Uninsured (UCB)	% Average Weekly Wage Provided	% Estimated Lifetime Earnings Provided under Workmen's Compensation for: Above Average Weekly Earnings	Below Average Weekly Earnings
United States			521,000	64.3			
Alabama	No	No	97	70.0	41	10	17
Florida	No	No	7,800	70.9	36	40	60
Georgia	Yes*	No	2,600	79.7	43	8	13
Kentucky	Yes	No	NA	67.7	46.75	11	18
Mississippi	No	No	1,300	80.0	41	11	18
North Carolina	Yes*	No	2,000	70.4	50	8	14
South Carolina	No	No	500	77.8	50	9	15
Tennessee	No	No	1,700	64.1	44	10	16

*State Minimum wage law lower than Federal minimum per Fair Labor Standards Act.

Sources: Column 1. *South Today,* II (November 4, 1970), 2.

Column 3, U.S.D.H.E.W., S.R.S., N.C.S.S. *Public Assistance Statistics,* Report A-2, 1970a, Table 9.

Column 4, The President's Commission on Income Maintenance Programs, *Background Papers,* 1970, Tables 2.2-1 and 2.2-2.

Column 5, *Ibid.,* Tables 2.3-4 and 2.3-5.

age protection for low-income workers), with the exception of Florida, states in the region afford extremely low levels of protection, ranging from 13 to 18 percent of estimated lifetime earnings for low-income workers. This range of percentages compares unfavorably to the 79 percent protection level afforded low-income workers under such programs in Massachusetts.

These data suggest that the states in the region have not been overpoweringly aggressive in matters of protecting the incomes of low wage earning workers. Recalling White's estimates of high levels of underemployment in the rural South, and the point that many of the occupations engaged in by rural Southerners are not protected by existing programs, it is safe to state that workers in these areas are in an even more tenuous position than is conveyed in our general observations. It may not be accurate to charge that such policies in the aggregate are designed to openly discriminate against less skilled, lower-income workers; but it can be stated with certainty that their overall impact limits the opportunities of such people to maintain an adequate standard of living.

Secondly, and more directly, social welfare policies define the employment and income opportunity structure of that portion of the poverty population applying for or receiving public assistance benefits. A variety of studies have documented how such policies prevent eligible persons from receiving benefits (Pomeroy, 1969; Meyers and McIntyre, 1969), and/or consign recipients to a status of "second class citizenship" (Chilton, 1968).

But here we are specifically interested in the values which seem to underlie program decisions of state level policy makers governing the employability and income of the public assistantance population. Two facts are of major importance. First, no state in the region has an AFDC-UP program currently while every state in the region is vigorously implementing the WIN program which focuses upon getting AFDC mothers employed and off assistance (U.S.D.H.E.W., S.R.S., N.C.S.S., 1970b).

Secondly, as Table 6-2 shows, the high level of interest being expressed in employability is not of recent vintage, nor simply a response to a change of emphasis in welfare programming at the federal level. As far back as 1967 states within the region were generally far out-stripping the national average in the use they were making of then established vocational rehabilitation programs.

The vigorous pursuit of employability and an equivalent neglect of income protection seem to generally characterize policy decisions affecting the lives of low-income less skilled workers in the South. At the same time that employment is emphasized as the way out of poverty, few of the supports needed to accomplish this feat are extended to those most vulnerable to becoming or staying destitute.

These contradictory policy emphases may well cancel out the potential effectiveness of employability programs; indeed, Genevieve Carter has concluded from her review of the literature on upward mobility among public assistance clients that in many cases movement or non-movement cannot be accounted for except in terms of policy affects on life chances (1970).

TABLE 6-2

Rates of Use of Vocational Rehabilitation Service per 100,000 Population, by States (1967)

	Number of Cases (in Hundreds)
United States	287
Alabama	413
Florida	479
Georgia	530
Kentucky	365
Mississippi	308
North Carolina	417
South Carolina	640
Tennessee	320

Source: The President's Commission on Income Maintenance Programs, *Background Papers,* 1970, Table 8.4-3.

One clear way that welfare policy influences the employability of AFDC mothers is in the matter of setting marginal tax rates, or the amount that public assistance is reduced in response to the amount of income a mother earns from employment. Hausman's analysis of data aggregated on AFDC programs for the states of Kentucky, Alabama, and Mississippi for 1967 yields information on the relationship between such deductions and the willingness of AFDC mothers to accept employment. His findings show that if the amount of deductions were reduced 16 percent from its present mean level (60.6 percent of earned income for the states analyzed), 5 percent more AFDC women would be encouraged to enter the labor market (Hausman, 1970). He concludes that

> if welfare administrators seek to provide a somewhat reasonable income floor and provide day care centers for children, low implicit tax rates will induce at least part-time labor force participation among recipient mothers. (*Ibid.,* 97)

In this and in many other ways, it thus would appear that current social policies tend to close off employment and income opportunities for low-income people, in the nonmetropolitan South as elsewhere (see, for example: Hausman 1969).

There may be another way in which public assistance policy limits such opportunities, namely, by inhibiting the geographic mobility, particularly of the rural Southern public assistance recipient. While no real data exist on this issue, it is possible that some of the rural poor in the South may be prevented from migrating because of fear of loss of their income supports upon relocation. The fact that residency requirements have been struck down for several forms of public assistance would not necessarily diminish such fear, particularly if the rural poor are ignorant of these relatively recent Supreme Court decisions. This clearly is an area deserving further exploration and research.

In any case, rectifying policy inadequacies and program limitations might not unlock the doors to opportunity for those affected. Such action would, however, allow a clearer determination of the extent of discriminatory practices in social behavior beyond the reaches of social policy. For example, evaluations of various vocational rehabilitation and work programs often yield conclusions that results are disappointing: success in achieving employment is rarely found to exceed 50 percent among post trainees, often much less (Goldin, 1970; Kunce, *et al.,* 1969; Carter, 1970). Goldin attributes such lack of success to wider social practices:

> Rehabilitation efforts, no matter how successful initially, are only wasted if the skills provided must go unexercised in a society that has no use or desire for the individual who has worked so hard to acquire them. (Goldin, 1970, 19)

But surely this is a shot in the dark, if not a rationale for program failure. Until we can be assured that discriminatory policy effects on opportunity for the poor are controlled—and this is the area most directly amenable to control—it cannot be stated with any certainty that the main barrier to equal opportunity rests in social practices over which there is little direct control.

This is not an idle issue as Landes' research on the impact of state fair employment practice laws shows. Utilizing data from the 1950 and 1960 U.S. Census, Landes grouped data on wages and employment for non-whites and whites—mostly urban residents—for the 22 states having fair employment laws in 1959 and the remainder that did not. He was able to show that wages for non-whites tended to be 5 percent higher and discrimination in hiring 11 to 15 percent lower in states with such laws. This seems to be a meaningful difference because similar comparisons using 1949 data when no state had such a law yielded no differences between the same two groupings of states. It also appeared that discrimination declined as a simple function of the existence of the law rather than a state's capacity to enforce it: degree of compliance was not positively correlated with the length of time the law had been in effect or the size of a given state's Fair Employment Commission's budget (Landes, 1966).

At best these materials illustrate *how* policy works to directly limit the employment-income opportunities of low income Southerners in general. With the possible exception of Landes' work and that of a few others, we are without the data needed to make sound estimates of the size of the role played by policy in such matters. Research is badly needed in this area to lend greater precision to the Opportunity Thesis.

This problem, of course, does not prohibit us from reporting what a variety of researchers estimate to be the overall contribution discriminatory employment practices make to nonmetropolitan Southern poverty.

Several researchers have warned that the trend over the last few decades has been toward a widening rather than a lessening of the income gap between black and white, rich and poor (Lampman, 1966a). Cowhig and Beale have shown in particular that the socio-economic gap between blacks and whites in the rural South increased in varying degrees during the 1950-60 decade, both in terms of farm and non-farm populations (Cowhig and Beale, 1964; Hoover and Crecink, 1962). Several writers have, in turn, attempted to trace these differences to their sources in the nature of Southern agriculture economy and the intertwined historical effects of racial discrimination (Maddox, 1968; Tang, 1959).

Persky and Kain recently reported on a major study of the effects of racial discrimination in nonmetropolitan Southern employment during the 1950's. Utilizing U.S. Census data, they isolated all nonmetropolitan counties in 6 Southern states* having more than 5,000 blacks as of 1950 (N=250) counties. They then proceeded to examine the employment progress of all males who could be classified as entrants to the labor force during the decade of the 50's (i.e., all males who were between 10-20 years old in 1950). Examination of racial patterns in employment in seven major categories of non-agricultural industries disclosed that only 21 percent of all new non-agricultural jobs in the 250 counties went to blacks during the decade whereas blacks comprised 43 percent of the total population and 47 percent of the potential entrants to the labor force in the counties studies. They concluded that "no industry showed blacks significantly improving their representation." Furthermore, "There seemed to be neither gains nor losses, except in manufacturing, where blacks showed losses [over the decade]" (Persky and Kain, 1970, 274-75).

While some observers of the situation in the nonmetropolitan South suggest that migration is the answer, particularly for the poor blacks (see: Clawson, 1967), Perky and Kain argue that this is not likely to be a successful out for many (1970, 268). Osburn's study of 254 white and black rural North Carolina in-migrants to the cities of Greensboro and Winston-Salem since 1960 tends to bear out this impressionistic conclusion. Although the distance of the move was not great, Osburn found that whites on the average incurred costs of $266.00 and blacks $283.00 related to relocating. This financial drain was coupled with the fact that about 32 percent of the whites and 53 percent of the blacks experienced no increase in earnings as a result of relocation, and many in fact experienced reduced income.

Utilizing regression techniques to project the effect of migration on lifetime earning prospects, and controlling for race, education, and other factors in the process, Osburn found that whites could expect a 106 percent return and blacks a 132 percent return as a consequence of relocation. That is, blacks could expect to do 32 percent better than they might have had they not moved. This greater potential, however, is obviously a function of the lower incomes blacks ordinarily have: while white potential seems smaller in a comparison of percentages, data suggest that whites will receive $9.00 for every dollar expended in moving over their lifetimes while blacks can expect a $4.00 return for equivalent investments.

Another study of intra-regional migration by Truett examined the flow of rural blacks into Miami-Dade County during the 1950-1966 period (Truett 1969). His findings show that about 15.9 percent of the Dade County labor force in service-labor types of occupations in 1960 was black, and that at present rates of in-migration this percentage figure could be expected at least to be the same and probably much greater by 1966. At the same time, direct analysis of the percentage of blacks employed in such jobs showed virtually no growth during the 1960-1968 period. Black males held 55.4 percent of such jobs in 1960 and 56.9 percent in 1966. Females showed a substantial percentage decline in the same period from 78.8 percent to 65.1 percent, probably as a result of fewer black females finding work in domestic types of labor. In any case, while rural in-migration is swelling the size and proportion of the black labor force, there seems to be no equivalent increase in the number and proportion of service and labor jobs held by blacks in recent years.

All of this may well reflect the effects of discriminatory employment practices and how they work to undercut advancement for nonmetropolitan Southern blacks even when they exhibit the initiative to relocate in hopes of improving their circumstances. These latter studies in particular help illustrate how racial discrimination in employment practices may contribute to converting the ever accelerating intra-regional rural to urban migration of poor people into more of a problem than it need be for the South.

The Impact of Discriminatory Practices in Education

The number of "experts" who proclaim education to be the answer to poverty (Ribich, 1968; Dailey 1964; Tweeten, 1967; Schwarzweller and Brown 1962) is matched only by the number who proclaim that even if this were so, discriminatory practices prevent blacks especially from advancing by this route.

Dailey, for example, concludes that education is the answer to poverty on the basis of his study of a national sample of 450,000 school children in grades

*Alabama, Arkansas, Georgia, Louisana, Mississippi and South Carolina.

9-12 done in 1960. He bases this conclusion on the observed link between level of education achieved and subsequent occupational and income success.

Yet his findings showed that with the exception of the top 2 percent in ability, entrance into college is most directly related to family income (Dailey, 1964). Since blacks generally have less income than whites, this obviously means that blacks have less access to opportunities in education.

It should be noted that while average levels of educational achievement among blacks now almost parallel that of whites (Deuterman, 1970), blacks in poverty remain a considerable and perhaps growing number.

In any case, the income barrier to education is one that can be passed off as not being directly reflective of discriminatory practices in educational establishments. It is more difficult to evade such a charge, however, when confronted with gross racial imbalances among student populations in college and professional level educational programs. For example, Neil McBride, Southern Director for the Law Students Civil Rights Research Council, recently reported that of 12,340 current students in Southern law schools, only 208 are black. This disparity is put into sharp focus by examining black-white student ratios in law schools in some of the states in the region, as shown in Table 6-3.

TABLE 6-3

Ratio of Black-White Enrollment in Southern Law Schools, by States (1970)

	Total Enrollment	Number of Blacks
Alabama	776	8
Florida	2514	31
South Carolina	648	4

Source: *Athens Banner-Herald,* "Black Lawyers Remain Sparse in the Deep South," (November 26, 1970), 40.

The educational selection processes which are in part implied by these imbalances contribute directly to the fact that of 42,448 attorneys now practicing in 12 Southern states, only 423 or less than 1 percent are black. In Georgia, for example, the Southern state with the largest black population, only 30 black lawyers exist, 10 of which are in private practice (*Athens Banner-Herald,* 1970a).

Discriminatory educational practices are evidenced in the differential quality of education at lower levels provided the races in the South as well as in admissions practices in higher education. Prior to the advent of extensive school integration in the South, it was possible to directly compare the differential in resources invested in education of blacks and whites in the region.* Welch has computed some measures of educational quality in rural Southern schools for the 1955-56 school year which are presented in Table 6-5.

Applying these and other measures of quality, Welch concluded that blacks at that time were getting only 73 percent as much education as whites for the same amount of time spent in school in the rural South. He suggests that this partly explains why blacks attend school only 91 percent as much as whites and why they drop out of school more often (Welch, 1967; Wilbur, 1964).

TABLE 6-4

Number of Black Lawyers to Total, by States (1970)

	Total	Number of Blacks
Alabama	2712	24
Florida	7801	60
Georgia	4824	30
Kentucky	3353	22
Mississippi	2201	23
North Carolina	3637	70
South Carolina	1896	11
Tennessee	4251	35

Source: *South Today,* January 2, 1971.

Also, since by his figures equivalent education returns only 32 percent for blacks of what it returns for whites in terms of subsequent income, Welch reasons that it is quite rational of rural Southern blacks to decide not to continue their educations. He concludes that blacks may

> simply devalue schooling since it is perceived to be either of poorer quality or of less instrumental use in obtaining income rewards than for the white. (Welch, 1967, 233)

Albin holds with Welch that the poor black's decision to terminate his education is quite rational in

*Parenthetically, it should be noted that other forms of discriminatory practices persist in public elementary and high school education in the South even though it was proclaimed officially that all but 76 of 2,700 school districts in the region (97%) had been desegrated by the Fall of 1970 (Southern Regional Council, 1971, 1).

One form in the public school tends to racially separate children in classrooms by imposing an "ability tracking" program. A recent NAACP sponsored study found that this and other devices produced segregated classrooms in 273 of 467 school districts monitored in September, 1970 (*Op. cit.* 8-9). Finally a rapid rise of segregated academies has occurred in response to demands for integration. While there are some indications that the movement is losing steam, enrollments for Fall, 1970, were up to between 450,000-500,000 from 400,000 the previous year (*Op. cit.,* 16).

TABLE 6-5

Quality of Rural Southern Elementary and Secondary Education for 1955-56 for 10 States, by Race*

	Average Per Pupil Costs	Instructors Per 100 Pupils	Average Staff Salary	Average Number of Pupils Enrolled in Secondary Schools
White	$230.00	4.6	$3,300.00	230
Black	$120.00	4.0	$2,310.00	175

*The 10 states are Alabama, Arkansas, Georgia, Louisiana, Mississippi, North Carolina, South Carolina, Tennessee, Texas and Virginia.

Source: Finis Welch, "Labor-Market Discrimination: On Interpretation of Income Differences in the Rural South," *Journal of Political Economy,* LXXV (June 3, 1967) 237, Table 3.

most cases. But he adds another ominous dimension to his analysis in taking into account the likely effects of the increasing necessity to master complex technological processes in preparing for work opportunities on the decisions the poor make about their educations. He suggests that these increasing technological demands require more extended investments in education, but for the black in particular, such extended investments do not yield the greater income benefits which should be associated with such investments. Therefore, as the required investment becomes greater, the likelihood that blacks will discontinue their educations increases (Albin, 1970).

Lassiter has shown this to be the case very clearly in his study of a 5 percent sample of all Southern males over age 25 drawn from the 1960 U.S. Census.* His analyses disclosed that there is a closer relationship between level of education achieved and lifetime earned income for Southerners than for Northerners, and that, regardless of location, there is less income return for blacks as educational achievement increases than for whites.

No doubt Albin would warmly endorse Lassiter's conclusion that

> on the basis of the lower additions to lifetime income through investment in education by the non-white, . . . such a failure [to continue in school] may be economically sound from a private standpoint. (Lassiter, 1965, 22)

*Southern here includes 16 states and Washington, D. C.

All of this helps support the notion that the poor are indeed rational, pragmatic decision-makers but it does so at the expense of raising considerable doubt about whether and to what extent education is, in fact, the most promising road out of poverty. Put simply, are the poor, particularly blacks, limited in their opportunities because of a lack of education and skills, or are they arbitrarily shut out of such opportunities regardless of their established levels of accomplishment?

A variety of studies have been carried out in recent years in the hopes of resolving this question. Expectedly, the results are as contradictory as the interpretations made by their authors.

David concludes evenhandedly on the basis of interviews with 3,000 whites and blacks in New York State in 1966, that the liability of being born black penalizes earnings almost as much as dropping out of school (1964, 257). Galloway makes a similar claim in asserting that educational differences between the races and discrimination exert about the same amount of influence on limiting opportunities for blacks (1967).

TABLE 6-6

Rates of Return over Opportunity Cost (Perceived Investment) of Completing Specified Years of School, by Race and Location (1959)

	Percent Lifetime Return for Completing:			
	10th year	12th year	13th year	16th year
Non-South White Males	13	12	13	9
Non-South Black Males	8	8	8	5
South White Males	15	14	15	10
South Black Males	10	9	10	6

Source: R. L. Lassiter, Jr., "The Association of Income and Education for Males by Region, Race and Age," *Southern Economics Journal,* XXXII (July 1965), Table VI.

These "middle-of-the-roaders" are flanked on either side by those who favor one factor or the other. Gwarthey, utilizing a sample of all males over 25 years old recorded in the 1960 U.S. Census who were urban and/or non-farm, found that education was the major factor limiting income opportunities. He controlled for age, region, city size, education, and scholastic achievement in order to test the extent to which race made a difference in earnings. His findings indicate that quality of education and scholastic achievement accounted for as much as 23 to 27 percent of the differences in incomes between the races in 1959. Even if discrimination were totally eliminated such educational differences would continue to influence income differentials to the extent that black income would only come up to between 70 and 80 percent of white income. Fourteen to 25 percent of the income differences between the races for urban males is unexplained by educational factors. Gwarthey concludes that these percentages represent the amount of income difference caused by racial discrimination (1970).

Rasmussen produced a similar result in a recent study which also utilized a sample drawn from the 1960 U.S. Census. He reasoned that differences in income between the races trace to differences in productivity. Lower productivity among blacks, in turn, is principally determined by their lack of skills and income. His statistical maneuvers yielded the estimate that only about 19 percent of income differentials can be accounted for by racial discrimination with the remainder mostly accounted for by educational differences (Rasmussen, 1969).

Welch and others, on the other hand, provide data which directly contradicts these findings (see also: Smolensky, 1966). In his previously cited study he examined the income levels for rural Southern blacks and whites having equal levels of educational achievement. He found that

> a non-white with no schooling will receive 81 percent of the income of a similar white. Yet, for nonwhites, school attendance increases income at a rate which is only 28 percent of the corresponding increase for whites. (Welch, 1967, 235)

He concludes from this that racial discrimination, particularly the long history of overt discrimination in the rural South, actually is the major factor in low incomes among rural Southern blacks.

Duncan's elegant study also concludes with the view that racial discrimination above all else leads the black to poverty. His analysis of data on a national cross sectional sample composed of 90 percent whites and 10 percent blacks showed that even after adjusting for such factors as family size, family background, occupation, education, and age, 37 percent of the dicerences in income between the races remains unaccounted for. This amount is attributed to racial discrimination (Duncan, 1969). He suggests that

> Negro families with better than average educational levels do, in general, succeed in passing along a comparable level of *educational* attainment to their children . . . [but they] are less able to convert such attainment into occupational and . . . monetary returns. (*Ibid.*)

Finally, data can be found which seem to show that neither factor makes a large difference in the matter. Michelson's analysis of data on a 1/1000 sample of the 1960 U.S. Census concludes with the estimate that about 15 percent of the difference in income between low income blacks and whites is traceable to educational differences. Secondly, only about 12 percent of such income differences could be accounted for by equalizing the number of weeks worked per year across the races. His view is that equalization in education and employment would have some effect on raising those of both races above the poverty line, but such measures would be of greater benefit to whites in poverty than blacks (Michaelson, 1968).

This is an interesting conclusion, one directly opposite of that expressed by Willie, who proposes that equal opportunity programming would have a differential effect favoring blacks, largely because the black poor would be responsive to such opportunities whereas the white poor would not (Willie, 1963). Willie bases this point on the assumption that white and black poverty have different causal explanations:

> White poverty has been reduced to the point where probably individual and family character are the bedrock problems whereas Negro poverty continues to be largely economic deprivation (*Ibid.,* 18)

One issue upon which studies seem to yield general agreement is that the better educated rural Southern poor—black or white—tend to relocate in greater numbers to seek more opportunities than do their less well educated cohorts (Schwarzweller, 1964; Hines and Tweeten, 1968). This at least suggests that education does play a part in increasing the expectations of the rural Southern poor. Whether the quality of their education is technologically inferior thus preventing them from converting their expectations into real gains by moving, or whether they simply are arbitrarily excluded from opportunities regardless of educational achievement because of their race, background, and so on, is another matter, one which available data do not resolve.

A Note on Stigma

The wealth of data presented in this chapter on the Opportunity Thesis is, as was stated at the outset, purposely limited in scope. A variety of ways that those in poverty are discriminated against because of the statuses assigned them by officials or others in society has been virtually ignored.

Some of the ways in which those in poverty may be arbitrarily excluded from opportunities for advancement because of the labels they bear can only be hinted at as we approach the end of this chapter. For example, a dual system of law and justice has long been recognized to operate in this nation, one for the poor and one for the better-off (ten Broek, 1966). Lack of legal representation for the poor black has been especially acute, and when we recall the fact that few black lawyers exist in private practice in the South, we can assume that such representation by members of their own race in the South is almost non-existent.

In addition to law and justice, the stigma attached to being a public assistance client demonstrably restricts such persons from full access to public housing, credit, and other resources (Block, *et al.,* 1970; Caplovitz, 1963 and 1965; Dixon and McLaughlin, 1970). Being unemployed in itself imposes substantial limitations upon a person's access to such resources; however, being unemployed in association with deviant status (e.g., being a felon, delinquent, mental patient, public assistant client, etc.) compounds the number of ways a person is restricted from the mainstream of socio-economic processes (Goodchilds and Smith, 1963; Kutner, 1970).

Again, the poor—particularly in racial minorities—may not utilize existing opportunities to obtain services simply because they expect to be treated so badly by agencies providing them that they avoid making contact (Manning, 1960; O'Reilly *et al.,* 1965; Marsh and Brown, 1965).

The importance of these factors in influencing the amount of opportunity available to the poor in the nonmetropolitan South is not minimized by my failure to treat them fully. Rather, I have placed greatest emphasis on the factors of education and employment in this section because that group of theorists and researchers who seem to assume the validity of the Opportunity Thesis have done so.

Summary Points

What then have we established about the Opportunity Thesis as a causal explanation of nonmetropolitan Southern poverty?

On the matter of whether the rural Southern poor are rational, pragmatic decision-makers, it does seem possible to conclude that many exhibit beliefs in the same values about individual striving and initiative supposedly held by the better-off majority of our society, even though the rhetoric and types of behavior (e.g., violent words and militant behavior) following from these beliefs may differ radically.

The better educated among the rural Southern poor may be exhibiting higher expectations for themselves and their families than are commonly associated with them in other theoretical views about poverty, by virtue of the fact that they relocate geographically in large numbers seeking advancement.

It does seem also that unfortunate or inadequate life decisions made by these people stem at least in part from lack of access to full and appropriate information needed to make better decisions.

Finally, there is conflicting and limited information about the extent to which the nonmetropolitan Southern poor are predisposed to or capable of organized activity, either in their areas of origin or upon becoming residents of urban areas.

Throughout all of this, blacks and the young among the nonmetropolitan Southern poor tend to be evaluated more favorably; that is, they are found to exhibit more self initiative, higher expectations, and greater predisposition toward joining in collective efforts.

On the matter of the degree of arbitrariness embedded in current employment and educational policies and practices, there is little question that, in various ways discrimination operates to limit the economic opportunity of the nonmetropolitan Southern poor.

Intentional or not, it does seem clear that current social policies which emphasize some programs and neglect others, particularly in regard to income protection, penalize the poor in the nonmetropolitan South, whether they remain there or relocate to urban areas in the region. They may also directly affect decisions made by nonmetropolitan poor people about remaining in or vacating their current residences.

Discrimination in employment practices seems widespread and partly at least explains the lack of advancement occupationally of rural Southern blacks. Again, racial imbalances in enrollments in higher education programs and measures of equality in education provided the two races in the South suggest some of the ways that advancement through educational achievement is denied.

Through all of this, the black seems to suffer more from these practices than the poor white in the nonmetropolitan South, and it is perhaps the older Southern black who has suffered and continues to suffer most of all.

While there is, as we have noted, controversy over which race suffers the most from arbitrary exclusion from the goods and services needed to advance out of poverty, most of the evidence in this chapter points toward the black in the nonmetropolitan South as being most directly affected by such exclusions.

The Opportunity Thesis may have greatest applicability to understanding the plight of youth—particularly black youth—now living in poverty in the South. All of our indicators reveal that this age group is growing in numbers in proportion to the size of other age groups now living in poverty in the nonmetropolitan South, that they are more self assertive, prone toward action, and better educated than their elders. Substantial changes in social policies and programs coupled with rapid expansion of educational and employment opportunities in the nonmetropolitan South might well prevent widespread poverty for this group and produce a new generation of leadership committed to improving the quality of life for those residing there.

Chapter 7

ASSESSING THE MALDISTRIBUTION THESIS

The case for the Maldistribution Thesis rests squarely upon whether a maldistribution in skilled manpower, accumulated wealth, and their implied production of income, goods, and services is demontrable. Secondly, the extent to which the thesis explains poverty is at least in part testable in terms of the amount that redressing old imbalances contributes to the increased income, improved life circumstances, and diminishment of out migration of the nonmetropolitan Southern poor.

Reductions in the rate and persistence of poverty and in the migration behavior of the nonmetropolitan poor directly associated with geographic and/or socio-economic advances toward greater balance in the distribution of resources can be taken as supportive of this causal explanation.

The Case for a Maldistribution of Resources: Geographic and Socio-Economic

The Maldistribution Thesis has an important place in American folklore about poverty as reflected in such commonplace adages as "the rich get richer and the poor get poorer." Socio-economically, those born to or otherwise enjoying a competitive edge in acquiring resources are simply in a better position to accumulate more and more over time. Geographically, the old saw, "them that's got gets and them that don't gits," bespeaks the belief that the only way up under such circumstances is out.

The academic equivalents of this more colorful terminology are found among a variety of poverty theorists. Seligman, among many others, proposes, for example, that poverty and its intergenerational transmission are chiefly caused by the inadequate distribution of medical care, skills, retirement programs, education, and the like, within the socio-economic structure (Seligman, 1968, 35).

Others have attempted to explain geographic concentrations of poor people in the rural South as a consequence of larger national changes in overall productivity stemming from technological advances which have had particularly strong impact on impoverishing the Southern agriculturally oriented economy (see: Hendrix, 1959 and 1967; H. A. Henderson, 1960; Bachmura and Southern, 1965). These views are adequately summed up by the following quotation:

> Rural poverty is caused mainly by a long-term secular, structural change that has reduced employment in farming and in relatively stable or even declining area non-agricultural jobs. This situation has been accompanied by high birth rates. Adjustments requiring mobility by rural people are made more difficult by limited occupational experience . . . and by problems of a shrinking rural population and tax base. . . . These conditions have created the large geographic areas in which the major proportion of the population suffers from prolonged poverty. (U. S. D. A., E. R. S., 1966, 66)

Whatever the reasons, analyses have yielded estimates that rural Southern poverty is changing little within the context of growing national affluence, and over time the income gap between the rich and poor has widened (Lampman, 1966b). The accuteness of this maldistribution in rural areas is illustrated by Coffey's findings that farm income is most unequally distributed precisely in those states having the highest overall farm income (Coffey, 1968, 1389).

Income statistics are, of course, the data most commonly used to show graphically how imbalanced resources are, both geographically and socio-economically. As often as not a formula is applied to the present distribution of incomes to illustrate how redistribution would have to occur to eradicate poverty. The extensive literature on guaranteed annual income schemes, which should be known to the reader, illustrates this point.

In its most straight-forward form, the Maldistribution Thesis explains poverty in terms of an inadequate distribution of national personal income. Yet there is considerable substance behind this apparent simplicity in the sense that the obvious imbalance in incomes is often directly or indirectly attributed to imbalances in existing skilled manpower, industrial investment capital, program benefit, and movitational distributions among the various geographic regions and social strata.

The important points to bear in mind are that current national resources are assumed adequate to resolve nonmetropolitan Southern poverty and that insuring equal opportunity to access under the current maldistribution of resources will *not* yield this desired resolution.

Income Protection Programs

Income protection programs are a good place to begin in marshalling evidence for the Maldistribution Thesis. As noted in the previous chapter, a variety of state administered programs of this type are neither redistributive in nature, nor are they capable of preventing previously non-poor people from falling into poverty should they need to rely upon them.

Unemployment Compensation programs in the several states, for example, do not pay above 50 percent of average weekly wages; moreover, all have maximums which further limit the size of benefits. As a general rule, therefore, the lower the earnings, the lower the benefits.

Workman's Compensation programs have been shown to have at least minor redistributive properties in the sense that the percentage of projected life-time earnings covered under the programs is slightly higher for low-income earners. However, many rural poor people are not covered by this program; and, even if full coverage is obtained, the percentage benefits are so low in all the regional states except Florida that it is unlikely that such benefits would either prevent entrance into or facilitate escape from poverty.

In public assistance programming the total inadequacy of General Assistance provisions and the total absence of an AFDC-UP program within the region have already been noted. Additionally, average failed to meet their own definitions of basic need under Old Age Assistance programs at that time, as shown in Table 7-1. The reason for this interpretation is that it is generally conceded that income programs for the aged are more acceptable to the public than those for women with children. Hence, if resources were available, it is likely that the states would meet their own definitions of need for their elderly citizens.

These programs in the aggregate are neither redistributive nor capable of delivering income to poor people in the several states at levels above current poverty lines. It is clear from this that even if all these programs were operating at optimum levels (full coverage and full provision of benefits) the impact upon poverty would be negligible.

Schooling and Vocational Training

Throughout the rural parts of the nation school consolidation proceeded at a rapid pace in recent years in part because it was the only reasonable way to meet educational needs under conditions of spiraling costs and shrinking local tax bases. By the mid

TABLE 7-1

Basic Needs Standards and Percentage Met by the States for AFDC and OAA Programs, April 1968

	AFDC Basic Needs Standard	% Met	OAA Basic Needs Standard	% Met
	177	50	125	66
Florida	189	45	111	68
Georgia	198	63	80	90
Kentucky	216	86	90	100
Mississippi	201	27	96	52
North Carolina	144	100	94	100
South Carolina	172	54	82	92
Tennessee	198	61	92	98

Source: The President's Commission on Income Maintenance Programs, *Background Papers,* 1970, Tables 6-2-7 and 6-2-8.

AFDC monthly case payments in all states in the region have been shown to be well below the national average. In no state in the region do the basic need formulas used to compute monthly benefits yield a figure exceeding the SSA poverty line for female headed households of a given size.

By 1967, 29 states continued to pay less than their own definitions of basic needs under their AFDC programs and, for the nation as a whole, AFDC payments averaged only 58 percent of the poverty line (Lurie, 1969). As of mid-1968, 7 of the 8 states in the region continued this pattern.

The Maldistribution Thesis gains some support from the fact that several states in the region also 60's school consolidation had occurred in well over half of all rural school districts. Local government investment in education continued to be substantial during this time: expenditures on education were estimated to exceed 7.3 billion dollars, or over 54 percent of all local revenues (U.S.D.A., E. R. S., 1966, 23 ff.).

Something of the crisis facing rural education can be seen in the estimates that it takes a base of 3500 people to provide the tax revenue to economically run a school, and that in many states up to 95 percent of local school revenues derive from one form of local property tax or another (*Ibid.*). Shrinking populations in some rural areas obviously are contributing to increasing the severe shortage of resources for education.

The situation likely is worst in the most heavily poverty stricken areas of the rural South. Recalling that it is in precisely these areas that the proportion of youth in the population is growing rapidly, it is clear that we have a rising demand for education coupled with extremely limited capability in terms of tax revenues.

Moreover, state administered federal programs set up to assist local school districts are contributing to the problem rather than relieving it. In a study of 3,081 U.S. counties all having some rural population, Zimmer discovered that present formulas for assisting local school districts tend to favor the more urban, better-off districts. This is so because federal programs provide matching funds on a per child estimate of operating costs. Since such expenditures tend to be higher per child in more affluent districts, those districts receive a disproportionate share of available assistance funds (Zimmer, 1967). This literally is a case of the rich getting richer and the poor falling further behind.

Vocational training and rehabilitation programs in the rural South also are hard pressed by existing maldistributions in resources, although of a different sort. Program financing is not so much the problem; rather such programs often face a critical lack of locating available employment placements for post trainees. There seems to be general agreement and concern that in the absence of employment placements such programs will become perceived by rural Southerners as just more welfare programs (see: Meenach, 1969; Bird and McCoy, 1964; Street and Meenach, 1967; Burkhart, 1969; McPhee, 1969). In fact, a review of the lack of success of various programs of this type has caused one authority to question whether realistically, these programs can be other than "make work" in nature (Carter, 1970).

Finally, the question of the availability of employment in rural areas is compounded by the great distances rural people often live from such employment. That is, even if work were to be located in rural areas, this does not mean that rural people would have ready access to it (Bird and McCoy, 1964; McPhee, 1969).

In sum, there is some basis for concluding that resources necessary to provide adequate education and insuring the success of vocational training are not distributed properly enough to accomplish such goals for the poor in the rural South.

Farm Income Supports

We have already noted that those states with highest aggregate farm incomes are also those with the most unequal distributions of farm income. Much that is paradoxical in this finding is explainable in terms of federal farm income support programs which were originally set up to hasten the change from subsistence to commercial farming (Bonnen, 1966). Clearly, these programs reward the successful commercial farmer and benefit the small farmer—who constitutes a large proportion of those still in farming in the South—very little.* Moreover, even if these programs were altered to be redistributive, two thirds of the rural poor would not be affected because they have no direct connection with farming (*Ibid.*). For both these reasons, the rural Southern poor benefit little from present farm income support programs (Booth, 1969).

Rural Housing

Credit and loan resources available for home construction, repair, and purchase are in woefully limited supply in rural areas—particularly the South—from private banking and lending institutions. While 57 percent of all mortgage funds invested in real property came from Savings and Loan Associations, for example, only 15 percent was invested in rural areas in 1959 (Yeager, 1962). Moreover, as late as 1965, only 3 percent of all Savings and Loan Institutions served rural areas in the South, representing about 1 percent of all such service activity carried out by such businesses (Southern Regional Council, 1966).

The record of other lending institutions was no more enviable. Insurance companies invested 22 percent of all mortgage funds in real property in 1959, only 10 per cent of this in rural areas. Commercial banks did a little better, investing 21 percent of all its mortgage funds in real property, 50 percent of which was in rural areas (Yeager, 1962).

Federal Programming in the matter of subsidizing rural housing has shown improvement in recent years. In fiscal 1965, 133 million dollars in loans to individuals were made under the Rural Housing program. As of 1968, the dollar figure had risen to a combined outlay of 1.4 billion under Title V of the Housing and Urban Development Act of 1968. Eight hundred and three million dollars of this figure went in loans to individuals for home purchase and farm improvement benefiting a total of 400,000 low income rural residents (The President's Commission on Income Maintenance Programs, *Background Papers,* 1970, 347).

Small comfort is afforded by these impressive increases in funding in recent years, however, when note is taken of the fact that rural housing programs —from the New Deal to the present—simply are not open to use by the very poor. This is reflected in the fact that although the Farmers Home Administration was set up in part to make loans to low-income families, it has historically had less than a 1 percent loss rate. This clearly indicates that the very poor have never forgotten an appreciable number of loans; if they had, no doubt the loss rate would

*This seems historically as well as currently true. Professor Holly's analysis of New Deal programs aimed at rural areas in the South reveals that while the black farmer was uprooted in large numbers (est. 200,000), only 9 of the total of 150 rural resettlement programs were aimed exclusively at this group through the F. S. A. programs. Address by D. Holly at American Historical Association, Boston, as quoted in the New York *Times,* 1-17-71.

have been considerably higher (Cochran, 1971, 7). Also as late as January, 1971, testimony by HUD officials before the Senate Select Committee on Nutrition and Human Needs revealed that present housing programs simply were not doing an equitable job for the rural poor (U.S. Congress, Senate, Select Committee on Nutrition and Human Needs, 1971). Among other facts brought out were that rural America has received less than 20 percent of the nation's public housing to date although 50 percent of the nation's poor reside there and 67 percent of all inadequate housing is rurally located (*Ibid.,* 5).

One of the major program gaps illuminated by the Committee related to the fact that the Federal Housing Administration does not operate effectively in communities of less than 25,000, while the Farmers Home Administration cannot operate in towns larger than 5,500 (*Ibid.*). Hence, large numbers of people in communities of intermediate size go totally unserved. After 30 years of programing, it remains that almost 1,200 counties, mostly nonmetropolitan, do not yet have a federal housing program (*Ibid.,* 23). In nonmetropolitan areas, moreover, 34,000 communities lack modern water facilities and 44,000 communities do not have adequate sanitation facilities (*Ibid.,* 11). In all of this, the rural South seems to suffer more severe inadequacies than other rural parts of the nation (*Ibid.,* 23 ff.). Hence while allocations are up, subsequent testimony reveals disappointing details about the extent to which the rural poor are actually benefiting. The picture is rather dismal in that it suggests that increased appropriations under the existing system of allocating funds simply will not be of major assistance to the rural poor. This lends more credence to the basic proposition of the Maldistribution Thesis that resources are available but poorly allocated.

Rural-Urban Allocations in Other Federal Programs

A review of federal program expenditures in 1966 accomplished by the Advisory Commission on Intergovernmental Relations disclosed that, by and large, program allocations aimed at helping the poor were being disproportionately invested in urban areas. For example, of $6.8 million granted by the Office of Economic Opportunity (OEO) in 1965 for small business loans, 65 percent of all loans representing 56 percent of all such expenditures went to individuals in 3 Northern urbanized states (Michigan, Illinois, Pennsylvania) and the District of Columbia. Again, only about 20 percent of the total cumulative expenditures under the Manpower Training and Development Act of 1962 (MTDA), the Vocational Education Act of 1963, and the Economic Opportunity Act of 1964, had found their way to rural areas by mid-1965 (U. S. Advisory Commission on Intergovernmental Relations, 1966).

All of this suggests gross imbalance in the distribution of resources through federal programing, coupled with severe lack of resources in rural areas, particularly the South, in reference to financing for housing, education, and other matters. These data should be born in mind in evaluating a recent report which shows that every Southern state except Florida currently receives more federal aid annually than they individually pay out in the form of federal taxes (Floyd, 1970). This apparent redistribution through the medium of federal programing is less than reassuring when we examine, as we have, the extent to which these program dividends actually benefit the rural Southern poor. Moreover, the widening gap between federal program authorizations and appropriations suggests that these programs, however ineffective presently, are likely to be even less effective in correcting resource imbalances in the near future. A full analysis of congressional program authorizations and appropriations for the years 1966 and 1970 shows that appropriations were 80 percent of authorizations in 1966 but fell to 65 percent by 1970. Hardest hit by underfinancing were precisely the programs most likely to be of benefit to the poor, those administered by the Department of Health, Education and Welfare, and the Office of Economic Opportunity (U.S. Advisory Commission on Intergovernmental Relations and Council of State Governments, 1970).

Professional Services: Health, Legal and Social Services

Health Services

Major support for the Maldistribution Thesis comes from a recent HEW report on health services for the poor, as follows:

> Given current estimates that about $200 per year per person would purchase 'good' health care, if resources were applied for maximum benefit, current governmental expenditures (about 4.6 billion by state and local government in 1968) would cover the major costs of health services for the poor. While this degree of efficiency is rarely found in any system, it seems clear that much room for improvement exists in the delivery of health services and in the structure of federal programs impacting on the health of the poor. (U.S.D.H.E.W., *Delivery of Health Services for the Poor,* 1967, 41)

The moral of this passage is, of course, that facilities, financing, and manpower in the health field may be adequate to overall need but inadequately distributed. This seems to be the case for the rural South when an overall impression is drawn from a scattering of data on health facilities, manpower, and unmet need.

Regarding health facilities, Table 7-2 presents recent data on hospitals, licensed nursing homes, and Neighborhood Health Centers.

In general terms, the South appears to be keeping pace with national rates for hospital beds per 1,000 population, while falling somewhat behind national rates in provision of nursing home facilities (see: U.S.D.H.E.W., S.S.A., *Health Insurance Statistics,*

TABLE 7-2

Hospital, Nursing Home, and Neighborhood Health Center Capacities, by State (1968)

	(1) No. Non Profit General Care Hospital	(2) No. Hospital Beds per 1,000 Population	(3) No. Nursing Home Beds per 1,000 Population over 65 Years	(4) No. Neighborhood Health Centers	Total Size of Potential Service Populations
United States	4305	7.9	44.5		
Alabama	87	7.5	29.2	2*	32,000
Florida	106	6.7	28.9	1	20,000
Georgia	98	7.3	33.2	1	30,000
Kentucky	82	6.9	36.5	3**	50,000
Mississippi	70	7.3	17.8	2**	24,000
North Carolina	105	6.6	37.4	NA	—
South Carolina	56	7.5	26.8	1	25,000
Tennessee	81	7.5	23.6	1	18,000

*One rural Center

**Two rural Centers

Sources: Column 1, Planned Parenthood—World Population, Center for Family Planning Program Development, *Need for Subsidized Family Planning Service,* 1968, Table 1.

Columns 2 and 3, U.S.D.H.E.W., P.H.S., *Health Resources Statistics,* 1970, Tables 174 and 182.
Column 4, The President's Commission on Income Maintenance Programs, *Background Papers,* 1970, Table 9.6-1.

1971).* At the same time, neighborhood health centers are extremely scarce. While these data are not overly impressive to begin with, they mask the extent to which facilities are probably deficient in rural areas. For instance, as late as 1962 urban areas actually had twice the number of hospital beds per 1,000 population comparing to rates in isolated beds per 1,000 population comparing to rates in isolated rural areas (U.S.D.H.E.W., P.H.S., *Health and Manpower Source Book,* 1965). A glance at Table 7-2 also discloses that only 5 health centers were serving the rural population of the region as of 1968. Professional manpower in the health services in the South are also lagging according to the figures in Table 7-3.

Every state in the region is well below national averages in all three categories of professional manpower per 100,000 population, with the lone exception of the large number of registered nurses practicing in Florida. Only Florida and Tennessee exceed the National Medical Association's (NMA) estimate that a minimum of 100 doctors per 100,000 people is necessary to deliver adequate health care (Terjen, 1970). Production of health service professionals within the states with few exceptions may not be adequate to keep pace with present ratios of personnel to population let alone improve upon them even in the unlikely event that population growth were held to zero. Take, for example, Mississippi's record of producing no dentists, only 17 registered nurses, and 65 medical and osteopathic doctors during the year of 1968.

And this is not the whole of it, since for various reasons professionals leave practice and locate in places where the best facilities and remuneration prevail. Therefore, even if personnel were being produced in numbers adequate to match the needs of growing populations and replacement, a clear possibility exists that their distribution would continue to produce inadequate services, particularly for the rural poor in the region.

There is, of course, more to go on here than supposition. For example, it has been recently estimated that at least 5,000 rural communities in the U.S. have no access to a doctor (*Time,* January 18, 1971, 35). This clearly suggests that professional health personnel are not flocking to rural areas.

Racial discrimination may well be a continuing factor in this geographic maldistribution of medical personnel both within the region and in comparing the region to the remainder of the country. Blacks have been virtually excluded from medical education in the past with the result being that of 317,000 doctors in the U. S. today, only about 2 percent, or 6,000, are blacks. The National Medical Association has estimated that about 30,000 black doctors

*Consistent with these data are recent data on amount of participation in the Medicare program as reflected in the number and distribution of manpower and facilities utilized. Data indicate the South compares favorably in such matters as number of hospitals and number of nursing beds, but lags in professional technical manpower (see: U.S.D.H.E.W., S.S.A., Health Insurance Statistics, 1971).

TABLE 7-3

Professional Health Service Personnel, by States (1968)

	Non Federal Dentists (per 100,000 pop.)	Production of Dentists 1968	Non Federal Physicians (per 100,000 pop.)	Production of Medical and Osteopaths 1968	RN Nurses Employed 1966 (per 100,000 pop.)	RN Grads 1968
United States	53		132		313	
Alabama	29	42	75	71	168	85
Florida	45	—	126	132	369	171
Georgia	28	67	93	159	156	69
Kentucky	33	94	90	150	198	100
Mississippi	25	—	69*	65	157	17
North Carolina	28	45	91	203	244	183
South Carolina	22*	45**	72	66	217	43
Tennessee	36	141	102	240	175	116

—Represents none.
*Lowest in nation.
**1st graduating class 1971.

Source: U.S.D.H.E.W., P.H.S., *Health Resources Statistics: Health Manpower and Health Facilities,* 1969, 1970, Tables 37, 40, 85, 87, 93, and 98.

are currently needed to service the primary medical needs of black citizens. The situation is most stark in the South where, for example, in Mississippi there are currently an estimated 900,000 black people but only 46 black doctors, or 1 per 19,000 population (Terjen, 1970, 2).

The outcomes for the nonmetropolitan poor in the South of this maldistribution of health personnel are perhaps best illustrated by citing some recent studies of unmet medical needs among this part of the region's population.

Pearman has reported on a study of the unmet

TABLE 7-4

Number of Public Family Planning Programs and Unmet Needs Among Nonmetropolitan Medically Indigent Women, by States (1968)

	No. of Hospitals with Family Planning Programs	No. of Counties with OEO Family Planning Programs	No. of Women in Need (Millions)	% Unserved Total States*	% Unserved outside SMSA's	% of Total State Need outside SMSA's	% of Total Services Rendered outside SMSA's
United States	435	170	5.367	861	950		19
Alabama	2	5	.175	81	85	57	45
Florida	7	2	.229	79	82	40	33
Georgia	7	2	.205	88	94	65	32
Kentucky	6	1	.142	92	95	81	50
Mississippi	2	5	.136	90	90	87	89
North Carolina	6	8	.231	87	92	75	47
South Carolina	3	8	.133	84	85	67	63
Tennessee	10	1	.186	94	100	64	.05

*All percents rounded for clarity of presentation.

Source: Planned Parenthood — World Population, Center for Family Planning Program Development, *Need for Subsidized Family Planning Services,* 1968, 34 ff., Table 1.

medical needs of 1177 black and white children in 389 families associated with Head Start programs in 6 rural north Florida counties (Pearman, 1970). All these families were in poverty because their income had to fall below $3,000 per year in order to participate in the program.

His findings show that infant mortality rates did fall in these families between 1960-67 but that 70 percent of the children needed dental care, hypochromic anemia was common, and over 50 percent had not been immunized against smallpox, diptheria, tetanus, pertussis, and poliomyelitis. Health care was notably less for black than for white children, and, by and large, medical services of all sorts within the counties fell well below national averages.

Unattended medical needs among adult family members in nonmetropolitan poverty are to some extent estimable from a recent study of unmet family planning needs among nonmetropolitan, medically indigent women. Table 7-4 shows the number of such programs currently in operation in the South and the extent to which they appear to be reaching nonmetropolitan poor families.

These data show how limited programing is within the region on matters of family planning for the poor in or out of the cities. While services are somewhat limited throughout the region, those that are being delivered are disproportionately delivered to metropolitan residents in most of the states, as comparison of the figures in the two extreme righthand columns in the table disclose. While all states—with the exception of Tennessee—exceed the national average in delivering such services to the nonmetropolitan poor, only Mississippi and South Carolina are doing so in proportion to the size of the need represented by people in nonmetropolitan areas.

Other studies could be cited to support the point illustrated here that the nonmetropolitan poor are the recipients of grossly inadequate medical care. Combined with other data showing imbalances in the distribution of manpower and facilities between the South and the rest of the nation, it is possible to speculate that maldistribution makes a substantial contribution to the unmet medical needs of the nonmetropolitan Southern poor.

Occasionally in this manuscript we get to end a discussion with a hopeful note. In this case hope stems from the fact that the Emergency Health Personnel Act of 1970 was signed into law December 31, 1970. This act authorizes Public Health Service doctors to dispense medical care in areas where local officials request their presence. The $10 million appropriated for the first year may be used to recruit more professional personnel to this service (*Time*, January 18, 1971, 35). This approach could improve medical services for the nonmetropolitan poor in the South almost immediately. However, much depends upon the enthusiasm of local officials for the program.

Legal and Social Services

Good data on the availability of legal service for the poor in the South are hard to come by. Inferences can be made from previously cited data showing less than 1 percent of Southern lawyers to be black, that representation of poor blacks may suffer from a lack of legally trained personnel within their racial group (*Athens Banner-Herald*, 1970a).

We can also infer inadequate legal counseling from the fact that Southern states have been notable in their apparent antipathy toward implementing Legal Aid Services provided for in the Economic Opportunity Act and administered by the OEO.* The "Store Front Lawyer" is apparently not as much of a fixture in the nonmetropolitan South as he is in other parts of the country or on TV (Neighborhood Legal Services).

Finally, major fact-finding and planning studies which have focused on the rural U.S. rarely mention legal services as a component instrument in eradicating poverty (see: The President's National Advisory Commission on Intergovernmental Relations, *Urban and Rural America: Policies for Future Growth*, 1968). While we have ample evidence as to how our system of law and justice may work against poor people (see: Ten Broek, 1966), it seems little effort has gone into assessing how much legal service is available to the poor, especially in nonmetropolitan areas. This matter is a fit subject for further exploration and research.

Estimates of the availability and distribution of social services in the South are no easier to come by. For some reason the best minds in the field of social services in rural areas have concentrated on producing doomsday predictions and/or grandeloquent plans rather than documentation of need and service delivery capacity.

Ginsberg, for example, writes that there is a great need for community organization activity in rural America and that "it is evident, a major need [exists] for the basic social services in rural communities" (1969a, 183). But from his writings—and those of others—we do not discern what these basic service needs are, where they exist or do not at present in rural areas, and what kind, how many, and where needed professional service personnel currently practice.

Moreover, statistics on social services provided to poor people in rural areas through volunteer agencies and programs simply do not exist. Statistics for public agencies are, on the other hand, basically aggregated for states, thereby making it difficult to assess the extent to which available service provisions reach nonmetropolitan and rural poor residents.

From such state statistics we can at least gain a rough impression of the quantity of service delivered for some kinds of programs through public assistance departments. The kinds of social services most concretely measurable are those related to the provision of institutional care for the elderly, disabled, blind,

*See the recent article in the New York *Times* on OEO legal aid program for Jackson, Mississippi to witness both the politics involved and the program results of same in a Southern state (New York *Times*, 1971a).

TABLE 7-5

Institutional Services and Community Action Programs, by States

	(1) No. CAP Programs (1968)	(2) No. Aged, Disabled Blind Receiving Residential Care Funded by Welfare Payments (Nov. 1970)	(3) No. AFDC Children in Foster Homes (Nov. 1970)	(4) No. AFDC Children Penal Residential Receiving Non-Penal Residential Care (Nov. 1970)
United States	2,016	155,000	43,400	3,400
Alabama	44	840	960	0
Florida	38	1,100	420	0
Georgia	130	470	1,100	0
Kentucky	97	NA	980	76
Mississippi	37	NA	NA	NA
North Carolina	80	NA	1,600	0
South Carolina	46	590	69	0
Tennessee	86	5,400	1,100	130

Source: Column 1, *Need for Subsidized Family Planning Services,* Table 1.
Columns 2-4, U.S.D.H.E.W., S.R.S., N.C.S.S., *Public Assistance Statistics,* 1970, Tables 11 and 14.

and young among the welfare client population in the South.*

Table 7-5 presents recent case tabulations of such services delivered by public assistance departments, including an accounting of Community Action Programs (CAP's) which are funded by OEO.

The 558 operating CAP programs represent about 27.5 percent of all such programs operating in the U.S. at the time the data were gathered. In the matter of public assistance supported institutional care services, the data are spotty but would seem to support a tentative conclusion that only Tennessee of the states in the South supports such services on anything approaching a large scale. And still the question remains unanswered as to the extent that the nonmetropolitan public assistance poor share in these limited number of programs of very limited size.

Not a great deal can be inferred from this limited information, and anything beyond what we can infer is pure guess work. This is so because leaders in the field of social welfare have yet to declare precisely the nature of social services (as distinct from health and economic services, for example). It is difficult under these circumstances to establish meaningful estimates of the extent of unmet need among the nonmetropolitan poor and how many and how qualified need be the personnel to deliver required services.

No worthwhile purpose would be served by grouping further. It seems sufficient to say that insofar as Maldistribution Theorists link inadequate legal and social services to the rate and persistence of poverty, their position suffers by inadequate conceptualization of the nature of such needs among the nonmetropolitan poor in the South and insufficient documentation of the scope and degree of imbalance extant in the financial and manpower distributions within such service programs.

*However, there are serious problems in gathering statistics on institutionalized persons related to institutional reporting techniques and other matters. See: The President's Commission on Income Maintenance Programs, *Background Papers,* 1970, 158-160.

Regional Industrial-Employment Growth and Distribution

The South not only exported great numbers of people during the decade of the 50's, it also experienced a deterioration in its aggregate wealth during that period. This deterioration was reflected in a relative decline in per capita income *vis a vis* other regions in the nation. This decline in turn, has been attributed to the nature and quality of industrial productivity in the South which required less skilled manpower and was less mechanized than was true of other regions.

Export of the products of such low technology processes yielded a trade imbalance for the South largely because higher priced goods and services needed to satisfy consumer demand had to be imported. Costello shows that this import-export trade deficit increased during the 50's. Using a standard import-export trade index of 100 for the year 1947, he indicates that the index declined to 77.2 by 1958, a trend reflecting an increasing drain on regional resources already less than adequate to meet regional needs (Costello, 1966).

With the advent of the 60's the South experienced something of a change in fortunes. Per capita income, as previously noted, rose more rapidly in most areas of the South during the 60's than was the case for the nation as a whole. Productivity in manufacturing industries, a bellwether indicator of the economic well-being in a geographic area, also showed some dramatic increases in the South. For example, the total value of shipments in manufacturing industries in the 8 states in the regions rose from roughly $53.6 billion in 1964 to $72.2 billion by 1967. Investment in expansion and improvements also advanced noticeably during the decade as evidenced in the fact that new capital expenditures in manufacturing industries rose from approximately $1.3 billion in 1960 to $3.2 billion in 1967 (U.S.D.C., B. of C., *1967 Census of Manufacturers,* 1970).

Table 7-6 introduces some measures of industrial progress in manufacturing in states within the region in recent years.

half of the outlay in North Carolina during the same year ($664.6 million).

We are concerned with measuring the extent and distribution of industrial growth in the region in the 60's for two reasons: first what does such growth mean in terms of revenue yields for local governments necessary for the underwriting of new and expanded services and, secondly, what does it mean in terms of new jobs and improved incomes for the people of poverty?

On the first matter it is clear from a recent study of property tax assessments within the states of the region that business expansion has not produced a horn of plenty relative to tax revenues during the last decade. Davis and Miller, concluding that property taxes will remain the basic source of tax revenue for local governments in the Southeastern states for the

TABLE 7-6

Some Indicators of Industrial Gains in Manufacturing Activities, 1960-67, by States

	% Increase in Cost of Materials (1960-67)	% Increase in Value Added (1960-67)	1967 Rank by Amount of Value Added	1967 Rank by Total Value of Shipments	% Increase in New Capital Expenditures (1960-67)	1967 Rank by Amount of Capital Expenditures
Alabama	29.0	80.4	6	6	87.6	5
Florida	30.2	105.5	4	7	96.7	7
Georgia	27.2	87.9	3	2	144.7	2
Kentucky	22.4	87.1	5	5	196.5	6
Mississippi	30.6	133.9	8	8	573.1	8
North Carolina	26.5	73.7	1	1	177.0	1
South Carolina	20.5	76.1	7	4	188.8	3
Tennessee	35.1	92.1	2	3	93.4	4

Data Source: U.S.D.C., B. of C., *1967 Census of Manufacturers,* Area Series MC67(3), 1, 10, 11, 18, 25, 34, 41, and 43, Table 2.

These figures, given that they no doubt incorporate the effects of inflation over the decade, lend a glimmer of optimism: increases in the costs of materials and the value added in processing operations imply at least some increased sophistication in manufacturing processes as well as volume of output.

However, there is also need for caution when the distribution of such gains among the states in the region is examined. Impressive percentage increases over the decade among the least industrialized states in the region have not led to any obvious trend toward equalizing the distribution of industrially related resources in the region. For example, Mississippi remains last in the rankings even though value added more than doubled during the decade and new capital expenditures increased almost sixfold (from $40.9 million in 1960 to $276.2 million in 1967). New capital expenditures in Mississippi in 1967 remained less than

foreseeable future, made a study of property tax assessments in the various states for the 1956-66 period.

Drawing on data from the Census of Government Reports for 1957, 1962, and 1967, the authors constructed elasticity coefficients for tax assessments on property, which reflect the likely growth in tax bases *vis a vis* a corresponding growth in state income. An elasticity coefficient larger than 1.0 indicates that the percentage increase in the tax base is greater than the percentage increase in income over a given time period. Thus, if the income elasticity of the property tax base is 1.5, then a 1 percent increase in income will increase the tax base by 1.5 percent (Davis and Miller, 1970, 22).

Table 7-7 indicates that the property tax revenue base for commercial-industrial properties did not increase over the 1956-66 decade at a rate exceeding the base for residential properties, except in South Carolina and Mississippi.

The picture is not overly bright on a number of counts. In 4 of the 8 states, the total property tax revenue base did not even keep pace with income growth during the 1956-66 period, and in all but two of the states the major burden continues to fall upon residential property holders, indicating revenues from commercial-industrial sources are not relieving the intense tax pressures on home owners.

Several reasons are advanced for the apparent shrinkage in local tax revenue bases which have to do with policy and assessment procedures surrounding property tax operations in the Southeastern states. For example, tax exemptions are high in these states comparing to states outside the region. In Mississippi 23.9 percent of gross valuation is exempted, the figures for Georgia and Florida being 18.8 and 18.0 percent respectively. Most of these percentages are accounted for by homestead exemptions.

not provided the tax revenue necessary to the creation and expansion of public services within the jurisdictions of local governments in a great many communities in the Southeast.

This section started on the bright note that the South has shown encouraging growth and increasing sophistication in industrial activities in recent years. It proceeded to show that such growth has not necessarily proven a boon to local governments trying to finance needed services. Finally, we may ask, to what extent has such activity benefited the non-metropolitan poor directly in terms of employment and income?

The probable conclusion here is, not a great deal. The more rural areas of the South simply do not appear to have the resources to attract enough industry of the necessary quality to assist in alleviating poverty. Nixon and Thompson have shown in a recent study of 159 coastal Southeastern counties in three states (Georgia, North and South Carolina) comprising one of 6 national Economic Development areas, how the regional

TABLE 7-7

Income Elasticities of Gross Assessed Values of Locally Assessed Taxable Real Property, by Classes of Property, 1956-66

	Total	**Residential**	**Acreage-Farms**	**Vacant Lots**	**Commercial Industrial**
Alabama	.95	1.21	.79	.07	.62
Florida	1.88	1.82	.61	2.28	1.65
Georgia	1.40	1.40	1.48	1.34	1.34
Kentucky	3.08	3.31	3.10	2.74	2.65
Mississippi	.70	.80	.58	.81	2.57
North Carolina	1.27	1.56	1.08	1.79	1.12
South Carolina	.47	1.29	-.44*	.00	1.61
Tennessee	.88	1.11	.11	.76	.84

*Value declined during time period.

Source: L. Davis and R. Miller, "Trends in the Growth of the Property Tax Base in Georgia and other Southeastern States," *Atlanta Economic Review*, XX (November 4, 1970), 23, Table 2.

Secondly, beside the fact that commercial-industrial properties are in short supply within the region, such properties have been "notoriously undervalued," partly as an inducement to relocate in economically depressed localities. Overall, those states which show the most healthy total property tax bases (Florida, Georgia, and Kentucky) are those which undertook revaluations of property during the decade (Davis and Miller, 1970, 24).

This latter fact suggests that property tax policy has been self defeating in some states and that revaluations could add substantially to local revenues needed to provide services. As things stand, however, it is fairly clear that a simple increase in commercial-industrial activity itself would not and has

maldistribution of present resources reinforces the inability of a region to attract new resources (Nixon and Thompson, 1970).

For example, they show that as of 1967, only 7 cities in the entire region had populations over 50,000; therefore, it is not surprising that there is a virtual absence of a dispersed urban-industrial base throughout the region: there simply are few cities which could generate such a spread of activity into more rural parts of the region. And the region is heavily rural as well as poverty stricken: over half the counties had no city of 5,000 population or more and 20 percent of all employment was still agriculturally related—compared to 5 percent nationally, as late as 1967. Moreover, the 1965 per capita income of the region was

$1,000 below the U. S. level of $2,760, and during the 60's these counties gained only 41 new jobs per 1,000 population.

These figures show only part of a bleak picture. Further assessments of the region's rural counties yielded the conclusion that "local marketing channels, government coordination, and funds for public overhead expenditures are virtually non-existent" (*Ibid.*, 14).

These deficiencies—coupled with the virtual absence of urban centers—are having a deleterious effect upon the region's efforts to attract industry. In the absence of needed governmental assistance, a mounting number of industries are complaining about the prohibitive initial investment costs they must shoulder when they relocate (*Ibid.*; Sazama, 1970). As industries become more sophisticated in such matters, more will likely find the region's main attraction of a low wage labor pool insufficient to prompt relocation.

Moreover, the types of industries which have relocated to the rural South in recent years have not been the types which could profoundly benefit local economies. Lonsdale has shown this to be the case in his current studies on trends in industrial growth in rural Southern counties (here defined *rural* if 66.7 percent or more of a county's population was rural in 1960) over the last 20 years (Lonsdale, 1969). He concludes:

> The bulk of the rural South's new plants in the past decade have been drawn from the following industry groups: textiles, apparel, food products, furniture, chemicals, and electrical machinery. As a general rule . . . these firms are ones characterized by a low payroll per employee, a low value added per production worker, and low capital expenditure per employee. In brief, they are usually labor-oriented, low-profit-margin operations wherein lower labor costs are considered essential to maintain a competitive market position. (*Ibid.*, 2-3)

Secondly, Lonsdale shows that the heavily black rural counties have received little or no new industry during the 60's with industrial growth declining roughly as the proportion of blacks increases, as shown in Table 7-8.

Lonsdale suggests that manufacturing firms are avoiding heavily black counties in the rural South for three basic reasons:

1. Most of these firms are, as noted, low-profit types, thus locating in heavily black counties where the level of education is accordingly low, would require heavy training investments which might cancel out profits.
2. A fear of federal guidelines on fair employment practice exists, in the sense that a percentage employment mix and attendant costs might be forced upon them.
3. There is a widespread conviction that black workers are "easier prey" for union organizers. (*Ibid.*, 4)

These findings suggest that high-profit, high-technology industry, the kind that could give a pronounced boost to local economies, is avoiding particularly the rural South, and that the type of industry that is moving in is both seeking a low-skilled, low-cost labor supply and excluding the rural low income black in the bargain.

In another study of the responses of executives representing 32 plants in rural North Carolina, South Carolina, and Georgia, Lonsdale plumbed the reasons they gave as to why the rural South is unattractive

TABLE 7-8

Comparison of Industrial Growth and Percent of Population Negro, for 21 Rural Counties in North Carolina, Georgia, and Mississippi

Percent of Population Negro, 1960	Number of Rural Counties	Increase in Manufacturing Employment, 1958-66, per 100 of 1960 Population
0 - 9.9	45	4.66
10 - 19.9	19	4.77
20 - 29.9	26	2.77
30 - 39.9	34	3.22
40 - 49.9	37	2.51
50 - 59.9	24	2.11
60 - 69.9	20	1.50
70 and over	10	1.05

Source: R. E. Lonsdale, "Deterrents to Industrial Location in the Rural South," *Research Previews*, XVI (April 1, 1969), 4, Table 1.

to high profit industry (*Ibid.,* 5). The drawbacks the executives perceive coincide with the previous observations of Nixon and Thompson. But in addition to the lack of area resources, services, and skilled personnel, these executives suggested that there is high resistance to relocation among technically proficient personnel from other parts of the country based on their assumptions about the rural South. Chief among these are assumptions about the persistence of racial prejudice, dirty small town politics, and poor and ineffectual school systems.

Clearly, the rural South's image as a socially undesirable place to live plays a prominent role in perpetuating the maldistribution of industrial-employment resources within the region and *vis a vis* the rest of the nation.

In sum, it seems fair to conclude that the South is not receiving widespread benefits from its apparent industrial growth, partly because of the low-profit, low-skilled nature of the plants attracted, and partly because of the low tax revenues yielded by such plants as a result of the tax policies in many of the states governing their assessed valuation. Finally, data suggest in any case that the black in rural areas of the South is largely unaffected by current levels of industrial growth and its distribution throughout the region.

Area Development Versus Income Guarantees

Area Development

These data are convincing enough to conclude that industrialization in the South has not much influenced a redistribution of resources within the region and/or between it and the rest of the nation. In particular, it has had little impact on rural Southern poverty.

But this need not be the result according to a number of theorists who view industrialization as a basic key to regional progress. If industrialization has been ineffective in solving poverty problems in the South—and elsewhere—it is largely because government—particularly the federal government—has too long avoided playing a central role in guiding area development. A variety of plans are put forth in hopes of perfecting the process of redistributing industrial resources ranging from the federal government underwriting incentives to entice industry to relocate (Bredemeier, 1967; V. Fuller, 1965) to direct federal financing of new industry (Levitan, 1965; Fisher, 1966; Kaufman *et al.,* 1966).

While some of these views may be attractive, especially since redistribution has not occurred as a result of primarily unplanned, uncoordinated economic growth in the region, the record on federally sponsored area development programs is not overly impressive (Carter, 1970). The fact is, for the most part, such federally sponsored programing has not yet been sufficiently evaluated to yield a definitive conclusion on its overall impact (President's Commission on Income Maintenance Programs, *Background Papers*, 1970, 385).

In spite of this, we know enough to conclude that federal intervention is no simple panacea. For example, according to one evaluation of area development programs funded by the Economic Development Administration (EDA), it was found that

> a high proportion of the jobs provided by new plants under the EDA program are filled by existing employed workers, and by new entrants and returnees to the labor forces. Thus, the most difficult problem of the distressed areas, the hard core unemployed workers, remains. (*Ibid.*)

Moreover, centralizing the control and financing of industrialization programs in the federal machinery will not in itself resolve the major problems of high level initial capital investment needs previously cited as facing private industry when it contemplates relocating to the rural South.

High capitalization costs also have a substantial influence on the initial effectiveness of governmentally sponsored service programs. Sharansky demonstrated a few years ago the relationship between costs and service outputs, state and local, in governmental programing (1967). He applied correlational techniques to the analysis of 58 measures of service output (both quality and quantity measures) controlling for 6 sources of federal-state-local spending in each of the then existing 48 states. His aim was to compare spending at all levels of government between 1957 and 1962 to evaluate the effect of changes in spending on service outputs.

He found that spending increases do not yield immediate service output increases primarily because increased spending implies program expansion which in turn implies "tooling up" costs. In other words, a large proportion of increased expenditures must go to purchase equipment, recruit additional personnel, train existing personnel, and to acquire building facilities. Importantly, his findings disclose that such investments are proportionately heaviest in new service programs and in the least affluent states and localities. This latter point simply means that the more impoverished state and local governments have to apply proportionately larger shares of limited resources to tool up than do more affluent governments; hence, their cost burden is greater for a limited amount of immediate return, at least over the short haul.

These findings suggest that area development programing faces the same kinds of hazards (substantial initial capital outlays *vis a vis* potential for immediate returns) and has been productive of similar and unsatisfactory results (little meaningful impact on nonmetropolitan people entrenched in poverty) when compared to industrial development which has occurred in the rural South outside its scope of influence.

Finally, our concentration on the impact of industrial growth in manufacturing upon the economies and employment opportunities in poverty areas of the rural South may be misleading and slightly more positive in tone than is warranted, even though the reader may think the outlook is already dismal enough.

This is so because it can be shown that only manufacturing industries of the types previously cited (e.g., textile, furniture, etc.), have yielded rural areas in the South proportionately greater employment gains than those registered in Southern urban areas in recent decades.

Goodstein's study of urban and non-urban employment growth in the Southern states between 1940-60 shows this clearly (1970). During this time period, the urban share of manufacturing employment expanded greatly only in Florida among the regional states, while the non-urban share rose by a median of 4 percentage points in all other states.

However, the urban share of all non primary employment* exclusive of manufacturing rose from 48.4 percent to 51.1 percent throughout the region during this period (*Ibid.,* 399). Thus, we are led to the conclusion that however ineffective industrialization has been in improving the lot of the rural poor, it is the *only* aspect of economic-employment growth that has disproportionately benefitted the rural South in recent times.

Income Guarantees

There is, of course, another approach advocated by some theorists who hold that a maldistribution of existing resources is the root cause of most poverty. It is the approach of redistributing income through federal programing to secure for all families and individuals an adequate standard of living.

The main point made by advocates of this approach is not that industrialization has not worked, but rather that it cannot work because the vast majority of those in poverty are simply unemployable (see: Kahn, 1970). Thus, Kidneigh rejects employment as an answer to poverty because

> of the 20 percent [of all low income people] whose money incomes fall below $3,000 per year, three fourths of them are not likely to be restored to economic self support by re-entering the labor market. (Kidneigh, 1967)

It is possible that Kidneigh's remarks reflect a long-standing absorption in urban rather than rural poverty problems. The level of employability among the rural poor in the South may well exceed his estimates for the poverty poulation as a whole. White's previously cited work suggests that under-employment may be as crucial in the rural South as unemployability (White, 1969).

Urban-rural differences in these matters can be clearly seen in the results of a recent study of the employable AFDC population in Georgia, as shown in Table 7-9.

TABLE 7-9

Employment Status of Employable AFDC Mothers in Georgia by Urban-Rural Residence, 1969 (in Percents)

	Urban	Rural
Employed Full-time	53.5	34.2
Employed Part-time	19.3	40.1
No Marketable Skills or Suitable Employment Available	7.5	17.8
Actively Seeking Work	17.1	5.8
Not Actively Seeking Work	2.6	2.1

Source: Georgia Department of Family and Children Services, Division of Research and Publications, *The AFDC Family in Georgia,* 1969, 19.

These data indicate that 57.9 percent of AFDC mothers in rural areas are under-employed (part-time workers), unskilled, or can't find work, compared to 26.8 percent of AFDC mothers in urban areas who fall into these categories. But these figures simply point to qualitative differences between rural and urban poverty populations in the South; they do not refute the main contention that full time employment will not lift most of these women out of poverty (see: L. Hausman, 1969). After all, 53.5 percent of all AFDC mothers in urban areas of Georgia are already employed full time, testimony enough that work did not even place them above public assistance grant levels let alone lift them out of poverty.

In order to facilitate further analysis, let us concede for the moment the point that the employed as well as the unemployable poor may require income supplementation to upgrade their life circumstances. What then, can planned income redistributions deliver in terms of decreasing the imbalance in geographic and socio-economic resources?

First, if we consider human motivation a resource, there is heated debate over whether or not an income redistribution program would be accompanied by a collective decline in the will toward self improvement among the poor. Lekachman, for example, insists that such a consequence is an inherent and unavoidable property of any income redistribution plan:

> It is impossible to design a program which simultaneously eliminates financial poverty, stimulates incentives, and avoids 'unneeded' rewards to the moderately prosperous non poor. (Lekachman, 1967)

This is a crucial matter because proponents of income redistribution most often assume that increased income will stimulate rather than depress motivation toward self-improvement. Thus, redistributed income is viewed as "seed money" which will have a multiplier effect on reducing the social costs of poverty. Theorists

*The non primary employment sector excludes primary industries (fishing, forestry, agriculture) and includes employment in transportation, trucking, communications, finance, insurance, real estate, repair services, professional services, recreation, and public administration (see: Goodstein, 1970, 399).

differ widely among themselves on the scope of the multiplier effect envisioned as achievable through planned income redistribution. Some foresee increased income contributing to a decline in a variety of deviant behaviors associated with poverty such as crime, delinquency, unwed motherhood, and so on (R. C. Allen, 1970). Others proclaim more modestly that increased income would at least yield the following:

1. Greater family investment in itself (in terms of education, savings, etc.).
2. Greater geographic mobility (because of residence free income).
3. More practice in consumer choice making. (The President's Commission on Income Maintenance Programs, *Background Papers,* 1970, 14-15)

All of this is pure conjecture since we have practically no factual information on how the addition of unearned income actually affects the motivation and behavior of low income people. The one exception to this is the New Jersey Experiment, currently being funded by OEO to test this proposition.

The study itself is of limited usefulness to us because of the fact that it is being carried out on an urban sample.* In addition, the sample is heavily weighted with families having characteristics not commonly associated with the main body of poor people in the nonmetropolitan South. For example, almost all of the 1359 families selected were headed by working aged (20-58 age range) males, 66 percent of whom were employed full time. Only 8 percent of all family heads were totally unemployed. Again, while all families fell below an income line of $5,000 per year for a family of 4, many obviously already had incomes above the poverty lines reflected in the Orshansky index.

Thus, the study has really focused on a group of families already functioning and achieving at relatively high levels at the point of its initiation. It is in this sense only a very limited test of the incentive effects of income supplementation.

In spite of these reservations, what are the reported results to date? At one time or another, officials of the program have reported in various forms of the mass media the following results:

> Earnings increased for 53 percent of the families getting income supplements and for only 43 percent of families in the control group—those who didn't get income supplements but cooperated in the study. (New York *Times Magazine,* 1970, 23)

> Those receiving payments tend to reduce borrowing, buy fewer items on credit and purchase more durable consumer goods such as furniture and appliances. (*Catholic Charities Newsletter,* March 1970, 1)

> However, income supplements did not enhance family stability: "When testing began 92 percent of the control and 94 percent of the experimental groups had husbands in households." Data compiled less than 2 years later revealed that husbands present had dropped to 86 percent in the control and 85 percent in the experimental group. (New York *Times Magazine,* 1970, 112)

These limited returns are not overly impressive with such a sample; nonetheless, they have moved one high-level OEO official to exude that

> our findings are what we call in the social sciences 95 percent significant now. . . . The final results may show some slight changes, but we feel strongly that the disincentive theory has been laid to rest. We see absolutely no indication of it. (John O. Wilson, quoted in New York *Times Magazine,* 1970, 112)

Well, even if this conclusion were warranted, it would put aside only one problem related to the potential effect of planned income redistribution on the life circumstances of the poor in nonmetropolitan areas. If true, all we could say would be that we are not diminishing one resource (motivation) by adding another (income).

Carter has rightly pointed out that what we are really talking about when we talk of planned income redistribution is the translation of additional income by the poor into more and better goods and services (G. Carter, 1970, 40).

Throughout previous chapters we have recorded many deficiencies experienced by the nonmetropolitan poor in the South running the gamut from infant malnutrition to inadequate nursing home care. The problem is obvious—and probably unresolvable currently: to what extent could additional income be converted by the nonmetropolitan poor into more and better goods and services, given present circumstances in their environments?

This question raises a third and final question about the effect planned income redistribution would have upon redistributing resources geographically in the nonmetropolitan South as well as socio-economically. It is highly problematic whether planned income redistribution to the nonmetropolitan poor in the amounts now envisioned would provide enough of an attraction to entice large numbers of commercial establishments and professional service personnel into these areas. If this did not happen, and assuming the nonmetropolitan poor would desire col-

---

*Similar studies are now under way to test this proposition among rural people in parts of Iowa and North Carolina. According to a flyer received April 21, 1971, by the Regional Institute, these studies are being conducted by the Institute for Research on Poverty, University of Wisconsin, among 825 dispersed rural farm and non-farm families in the two states.

Statistically, 600 of the families are headed by a male between the age of 18 to 58, 110 by a female in the same age range, and 115 by a male or female over age 58. The first payments were made in the fall of 1969 and will continue for a 3-year period. Other features of the program are similar to the New Jersey design.

lectively to spend this additional income on goods and services, what might be the impact of planned income redistribution on rates of out migration among the nonmetropolitan poor in the South?

The question is an important one because if income redistribution programs stimulate out-migration by providing the poor with the funds needed to relocate, the programs would be self defeating: imbalances in geographic resources cannot be corrected by encouraging decline in so fundamental a resource as population. The flow, of course, might work both ways by underwriting the return migration of urban residents desiring to relocate to their places of origin (Tadros, 1968). It would seem easiest here to conclude with Christopher Green that planned income redistribution would likely

> reduce both the benefits from and the costs of migration. . . . Therefore, whether or not imposition of a negative income plan on balance will increase or reduce migration is an empirical question and cannot be answered on theoretical grounds alone. (C. Green, 1970, 115)

Truc enough, but there is sufficient empirical evidence on why the rural Southern poor migrate to warrant something more than a position of neutrality on the question.

For example, evidence is available showing that the better educated and more aspiring among the rural Southern poor are more likely to migrate in search of better life chances (Schwarzweller, 1964). Also, younger rather than older persons are more likely to relocate for economic reasons (Balch, 1968).

But not everyone moves for economic reasons. In a major study of population flows among poor blacks in 150 Southern counties between 1950-60, Stinner and De Jong discovered that racial discrimination and age also contribute to rates of outmigration under specific socio-economic conditions existing in their counties of origin (1969).

Counties were classified as being one of three types, agricultural, transitional, or industrial. In agricultural and industrial counties, black migration—especially for the young—was clearly related to declines in farm employment and increases in industrial employment respectively. However, in transitional counties where the above declines and increases were tending to balance out job opportunities, the major factor influencing outmigration among the young was white traditionalism, or racially discriminatory social practices.

Of equal importance, it was found that the rate of out migration among older people throughout all the counties was most directly related to the twin factors of non-ownership of housing and problems in personal management requiring family support. This last feature bears out the suspicion that older rural people may move primarily to be among familiar others and to receive the attention and care of family members not otherwise obtainable in their rural areas of origin (see: Marc Fried, 1969).

From this we get no answers, but we do get a couple of more specific questions:

1. Would planned income redistribution fulfill the aspirations of the young in the nonmetropolitan South, enough to make them want to stay?
2. Would additional income from such a program yield the quality and quantity of goods and services for the older nonmetropolitan resident necessary to make his continued residence in such areas possible?

In sum, we have labored over the details of what we seem to know about the potentials and actual impact of area development and guaranteed income plans and programs. We have done so because these are the major resolutions to poverty proposed by those theorists who hold that the dominant cause of poverty is the combined geographic and socio-economic maldistribution of existing national resources. The line of reasoning simply put is that maldistribution must be met by redistribution.

Thus far we have attempted to assess the extent of maldistribution of resources in the nonmetropolitan South and between it and the rest of the South and nation. Secondly, we have attempted to assess the redistributional effect of programs and plans set forth to aid the nonmetropolitan Southern poor by this means. It remains now to conclude by addressing the feasibility of redistribution on a scale which would end nonmetropolitan Southern poverty within the context of current political realities.

The Politics Of Maldistribution

Generally speaking, there seems to be no widespread commitment to the goals of resource redistribution in American society today. Materials presented in this chapter indicate employers do not develop hiring practices primarily to meet social goals, industries do not relocate where high investment in training or the imposition of fair employment practice demands are likely, professional service personnel do not dot the rural landscape in large numbers, income protection programs fall far short of poverty level needs, and so on. These less obvious signs are often accompanied by more direct and heated actions and sentiments as reflected in skilled labor union exclusions of black trainees, and the following editorial evaluation of Senator Holling's current interest in expanding food programs for the hungry poor. The Senator is implored to

> spend time listening to legitimate complaints of self-reliant working people who are squeezed by taxes for welfare programs and who pinch pennies while a horde of handout types pay for their groceries with food stamps provided by officeholders who politically advertise themselves as humanitarians. (*Athens Banner-Herald,* 1970 b, 2)

This overall "atmosphere" of antipathy toward redistribution probably helps sustain the inadequate property tax structures evidenced by many Southern state and local governments. Moreover, it probably has something to do with what planners perceive to be resistance to outside intrusion among officials of local rural governments (Hahn, 1970).

In the rural South, this resistance to planned redistribution of resources takes on distinct racial overtones among local officials. This is clearly evidenced in a recent report on the political reaction to an OEO program proposal aimed at improving the lot of poor black farmers in southwest Alabama by financing a rural farm co-op (Munk, 1967, 40).

Both Alabama senators and 4 of its 8 representatives lobbied strenuously against implementation of this program on behalf of "many of the county and city officials, . . . as well as the owners of the major packing companies in the area" (*Ibid.*). Ultimately they succeeded in delaying implementation and reducing overall funding by about one third. Redistribution apparently implied not only increased economic competition, but perhaps political and social status realignment between the races. For these and perhaps other reasons, responsible elected officials sought to impair the potential for economic progress among their fellow citizens.

The question does arise, of course, as to whether redistribution can come about for nonmetropolitan Southern blacks by reversing the process, that is, achieving economic redistribution by first obtaining a greater share of political power. At first glance, prospects seem bright. Black voter registration in the South has climbed dramatically in recent years, especially so immediately after enactment of the Voting Rights Act of 1965 (Feagin and Hahn, 1970, 45, Table 1).

But the effect of this additional political muscle has been pronounced only at the local level of government, and then only for certain types of elective office:

> Although the number of black elected officials increased dramatically from 72 in 1965 to 473 in mid-1969, they have been disproportionately represented in a limited number of local offices. The largest number . . . were municipal officials; but 93 percent of these positions were in city councils. In addition, 83 percent of the black law enforcement officers were justices of the peace or constables. . . . Only 5 of 30 black legislators in the South were in state senates. (*Ibid.,* 51)

These authors take the signs of progress in their research as evidence of a slow erosion of white political power in the South. Perhaps, but in noting that blacks have made greatest inroads in low-level local government positions, a question arises as to whether blacks are simply getting elected to offices within jurisdictions having black voting majorities. Since black dominated communities and counties in the nonmetropolitan South are among the most impoverished, black officials may simply be inheriting already ineffective government machinery. The extent to which blacks are gaining control over their own destinies through command of local elected offices may be more apparent than real, the erosion of traditionalist—and racist—white power more fiction than fact.

Concluding Remarks

The maldistribution theorist must first establish the nature and extent of the maldistribution of income, goods, and services. Insofar as national averages for income, industrial growth, service facilities, professional manpower, and so on, can serve as standards, it is clearly demonstrable that the nonmetropolitan South lags behind on almost every count.

Secondly, he must show whether efforts to reduce imbalances have had a noticeable effect on the level of poverty and destitution among nonmetropolitan Southern people. In this matter, the evidence is less than convincing. Efforts, sometimes major efforts, at rural industrialization, area development, income protection, and the like cannot be shown to have had much impact upon reducing the extent of nonmetropolitan poverty in the South or upon stemming the flow of the poor out of their areas of origin.

Whether planned redistribution is the answer to nonmetropolitan Southern poverty (that is, whether maldistribution is the dominant cause) or not, cannot be responded to definitively. Those programs that reach the nonmetropolitan poor (e.g., income protection) simply are not of a magnitude necessary to affect redistribution; therefore, they produce no measurable redistributive impact. Those programs which seemed to hold promise of major impact (e.g., industrialization and area development) on poverty have not and currently do not reach the nonmetropolitan Southern poor; therefore, they show no measurable redistributive effect either.

Since the entire Maldistribution Thesis rests on the premise that planned intervention in redistributing resources geographically and socio-economically is required, it will likely not be put to an adequate test until the political climate in the nation, and particularly the South, shifts away from the politics of maldistribution and toward the politics of redistribution.

Chapter 8

ASSESSING THE SCARCE RESOURCE THESIS

The Thesis through the 50's

The Scarce Resource Thesis has a long and varied history in Western thought. As a tree changes and cycles with the seasons, the Scarce Resource Thesis has known many forms and labels over the centuries, but remains today essentially the same in meaning: for one reason or another poverty has always existed because there simply is not enough to go around.

The main proposition has, of course, taken on more subtle and sophisticated meaning over time. Arbitrarily beginning with Malthus, we witness a relatively simple proposition that food production increases arithmetically while population expands geometrically; hence, sooner or later population will exceed supply and cause widespread poverty, disease, starvation, and rebellion.

Technological advancements in agriculture have time and again prevented the predicted disasters from taking place, at least on a grand scale worldwide, although neo-Malthusians, pointing to the current population explosion, hold that the point will eventually be proven (Ehrlich and Ehrlich, 1970; Ehrlich and Holdren, 1971).

Technological advancements have also led to a fundamental shift in responsibility for contending with the implications of scarce resource propositions. As industries—agriculture included—moved toward greater reliance upon machines to upgrade productivity, obviously they moved away from a reliance upon a large pool of low wage unskilled workers. In the mines, fields, and factories, the paternalism industrialists and land owners evinced vanished as the need for unskilled labor was replaced by machines. Tenant farmer arrangements, company stores, credit, and other forms of "charity" designed to keep the pool of labor breathing, indebted, and servile were no longer necessary. The job of keeping such people alive and employed was no longer recognized to be a direct responsibility by the owners and managers of private capital. When volunteer efforts became inadequate to meet demand, the responsibility finally fell upon government.

But in a nation of ever accelerating material abundance, the obligation to manage supply and demand, production and consumption, has rarely been keenly felt by governmental leaders. And, except in times of widespread economic stress such as the Great Depression or the world wars, the public has never been overly enthusiastic in supporting the governmental exercise of such responsibility in the form of direct and open intervention in such processes. A socio-economic system which has produced such abundance, it is reasoned, should not be tinkered with except under conditions of temporary necessity.

This is not to say that this brand of scarce resource theorist accepts a certain level of poverty as an inevitable by-product of our current socio-economic system. But it is to say that planned redistribution mechanisms of the estimated scale needed to end poverty are rejected as a solution. Such large-scale tinkering with the present socio-economic system is not only held to be politically unattractive because of the likely resistance and resentment it would generate among the better-off majority, but also because it would undermine the incentive system which motivates economic activity causing major declines in investment and productivity.

The solution to poverty obviously lies in large-scale and sustained economic growth. The point that large-scale planned redistribution is both inimical and unfeasible regardless of our current level of wealth leads to the conclusion that the continuation of poverty within a generally thriving society is proof of the existence of scarcity, not abundant but maldistributed wealth. The economy is simply not performing at maximum.

This theoretical position must make at least three important assumptions about the relationship between economic growth and poverty:

1. First, potential for increasing levels of economic productivity as reflected in our reserves of natural resources and technological ingenuity must be viewed as virtually limitless.
2. Secondly, it must be held that increases in economic activity will increase labor demand and to some extent "trickle down" to the poor in terms of more and better jobs and income.
3. And, thirdly, economic growth will produce sufficient growth in tax revenues to underwrite needed creation and expansion in governmental services and income supports to raise the unemployable poor out of poverty without having to resort to major planned redistribution mechanisms to achieve this goal.

Without any pretense to having treated these ideas and their development to a full historical review, it is still possible to suggest that they represent the dominant strain of thought on the subject through the late 50's.

The Tone of the 60's: The Affluent Society

With the advent of the 60's, a high level of optimism emerged—cynics would call it naivete—which signaled not so much a change in thinking as it did a growing belief that the affluent society had arrived. In short, it was assumed that productivity had already reached the level necessary to underwrite a total end to poverty. The economic imperative toward growth was absorbed by the moral imperative toward redistribution: it was held unthinkable that a society with the means to end poverty would not willingly and swiftly do so (see: Epstein, 1963; Myrdal, 1962; Ornati, 1966).

Optimism overrode some earlier warnings that affluence has its negative and costly by-products (see: Galbraith 1958, 231-269), and the various drains imposed on our socio-economic system by our escalating involvement in Viet Nam were dismissed with the insistence that we could have both "guns and butter." Fantastically costly schemes were put forth to aid the poor, not the least of which was a passel of proposals for whole new towns and cities for the poor, without the slightest hesitation about our capacity to make them a reality (see: Stein, 1967; Galantry, 1968).

Importantly, these were not true redistribution schemes. The optimism which supported the contention that affluence had arrived assumed in the bargain a pool of existing resources in excess of the overall level needed to sustain productivity and meet current consumer demand in society. In short, it was reasoned that the cream could be skimmed off the top and redistributed without the slightest restriction being placed on current levels of consumption or the slightest undermining of incentives to continue high levels of economic activity. In somewhat jargonistic cant, the economic line of reasoning on the matter can be witnessed in the following quotation:

> Where a portion of income is in excess of the remuneration necessary to induce existing supplies of labor and capital services, the income of some can be reduced and the income of others raised without affecting output. (President's Commission on Income Maintenance Programs, *Background Papers,* 1970, 24)

Thus, there was an apparent shift away from a simple belief that economic growth would by market processes "trickle down" to the poor and toward an insistence on a greater role for government as a medium for distributing existing resources. But the belief in affluence as a reality yielded the comfortable conclusion that major revisions in the socio-economic system were unnecessary to assist government in achieving the goal of ending poverty. Rather, government simply had to do what it was already doing but on a much larger scale by absorbing a greater portion of our excess productivity. Poverty would end and no one would feel the pinch; it would be painless; who could object under these circumstances?

Toward the 70's: The Myth of Affluence

This heady atmosphere began to evaporate almost before it was formed. Prophets in this strange land strained to be heard on the negative effects of economic growth on the circumstances of the poor. Theobald insisted over and over again that insofar as economic progress depends on technological advancements, the benefits of such growth for the poor would be reduced rather than increased (1965). Martin Rein summed up this point rather well in stating:

> It is not because our economy is not working well [as during the depression] that these people become dependent—but because it is working well. Efficiency has made them superfluous or branded them incompetent. They did not pass the tests—they had the wrong skills or backgrounds; they were too old; they were in the wrong place; they could not adapt quickly enough. They no longer fit and are rejected. Technical progress increases dependency. (Rein, 1965, 19)

In another vein, Steiner exposed the "withering-away Fallacy" to a penetrating analysis. He contends that much of recent policy and planning that has gone into the creation and delivery of income and social services to the poor has implicity subscribed to the proposition that such additions and expansions will result in reducing need to the zero point (Steiner, 1966, Ch. II). In reality, an unexpected and confounding result seemed to obtain in the affluent 60's: every increase seemed to be accompanied by increased demands by the poor. Rather than producing a sense of greater well being and satisfaction among the poor, each new program success seemed to stir desires among the poor for an even greater share of the good things of life.* Definitions of need seemed to be escalating faster among the poor than the pace by which government was funneling the leftover affluence of economic progress to them.

One of the major features in the line of reasoning advanced by the theorists of the 60's who insisted that we had reached a platform of affluence was the abiding—if implicit—assumption of social and economic constants. In order to compute affluence, for example, it was necessary to assume that consumer expectations among the better-off as well as the poor remained stable, that poverty could be determined in absolute dollar terms (an unwavering poverty line), and that economic progress did not create in its wake more problems (such as automation) which would intensify competition for existing resources and drain them away from an investment in ending poverty (see: The President's Commission on Income Maintenance Programs, *Background Papers,* 1970, 29). Assuming these constants made it a relatively simple

*See: *Report of the National Advisory Commission on Civil Disorders,* 1968, 226, on how legal-political success among blacks simply increased their demands.

matter to conclude that for every unit of increase in economic productivity there could be an equivalent unit reduction in poverty.

Moreover, the assumption that affluence had already arrived blinded these theorists to some of the basic underlying issues in the whole Scarce Resource Thesis. The rose cheeked—if sickly feverish—optimism which generated the assumption that affluence existed in sufficient supply to end poverty temporarily shunted off the ancient and unresolved debate on whether this society—or any society—has the wherewithal to sustain unlimited (in time or resources) economic growth. Since affluence had arrived, what point was there in debating whether we could ever achieve it?

Into the 70's: Overriding Issues

The beginning of a new decade has brought with it a renewed interest in these long-standing questions which in magnitude overshadow the issues and questions surrounding automation and rising expectations in the minds of some current theorists.

In a sense, we have come full cycle: the new issues are the old issues, the notion of scarce resources is in ascendency, that of affluence in decline. The issues about finite natural resources, population growth, and the by-product costs of economic progress are taking on new life. The implications of each and all for achieving the goal of ending poverty are indeed potent. If there is anything new in this renewed debate, it is the intensity now being evidenced over the issue of the ecologically despoiling effects—and the attendant social and economic costs—of economic progress.

Unrestricted economic growth, writes Alan Wagar, cannot possibly yield the utopia we envision as the end product of such growth. The planet is finite; resources must therefore be limited and unrestricted growth must lead eventually to the exhaustion of resources. As this approaches, the quality of life will be seriously diminished and international competition for what remains will intensify, throwing us back to a level of brute savagery in human affairs (Wagar, 1970).

Unrestricted population growth is viewed in the same dim light. Hardin suggests that for the well-being of man, the world's optimum population must obviously be less than the maximum that it could support at some minimum or survival economic level (Hardin, 1968).

The sweep of these views is enormous. The scope and the recency of their reassertion in contemporary thought make it understandable that there is little more than rhetoric and opinion to support their ad-advocates' claims to priority and accuracy of prediction. We can sympathize a bit with Hardin when he laments on the population issue:

> The difficulty of defining the optimum [population level] is enormous; so far as I know, no one has seriously tackled this problem. Reaching an acceptable and stable solution will surely require more than one generation of hard analytical work—and much persuasion. (*Ibid.*, 1244)

The pliants of those who might attempt to assess the ultimate limits of the world's—or the nation's—technological and natural resources can surely be heard to echo in the background. Perhaps part of the intensity attached to the issue of environmental despoliation can be attributed to this: theorizing about its causes and estimating the accompanying costs of rehabilitation may be far more manageable by men of ordinary imagination than are the dimensions of these larger, more timeworn issues.

The Scarce Resource Thesis and Rural Southern Poverty

The fact that we cannot provide hard, definitive responses to these issues at present does not reduce their relevance to any assessment of the adequacy of the Scarce Resource Thesis as the dominant causal explanation of poverty. In a limited way these issues can be boiled down to measurable dimensions to make the beginnings of their applicability to explaining poverty in the rural South.

For a start we can address three basic questions, as follows:

1. Has economic growth had the predicted impact on reducing rural Southern poverty?
2. Is the size of the rural Southern poverty population increasing at a rate which outstrips the pace of economic progress?
3. Are the consumer expectations of the rural Southern poor rising?

Economic Growth: Does "trickle down" Work?

There are two ways to approach this question. First, recalling materials presented in Chapter 7, we can conclude that the idea has not really been put to the full test yet. It has been shown that while the South experienced substantial growth in industrialization during the 60's, such growth was not of the magnitude or quality sufficient to enhance the region's export-import trade balance with the rest of the nation (Costello, 1966; Leary, 1969). Secondly, the kind of industrialization that occurred in concert with current state and local tax policies did not yield large gains in governmental revenues (Nixon and Thompson, 1970). Finally, industrialization did not occur in the most intensely poor areas of the rural South, those areas having high proportions of black residents (Lonsdale, 1969).

In the realm of governmentally sponsored area economic development it was suggested that high capitalization costs—especially in rural areas—may absorb a considerable portion of program inputs thus limiting the amount of "trickle down" that can immediately be expected from such activity (Sharansky, 1967). Moreover, evaluations of such programs show that they have mostly benefited the already employed or otherwise skilled person, not the truly destitute core of the poverty population (The President's Commission on Income Maintenance Programs, *Background Papers,* 1970).

But suppose all these "bugs" could be eliminated. Suppose that industrialization and area development could generate in concert an impressive leap forward in the quantity and quality of economic productivity within the region. Suppose also that a disproportionate emphasis were placed upon locating such activities in rural areas and that in the main they were targeted specifically at the poverty population. Under these conditions, to what extent would "trickle down" from sustained economic growth work toward ending rural Southern poverty? (See: B.J.L. Berry, 1967.)

The answer, of course, lies in estimating the extent of employability among the rural Southern poor. Those who look upon the effects of economic growth with a jaundiced eye usually support their cynicism by showing that the poverty population has become increasingly, over time, a population of unemployables. Estimates vary, but Seligman offers that constant high levels of economic activity will leave untouched approximately 10 percent of the population nationally composed primarily of the aged, the female headed family, and the otherwise unskilled and ignorant (1968, 38). Kelly has shown recently that this seems to be the case: during a decade of unparalleled prosperity for the majority, the composition of the poverty population showed declines in the number of male headed households and increases in the number of aged, female headed households, and black families in its ranks (Kelly, 1970).

But care must be taken in applying these national trends to the rural South. Under the more-or-less idealistic conditions stipulated above, economic growth might have an immediate and significant impact upon rural Southern poverty. This is largely because of the fact that economic progress has lagged in the rural South; therefore, it is likely that the poverty population in those areas of the South has a higher proportion of immediately employable persons within it than is true of the current poverty population nationally.

Anderson has shown that steady growth in economic activity has a declining effect on reducing the poverty population over time precisely because those who can advantage themselves of the employment opportunities which "trickle down" do so, leaving behind an ever growing proportion of unemployables in the poverty population (W.H.L. Anderson, 1964). Recalling the high levels of *underemployment* estimated to characterize the rural Southern poor currently (White 1969), the possibility exists that massive economic growth could yield an immediate and substantial reduction in rural Southern poverty.

But judging from the standpoint of past experience rather than an ideal situation, the picture is far from encouraging. Even for the employable poor, high and sustained economic growth in the South appears to have had only moderate impact at best.

Alabama is a good case example because it has distinguished itself by industrializing more rapidly in the post World War II period than its sister states in the region. Industrialization has had a substantial impact upon agriculture and agriculturally related employment in Alabama (Pearce, 1966), but what of its impact on the employable poor?

Joiner, in a review of a variety of economic analyses of the Alabama economy during the 1940-60 period, studied the relationship between economic growth and the occupational-income advances of minority groups in the labor force, primarily women and blacks (1968). His findings indicate that black women improved their occupational standing during the period comparing to their own previous occupational standing, and that only white women made any consistent income-occupation gains in the most rapidly expanding fields of employment.

In spite of these advances by women toward occupational parity with men, women's income actually declined during the 20-year period relative to men's income, and black men showed very little gain either occupationally or income wise. Joiner concludes that high economic development over the 20-year span did not significantly affect the relative occupational or financial position of minority groups.

Similar findings present themselves in evaluations of the economic impact of governmentally sponsored economic development programs in the rural South. While a multiplier effect does occur to some extent in the sense that such programs do seem to stimulate the creation of a number of jobs beyond those actually supported by such programs (C. Berry, 1968), only a highly selective group of persons within the area labor markets seem to benefit. Britt's study of the work histories of 1262 employees in 33 establishments associated with the Area Redevelopment Program (programs funded under the Area Redevelopment Act of 1961) indicates that such programs benefit mostly the young (Britt, 1966).

This finding was true for both sexes (the sample was about evenly split between men and women). One of the major reasons Britt gives as to why the young seem to absorb most of the newly created jobs is that the young are more geographically mobile, more capable of relocating and/or traveling long distances to work than the older employable resident. While he makes no definitive estimate, Britt concludes that Area Redevelopment programs would have to be expanded massively to reach the over age 45 unemployed but employable rural resident of both sexes (*Ibid.*).

Thus, we can conclude that economic growth in the South—through industrialization and Area Economic Development—has not been of the magnitude to adequately test how much "trickle down" would succeed. Perhaps because such massive input has not occurred on the scale it has elsewhere nationally, a reservoir of underemployed poor exists which indeed could respond to large scale economic growth in the rural South. In any case, economic growth would likely impact only the employable segment of the poverty population, and unless it was massive, only a select group within that population, primarily the young.

Does Economic Growth Create Revenue?

The second way that economic growth is supposed to benefit the poor is by creating expanded revenues for governmental programing. These expanded revenues could presumably be applied to ending poverty among the unemployable segment of the poverty population. The primary difficulty with this proposition is that state and local revenues do not grow in an accelerated fashion as economic activity increases, because of the nature of our present tax structure. As Galbraith has shown, federal revenues expand faster than the pace of economic growth because they are pegged to personal income taxes; however, state and local revenues are much less elastic deriving as they do mostly from property taxes (1958).

Additionally, state and local governments in the South are caught in the bind of having to guarantee low taxes to induce the relocation of industry into the region, thus undermining the revenue yield from economic growth. In turn, such inducements prove attractive primarily to low wage, low profit industries, the kind that yield the lowest valuation on assessment for tax purposes, even if tax inducements are terminated. High technology, high-profit industry, the kind that could afford to pay substantial taxes to local and state governments and still remain solvent, on the other hand, are not relocating to the rural South because, among other reasons, they find the rural South to be a socially undesirable environment for their personnel.

The fact that personal income growth does not yield equivalent revenue growth in the states in the region to underwrite expanded services is illustrated in Robertson's recent study. Robertson analyzed growth trends in higher education in 5 Southern states for the period 1940 to 1965. He compared growth trends in per capita income in these states to ratio measures of growth in higher education such as college enrollments/college age population, graduate enrollment/total college enrollment, enrollment, and earned degrees and financing of education/general state expenditures.

His findings indicate that per capita income gained in all states approaching the national norm toward the end of the 25-year period. In contrast, the number of institutions of higher education grew very little, and while enrollments increased faster than the national rate of increase in all states except South Carolina, expenditures for education did not keep pace with national norms and actually declined as a percentage figure of per capita income in all states except Tennessee (Robertson, 1968). In short, as per capital income was rising, the financing of higher education was suffering. It is not beyond the realm of possibility that a variety of less esteemed welfare services for the poor were caught in this bind as well, perhaps more severely than higher education. The paradox of growing wealth and diminishing revenues is one which faces every state in the region today.

Cost Estimates for Adequate Economic Growth in the Rural South

Throughout this section it has been suggested that a massive input of funds would be required to create an optimum impact on rural Southern poverty through the mechanism of economic growth. Some idea of the amount required can be obtained by an estimate made in 1965 that an investment of 90 billion dollars would be required by 1970 to create roughly 1.7 million full-time jobs in rural areas of the U. S. This number of full-time jobs was the estimate of need existing in 1965 in the rural U. S. among employable rural residents, and it is assumed in the estimate that .8 of a service related job would be generated by every job directly created by funded programs (U.S.D.A., E.R.S., 1966, 43). In other words, the 90 billion would yield directly slightly over half the needed employment, the rest being generated by a multiplier effect following from the initial investment.

If we estimate conservatively that the rural South represents one third of the problem, roughly 30 billion dollars, allocated under optimum conditions would be needed to yield enough economic opportunity for the employable poor in the rural South to lift them, as a group, out of poverty.

This is perhaps a minimum estimate in the sense that it is a direct investment in expanding economic activity, and through this an expansion of jobs. Programs which would center more on investing in human capital, such as some "War on Poverty" and other job training programs, may incur much higher capitalization or "tooling up" costs, thus yielding less immediate benefit in terms of employment for the rural poor per dollar invested than sponsored area development and industrialization (W.H.L. Anderson, 1964, 512-13).

Of course, this investment at optimum would directly reduce poverty primarily among the employable rural Southern poor and their dependents, a group which may not comprise the majority of the present poverty population.

How Fast is the Dependent Population Growing in the Rural South?

The effect of population size and rate of growth on the incidence of poverty is a resurging issue, as previously noted. At the moment, an estimate of an optimum population size and rate of growth based on an assessment of the limits of our natural and technical resources cannot be calculated. The issue can be scaled down to manageable dimensions, however, by assessing the relationship between economic growth and the size and rate of expansion of the dependent population. For purposes of this analysis, the dependent population includes all persons of working age (ages 15 through 64) who are unable to earn their own livings as well as those younger and older than this age group who are officially deemed outside the labor market.

On the grandest scale, poverty may well be a function of population out-striping consumable resources, but as David has pointed out, for the immediate years ahead it may be wise to conceive of poverty as a function of the growth of the dependent population within the context of economic progress (1964).

Natural Increase and Poverty

Nationally, the number of live births recorded yearly has been falling steadily in recent years, from a peak of 4.3 million in 1957 to 3.5 million in 1967 (U.S.D.H.E.W., P.H.S., *Natality Statistics Analysis,* 1970b, 9). This decline has been noted in every state of the region as well, with several states showing greater-than-national-average declines as noted in Table 8-1.

During the same period national fertility rates dropped from a peak of 122.9 live births per 1000 women aged 15-44, to 84.8 in 1968 (*Ibid.,* 2). Differences in fertility rates are noticeable when controlling for race. While both nonwhite and white rates declined during the 1960-65 period, nonwhite fertility was 36 percent higher than white fertility in 1960, 36 percent higher in 1965, and 44 percent higher by 1967 (*Ibid.,* 11). Importantly, fertility rates were most pronouncedly higher for nonwhites in the younger age brackets, as shown in Table 8-2.

The decline in birth rates and fertility have been taken by some as a hopeful sign that rapid population expansion is coming under control. For the most part these declines have been attributed to the fact that women who had high reproductive rates in the early 50's are growing older, and the concomitant possibility that younger people are either marrying later, delaying their families longer, or both (*Ibid.,* 3-5). The introduction of contraceptive pills was not seen as a major factor in this decline:

TABLE 8-1

Birth Rates and Percentage Change 1965-67, by States

	1967	1966	1965	Percentage Change 1965-67
United States	*17.8	18.4	19.4	— 8.2
Alabama	18.3	18.9	20.3	— 9.9
Florida	16.7	17.3	18.4	— 9.2
Georgia	19.2	20.1	21.5	—10.7
Kentucky	17.7	18.2	19.4	— 8.8
Mississippi	19.8	20.6	22.7	—12.8
North Carolina	18.4	18.6	19.8	— 7.1
South Carolina	19.2	19.6	20.8	— 7.7
Tennessee	17.5	17.8	19.0	— 7.9

*Number of live births per 1000 women aged 15-44.

Source: U.S.D.H.E.W., P.H.S., *Natality Statistics: U.S. 1965-67,* National Center for Health Statistics Series 21, No. 19, 1970, 15-16, Tables 4 and 5.

TABLE 8-2

National Birth Rates* for 1967, by Race and Age of Mother

	Total 15-44	10-14	15-19	Age Bracket 20-24	25-29	30-34	35-39	40-44	45-49
White	83.1	0.3	57.3	168.8	140.7	76.5	36.6	9.8	0.6
Non-White	119.8	4.1	135.2	212.1	212.1	99.1	52.4	16.8	1.2

*Live births per 1000 women in each age bracket.

Source: *Natality Statistics: U. S. 1965-67,* 13, Table 3.

> The pill was not licensed for general use as a contraceptive until 1960 and probably did not come into wide use until a year or more later. This means that if it has had any major influence on the birth rate, it would not have been detectable until 1962 at the earliest. [Yet] the decline in fertility, however, started in 1958, so it is not possible for the pill to have initiated the downward trend or contributed to its early progress. (*Ibid.,* 9)

Again, the number of women using the pill rose to an estimated 13 percent of the child bearing aged population between 1960-65 while the birth rate dropped 20 percent during the same period (*Ibid.*).

There are ominous overtones in these interpretations, particularly insofar as the notion that younger persons are delaying their families is accurate. Should this be so, once they begin their families, a noticeable upswing in the birth rate would occur.

Moreover, the number of women of child bearing age will increase nationally by about 30 percent during the 70's according to U. S. Census estimates, and the age group usually most prolific (20-29) will increase on the order of 48 percent (*Ibid.*).

The possibility of another wave of population expansion is imminent. In order for the rate of live births to remain constant at the 3.5 million figure for 1967, the birth rate would have to decline from 2,562 per 100,000 in 1967 to 2,100 in 1975 and less than 1,800 by 1985 (*Ibid.*). If the birth rate remains at roughly the current level of 2,500, the annual number of live births would rise from the current 3.5 million figure to 4.2 million in 1975 and to over 4.9 million in 1985 (*Ibid.*).

The problem of creating enough economic growth and services to meet demands inspired by a new explosion in the size of the population are likely to be facing us with renewed insistance in the immediate years ahead. Failure to meet these demands and/or check the population growth potential cannot but contribute to our pressing poverty problems.

But the implications of sheer growth for poverty are only part of the story. Examination of the data discloses the crucial factor that birth rates are highest—and increasing—among the youngest women. Johnson, in a recent review of the literature on the relationship between teen-age pregnancy and poverty raised the issue as to whether early pregnancy—whether the girls are married or not—may not be a contributing factor in producing a life of poverty for such women. Early pregnancy seems to contribute to undue financial stress for young married couples, may disrupt young women's educational and vocational training thereby limiting their future economic potential, and very likely indicates a future large family since early pregnancy is followed by long years of child bearing potential (C. L. Johnson, 1971).

While these points are raised as hypothetical, the fact that the poor have more children than the better-off segment of the population has often been noted. Jaffe, for example, revealed in an analysis of 1960 U. S. Census data that by 1962, 34 percent of all families with 6 children had incomes below $4,000 per year, compared to 20 percent of all families with 2 children and 22 percent of all families with three children (1964).

While we do not know for sure that AFDC mothers are on the average younger than they were a decade or so ago, we do know that the average size of AFDC families is growing. This trend among the states in the region is shown in Table 8-3, which also indicates that several of the most poverty stricken states exceed the national average for AFDC family size.

TABLE 8-3

Average Number of Children per AFDC Case, 1960-1968, by State

	Average Number of Children (1) 12/1960	(1) 5/1968
United States	2.95	3.05
Alabama	3.16	3.39
Florida	2.88	3.16
Georgia	2.88	3.03
Kentucky	2.69	2.84
Mississippi	3.05	3.48
North Carolina	3.07	3.09
South Carolina	3.15	3.18
Tennessee	2.82	3.04

Sources: Column 1 *Social Security Bulletin* XXIV (April, 1961).
Column 2 *Welfare in Review* VI (September-October 1968).

Another thing that pregnancy at any age portends is a withdrawal from the labor market. And this withdrawal may not be of temporary nature. In a recent paper by Contes and Brown, it was estimated that about 940,000 of the 25 million women currently employed full-time are in low income jobs, 60 percent below the poverty line (1970, 2).

Pregnancy for these women, especially those just beyond poverty may very well doom them to a life of poverty. Quoting from a 1964 HEW study on the effects of pregnancy on working women, the authors cite the following results:

> 1. Only 73 percent continue to work after becoming pregnant.
> 2. Only 47 percent work during the last 3 months of pregnancy.
> 3. No hard data are available, but the experience of industry is that a high percentage do not return to work at all post-pregnancy. (*Ibid.*)

Thus, preganancy itself may well contribute to increasing the number of women and children in the dependent population, many of whom would have been otherwise self supporting. Particularly for young women, early pregnancy may signal an increase in the dependent population both in an immediate sense and the long term sense that they are likely to produce many more children, prolonging dependence and swelling the dependent population. This contribution to the growth of the dependent population would not necessarily be reduced by high levels of economic progress.

Economic Growth and Dependent Populations

Processes of natural increase then, contributes to the growth of the dependent population in at least three ways:

1. By taking working aged women out of the labor market.
2. By increasing the probability among younger women that a succession of children will be born into a dependent status.
3. And, because of the sheer number, increasing the size of the youth population which must eventually enter the labor market and compete for available job opportunities.

The last point is perhaps best illustrated by citing a recent study by Paul Stone of the flow of employment in 35 primarily rural eastern North Carolina counties between 1950-60.

Projecting from U. S. Census data for 1950 and 1960, Stone estimated that the region would experience tremendous economic growth for the 1960-1975 period. Specifically, 78,995 jobs would be created due to economic expansion during that period representing a 20 percent increase over the number available in 1960. This further represents a growth rate 7 times larger than that which occurred in the region between 1950-1960.

In spite of these impressive economic advances, the region will face the need to export an estimated 46,000 people, or 4 percent of its 1960 population, during this 15-year period in order to *maintain* its 1960 employment ratio in 1975. This conclusion is based on the estimated pace at which the population of the area would grow through natural increase during this time span (Stone, 1969).

In one area of the rural South, at least, we are confronted with a sobering estimate that natural increase in the years immediately ahead will simply outstrip even substantial economic gains. It is a mute point as to what the situation will be in areas of the rural South not benefitting by such economic growth rates. The simple lack of employment for growing numbers of youth attempting to enter the labor market clearly portends prolonging their dependent status and, in turn, increasing the size of the dependent population.

Economic growth in itself may also contribute to the size and rate of growth of the dependent population in another way, namely, through automation and related processes. Economic growth depends in large part upon technological advancements. While it is an arguable point as to whether the automation of production processes has contributed heavily to the removal of low skilled, low income workers from the labor force or not,* there is considerable agreement on the point that improved technology delays the entrance of the young into the labor force because of the need to undergo ever more prolonged education and training in preparation for available employment.

And as yet nothing has been said about the growing input to the dependent population made by those at the other end of the life cycle, the aged and aging. The above mentioned trends associated with economic growth may well be leading to earlier forced retirements for workers thus yielding an increase in the dependent population by eliminating ever larger numbers of older workers as well as preventing the entrance of growing numbers of hopeful youth.

Additionally, medical science seems to be on the brink of new advances which would substantially contribute to prolonging the life span of the average American. Progress in this area has already contributed substantially to the rate of growth of our dependent population, and the prospects of further improvements have led at least one expert to conclude glumly that

> the problems posed by the possibility of unlimited prolongation of life are beyond estimate. . . . The demographic problem of over population is generally associated with increased birth rate. Yet the birth rate actually is falling in most nations; population increase is mainly due to reduced death rate. (Goldman, 1969, 6)

In sum, all of these factors, birth rates, termination of employment due to pregnancy, early retirement of the older workers, prolonged training of the young due to technological upgrading, and increases in the life span, contribute to the size and rate of growth of the dependent population.

On the macro level, the Scarce Resource Thesis tussels with the relationship between unchecked population growth and the ultimate limits of our natural and technological resources. At the more immediate level the issue can be reduced to the relationship between the growth of the dependent population and economic progress.

At this level two kinds of solutions present themselves: either reduce the dependent population, by preventing pregnancies, better training for the young, etc., or increase the revenues needed to support the dependent population at above poverty levels, primarily through economic growth. In reality, of course, it is not an either or matter, since efforts are being made to achieve both goals.

Pro: Theobald, 1965; con: Hamilton, 1967; Silberman, 1967; mixed: Zydislaw and Wesoloski, 1970.

In the rural South, the record of achievement has not been overly encouraging: data indicate that the size and rate of growth of the dependent population is outstripping economic progress. By 1960, the ratio of the dependent population to the total population in the rural areas of the several states in the region exceeded the ratio for rural areas of the nation as a whole. And it should be remembered, this ratio counted only those under age 15 and over age 65 as dependent (see Table 2-6, Ch. 2). Inclusion of the substantial number of under-employed and unemployed workers coupled with the higher-than-average birth rates occurring in recent years in the poverty pockets of the rural South would surely swell this ratio.

At the same time data suggest that economic growth in the rural South has neither produced a substantial increase in jobs available to the rural poor nor yielded the tax revenues needed to expand income and social services to them. At this level of analysis the Scarce Resource Thesis would seem to have some applicability to revealing the causes of rural Southern poverty.

Are the Consumer Expectations of the Rural Southern Poor Rising?

As previously noted, one of the major problems in the contention that we have achieved an affluent society is the need to assume a series of social and economic constants. In this section we are concerned with estimating the extent to which such assumptions bear merit.

The first order of business is whether the better-off majority come increasingly to recognize themselves as affluent as their benefits from economic progress increase. One cross-cultural study of the relationship between economic progress and attitudes in 12 nations reported that more modern and liberal attitudes do seem to prevail in the more advanced nations, at least on the matters of provision of education to the young and care for the physically handicapped (Jordon, 1968). Before too much is made of such a finding, however, it should be recalled that those who sit in judgment in the U. S. Congress have shown declining support in recent years (in terms of appropriations) for service programs which affect the nation's poor within the general context of rising affluence (U. S. Advisory Commission on Inter-governmental Relations, 1966).

It is probably closer to the truth to suggest that those who are better-off and experiencing even further economic gains recompute their standard of living to absorb additional monies rather than holding their living standards constant and considering additional income excess (The President's Commission on Income Maintenance Programs, *Background Papers,* 29). Simply put, as income rises, an ever increasing number of past luxuries become redefined as necessities.

Klingaman in a recent article on the impact of rising affluence on consumer demand identifies other mechanisms which likely occur to cancel out any substantial feeling of affluence among the better-off. He suggests that consumers take the route of increasing their consumption of a wider variety of goods as income rises, and, in conjunction, may change their tastes to conform to a different and higher standard of living. Another factor is that the number of new products competing for the consumer dollar increases along with affluence (Klingaman, 1970).

These factors in association with the higher taxes that accompany higher income probably work against any widespread feeling among the better-off majority that they can afford any substantial degree of income reduction required to support new and expanded income and social service programs for the poor.

Do the poor in the rural South follow this pattern of rising expectations? Systematically gathered data on the consumer practices of the rural Southern poor are in short supply. However, some things can be inferred from a variety of studies previously cited which reflect on the attitudes and expectations of these people.

In Chapter 5 on the Culture of Poverty Thesis, a number of studies were reviewed which suggest something of a generation gap exists between the young and their elders in the rural South. Youth seems to be demanding more of life, both in terms of control over their destinies and a greater share of society's goods and services. In the section on expectations in Chapter 6, a number of studies also indicate that the expectations of the rural poor in the South are rising relative to what they want out of life. This seems particularly true for youth and for the expectations their elders hold for them.

The collective impression is that the expectations of the rural Southern poor are on the rise, and that pressures are forming for fulfillment of these expanded expectations among youth in these areas. This may be particularly true for young blacks in the rural South who, Youman and Grigsby suggest, are oriented to the issues and demands embedded in the so-called black revolution now occurring in urban areas (Youmans, Grigsby, and King, 1969). Rising expectations among the poor black in the South has been given as both a cause and a consequence of their growing assertiveness dating from the beginning of Martin Luther King's activities in the early 50's (Report of the National Advisory Commission on Civil Disorders, 1968, 226-27).

The situation of the rural poor would seem to parallel that of the better-off majority in the South: expectations are rising across the board at a frenetic pace, one which probably outstrips the pace of economic growth in the South and most certainly outstrips the revenue gains yielded state and local government from economic expansion. The poor, in converting past luxuries (e.g., convenience foods, college education, TV's, autos, etc.) to necessities are expanding their perception of basic needs at a time when the rising expectations of the better-off majority cause it to conclude that it doesn't have the surplus necessary to meet much less elaborate definitions of need. This press is likely to become more acute in the immediate years ahead in the rural South as a consequence of the growing awareness among the poverty population of the extent of its deprivation and the increasing proportion of youth in that population intent upon being heard.

Summary Points

The Scarce Resource Thesis is difficult to assess in large part because of the magnitude of the variables employed to support its contentions. The "proofs" which can presently be marshalled to show that natural and technological resources have ultimate limits and that population is increasing at a rate that makes it impossible to meet its current and future needs consist largely of considered opinion.

In a limited way the major contentions of this thesis have been addressed in this chapter by assessing the relationship between economic growth and the growth in sheer numbers and expectations of the poverty population—the employable as well as the dependent—in the rural South. The general impression is that the pace of economic growth in the rural South has not substantially reduced the number of people in poverty even by an absolute dollar standard (e.g., the SSA index). To the extent that the definition of poverty is relative and increases in dollar terms as the expectations of both the poor and the better-off rise, it is possible to conclude that poverty is actually increasing faster than economic expansion.

Following from this it is also possible to contend that ours is a society of scarcity, not affluence. But if ours is a society of scarcity, we come full cycle to the proposition that the answer to scarcity—and the resolution of poverty in the bargain—is economic growth of the magnitude to create true affluence—that is, income which exceeds the satiation level of consumer demand among the better-off majority and the needs of society to sustain incentives supportive of continued economic growth. It is this excess which will "trickle down" to the employable poor in the form of new jobs and better income and to the unemployable poor in the form of new and expanded income and social service programs.

The evidence suggests, however, that major factors in economic growth, such as the kind and quality of industry, prevent any large-scale "trickle down" to the employable rural poor in the South, regardless of the overall pace of expansion. Furthermore, present tax structures make it unlikely that state and local government will be able to underwrite new and expanded programs for the unemployable poor as a consequence of economic growth in the region, whatever its magnitude. Finally, the fact that expectations appear to be rising in all social strata, in part at least as a consequence of rising affluence, yields the conclusion that consensus on the essential point that affluence exists may never be achievable. Without widespread acknowledgement of the fact of affluence, poverty could hardly be ended by means of allocating society's excess productivity to those in poverty.

Thus, serious questions are raised about the validity of a central assumption in the Scare Resource Thesis, namely, that poverty can be ended through massive economic growth without requiring in the bargain substantial revisions in our current socio-economic systems.

Chapter 9

SUMMING UP

Take a moment, a step back, a deep breath, a fresh look. Embedded within this mass of opinion and fact is the ultimate goal, an end to poverty in the nonmetropolitan South.

Perspectives on causation differ, sometimes radically; accordingly, so do the proposed remedies attached to them. Research findings brought to bear on the adequacy of each perspective are sometimes contradictory and interpretations drawn from them equivocal. The quality is uneven, and quite often major assumptions about why poverty persists in the nonmetropolitan South are found precariously perched on a single, fragile strand of opinion woven by a few self-proclaimed experts rather than a solid base of systematically gathered data.

But there is a general intent: an end to poverty in the nonmetropolitan South by achieving economic independence through employment for the employable segment of the population, and through income supports and self-management for the dependent segment of the population.* Above all, these goals should be achieved within the region in ways which yield a rebirth and renewed growth in the quality of life outside the cities rather than in ways which stimulate a further out-flow of population as a function of providing the wherewithal to relocate.

An end to nonmetropolitan poverty in the South thus holds out the promise of reducing public expenditures in support of the currently unemployed and otherwise dependent population to a bedrock minimum while increasing the self respect, enjoyment of goods and services, and command over personal and regional destinies to a maximum. To this end a staggering array of proposals have been advocated, and many, at least partially, have been implemented.

The Goal of Economic Independence

The elusive goal of economic independence through employment is being sought by various approaches, such as the following:

Enhancing individual employability by utilizing various vocational counseling, education, and job training programs as well as such supportive programs as day care.

Expanding employment opportunities by breaking down employment and union practices which are discriminatory in intent through such mechanisms as fair employment legislation, consumer boycotts, and the like.

Subsidizing individual and collective initiative through such mechanisms as economic co-ops, small business administration loans and expanded commercial credit.

Developing industrial capacity aimed at the creation and relocation of industrial and commercial establishment by means of local solicitation and/or federal-state subsidization.

Protecting the incomes of the low-wage, low-skilled employee through such devices as minimum wage laws, unemployment, and workman's compensation programs, expanded Social Security coverage, and similar measures.

Taken individually, our data suggest that each approach carries with it potential for creating negative consequences for the employable rural poor in the South as well as benefits.

An approach which aims at vocational training and education runs the risk of increasing competition among the nonmetropolitan poor for available jobs in a region already marked by high levels of underemployment, particularly if such programs seek to implant skills needed to handle the types of jobs already available. Training in skills which are more advanced than called for by currently available jobs may simply yield increased expectations and no work. Unless job opportunities increase in pace with the size and scope of such programs, the products are likely to be heightened disillusion, bitterness, and competitiveness among the rural poor. Under these circumstances, one likely outcome of such programming would be to spur the rate of out-migration of the employable poor.

Similarly, the achievement of equal opportunity in employment is nothing short of a cruel hoax for the nonmetropolitan poor if they are not prepared to qualify technically for the positions opened to them by such advances. Furthermore, unless the number and quality of jobs keep pace with the number and kind needed to absorb those who may be encouraged by equal employment regulations and practices to seek them out, the outcome is likely to be intensified cynicism and hostility among the poor. The same result may obtain in rural areas even if the

*Here we acknowledge that such goals may not immediately apply to some sub-groups in the non-employable population, notably those presently in mental and penal institutions and children in need of protective services.

growth in jobs matches advances in equalizing opportunity should the location of such opportunities be so remote from where the poor reside as to render them geographically inaccessable.

Subsidization of individual and collective initiative is of such recent vintage that it is not possible to envision the kind of negative consequences that could be generated by such program efforts. It is possible to conjecture, however, that such programs are of benefit only to those who are already instilled with the entrepreneurial spirit. While it may be possible to instill this spirit in a large number of the poor through educational and training programs, large-scale programing of this type prior to such training might well yield a frightening rate of small business failures (McClelland and Winter, 1969).

In the arena of industrialization and area development, it would seem that the creation and expansion of such enterprises may yield greater burdens than benefits to communities in terms of the costs incurred in underwriting their relocation and providing them needed public services. Moreover, such growth is accompanied by increased costs for public services for any addition to the population created by new employment as well as increased costs for controlling the environmental despoilation caused by industrial activities.

Finally, it has been reasoned more than once that some income protection programs such as minimum wage requirements and expanded employee benefit coverage programs may yield less employment for the already poor. The problem seems to be that low-profit establishments are the predominant employers of the low-wage, low-skilled employee and as the costs of employee coverage and wages rise, profits quickly disappear causing the closing, relocation, or mechanization of processes in these enterprises, all of which put such employees out of work.

The Goal of Social Self-Management

There is growing awareness that all proposals aimed at achieving social self-management among the dependent poor must begin with the provision of some sort of guaranteed minimum income. For those who are not yet or no longer employable, the provision of sufficient income to make self-management possible is the first order of business.

Growing agreement on this proposition does not portend an end to controversy. Two camps immediately appear creating the poles of debate: there are those who insist that the provision of sufficient income is an end in itself, that it will yield the desired result of self-management. On the other hand, there are those who protest that a guaranteed minimum income would make it possible for the poor to utilize a network of health and allied social and educational services which must be developed to assist the poor along the road to self-management.

The question therefore is not how much health, education, and social services can do to achieve this goal in the absence of sufficient income, but rather how much of this kind of assistance is needed beyond the provision of an adequate base income.

In other words, to what degree can the problems of self-management attributed to the poor be traced to economic sources? How much of the apparent isolation of the aged is attributable to a lack of funds necessary to underwrite transportation and participation? How much of the poor health, malnutrition, poor learning, poor school attendance, and so on, of the children of poverty is traceable to the insufficient incomes of their parents? How much adolescent deviancy—from auto theft to pregnancy and drug use—finds its causation in the long standing frustrations and growing expectations of youth raised in wretched circumstances deprived of most of the joyful pleasures of childhood, let alone the sense of decency that comes in part from adequate clothing and a little spendable income? How much of the depressed state of mind, indifferent mothering, and family desertion by fathers results from the intense pressures of trying to make do without money?

It is probably safe to say we do not know how much adequate income provisions would contribute to increasing self respect, improving home life, decreasing deviant and criminal acts, and raising the level of consumption of goods and services among the poor. Indeed, a goodly part of such a test may rest on how much income is provided. Certainly we cannot test whether the poor will adopt habits of saving, for example, unless income is sufficient for that purpose.

In any case, the idea that adequate income provision is the answer may not be testable on a large scale. Raising the standard of income adequacy enough beyond the basic needs level (i.e., food, clothing, shelter) to test the idea would probably create enough political resistance to condemn it to the status of a crackpot scheme. The history of public programing for the poor indicates that putting more money directly into the hands of the poor than they need for base subsistence has never been viewed favorably. The more accepted approach is to funnel funds into service programs over which there is more direct control of purposes and expenditures. Given that the financial resources available to end poverty are never unlimited, the extent to which funds are poured into sponsoring services likely diminishes the amount available for direct cash payments to the poor.

But to those who advocate the need for supportive services the basic question is not resolved or resolvable in terms of whether income provisions are at the subsistence level or beyond it. Instead, doubts are raised about the efficacy of improved income provisions *vis a vis* the lack of available services and goods and the hypothesized psychosocial orientations of the poor. In short, what good would more money be if goods and services were not available on which to spend it? And even if they were available, what assurance is there that the poor would exercise wise consumer choices?

In rural areas, for example, would increased income be a sufficient stimulus to attract commercial and service establishments into these areas, or would it simply underwrite the out-migration of larger numbers of poor persons seeking such services and goods? Would not the location of such services and transportation to and from them remain problematic regardless of increased disposable income, even if they should be attracted in sufficient quantity to rural areas?

Even if commercial and professional services were to increase in numbers and quality in rural areas, would the poor utilize them on their own initiative? To what extent would the self utilization of health services, birth control programs, and the like be affected by the reliance of the nonmetropolitan poor on folk remedies? How much malnutrition results from inadequate and deeply ingrained dietary and food preparation habits regardless of income level? How susceptible are the nonmetropolitan poor to the utilization of day care, head start, and similar programs which might challenge and attempt to change child rearing habits? How suspicious are the nonmetropolitan poor of counseling programs which advertise techniques promising to enhance family stability and parent-child relations? How resistent or wary of educational and job training programs given their common experience of being ignored and shunted aside in the past, and, how possible is it for the aged to negotiate great distances to obtain goods and services, in any case, regardless of their income level?

These and many other points are raised in support of the need to develop an effective network of health, educational, social, and recreational services in nonmetropolitan areas to assist the dependent poor to a status of social self-management.

Maximum social self-management is not possible without good physical health, reasonable education, and a sense of self worth. To the extent to which these are achievable, the degree to which society has to fund social supports and controls such as old people's homes, mental and penal institutions, foster care arrangements, and other costly devices is presumed to diminish.

It would be erroneous to conclude that anything like adequate tests of this proposition have been made involving the dependent segment of the poverty population in the nonmetropolitan South. For one thing, program efforts have been aimed mostly at the employable segment of the population. For another, the "ghettoization" of the poverty problem, so prominent a part of the theorizing of the 60's, further pushed the plight of the nonmetropolitan dependent poor into the background.

In large measure, commercial and professional services simply do not exist in any meaningful supply in the South outside the major cities. How then to test the relationship between the existence of such services and their utilization by the dependent poor, and the impact utilization might have upon moving the poor toward the goal of social self-management?

The Abiding Problems outside the Cities

Whatever approach one adopts, whichever set of questions one finds most important in the foregoing, several common factors must be confronted in addressing the question of how to end poverty in the nonmetropolitan South.

First is the problem of open spaces and small numbers of people even in the more densely inhabited spots in the region. This is an obvious problem in that it influences costs, and creates difficulty in service coordination. Problems of client access are compounded by the great distances they may have to travel, and coordinating and mounting collective actions among themselves for aims of self improvement no doubt are hindered by the distance factor. The difficulty in getting large numbers of persons together repeatedly to sustain collective action may well be insurmountable without substantial assistance from some type of organized service establishment.

Secondly, there is the prospect of a further drain of population toward the cities. If it is a selective drain of the young, the more vigorous, and the employable, the problems of nonmetropolitan poverty will be exacerbated by the growing proportion of dependent poor persons left behind in an ever more depopulated environment.

Thirdly, these problems in conjunction with current tax structures create immense difficulties for state and particularly local governments in confronting the urgent needs of the nonmetropolitan poor within their jurisdictions.

Finally, there is the problem of the general "image" of the nonmetropolitan South itself, its traditions, patterns of justice, and other social, educational, and political practices. Many needed professional services and commercial enterprises may resist relocating because of stereotyped or accurate assessments of the miserable quality of life in such areas. Indeed, if given the chance, how many native to such areas would not move out immediately? Local institutions and social practices need up-dating and revitalizing, and such efforts need wide public exposure to enhance the possibility of retaining the present population and attracting needed ousiders.

Where Can We Go from Here: A Proposed Strategy

The wealth of material reviewed in this work yields the first order if altogether prosaic conclusion that nonmetropolitan poverty in the South is not monolithic in nature nor subject to explanation by a single causal thesis. State by state, locality by locality, the data reveal substantial differences in social and age structure, racial composition, employability potential, availability of resources, political climate, and the like among and between groups of regional residents living in poverty.

But care must be taken to avoid constructing broad generalizations which have the false appeal of comprehensiveness and coherence. Such an approach creates the impression that the poor in the nonmetropolitan South can be described accurately in terms of a common set of traits and characteristics. In other words, it blurs the very real and meaningful differences found in the data.

Of equal importance, it leads to multicausal explanations of poverty. Generalizations about the common characteristics of the poor once made, constitute the "facts" about poverty requiring explanation in causal terms. Obviously, any particular causal thesis could account for only a part of the multiple features of poverty at any point in time. Equally obvious, and just as misleading, is the simple-minded solution that nonmetropolitan poverty is therefore caused by the simultaneous interaction of the full range of causal factors.

This kind of approach is intriguing in the sense that each added generalization aimed at the admirable goal of conceptual simplicity, yields instead less definitive knowledge and more intricate, unfathomable and less useful causal arguments. The grandeur of its sweep is matched only by the spectacular nature of the program design embedded within it for ending poverty in the nonmetropolitan South. Clearly, such a goal can only be achieved by developing a massive array of programs addressed to the full variety of deprivations and inadequacies commonly experienced and demonstrated by the nonmetropolitan poor. This full array of programs must then be adequately funded and controlled in order to insure its simultaneous and uniform implementation throughout all nonmetropolitan parts of the region.

Questions of economic and political feasibility aside, such an approach if fully operationalized could be predicted to produce monumental waste in conjunction with whatever effective impact it yielded. Some programs might be more effective if implemented in time sequence rather than simultaneously; others may be unneeded in some locations indicating selective rather than uniform implementation.

A more promising approach would seem to be a rank ordering of priorities by localities based on assessments of the data and what they indicate as the dominant and, in declining order, the less influential causes of poverty. Assuming that an end to nonmetropolitan poverty in the South is to be sought in ways which retain and perhaps increase the population in these areas, the question becomes which localities are capable of yielding the most immediate and large-scale gains towards the goals of economic independence through employment and/or social self-management from various kinds of programs. Where could the greatest immediate gains be obtained from industrialization, tax reform, equal opportunity efforts and legislation, birth control programs, better vocational and other education, increases in health and social service manpower and facilities, improved environments (e.g., roads, water, sewers, and housing), and so on?

In pursuing an answer to this question much depends upon a more precise analysis of the resources and characteristics (not necessarily the "needs") of target localities. For convenience, localities shall mean a county or set of counties lying outside major metropolitan areas which comprise the definable geo-political targets.

Two essential dimensions of the analysis of localities are advanced, as follows:

1. *The geographical and cultural remoteness of* a locality from the nearest major metropolitan area.
2. *The existing socio-economic and political mobilizability of the population*—poor and nonpoor, within a locality.

Measuring Geo-Cultural Remoteness

For purposes of illustration, a partial list of factors bearing on geocultural remoteness which are patently measurable are offered, as follows:

1. *Actual Physical Distance and Linkages*

A major feature of remoteness is the physical distance of a locality from the nearest major metropolitan center and the extent of its trade, transportations, and communications ties with it and surrounding localities. The greater the distance and the fewer the links the less likely the exposure of the locality to some of the "winds of change."

2. *The Degree of Localization of Local Institutions*

This factor covers the degree to which local religious, educational, police, justice, government, commercial and other operations are influenced in their financing, staffing and employment practices, and policy making and implementation procedures from the outside. To what extent, for example, are churches independent of connections with major denominations, and to what extent to they utilize self proclaimed "home grown" preachers? To what extent are commercial-industrial establishments tied to or owned by regional or national cooperations? Conversely, to what extent are hiring practices controlled by absentee owners rather than the personal preferences of local managers or owners? To what extent does local government participate in cooperative planning and financing of projects and services with surrounding localities, the nearest major metropolitan center, and state and federal governmental agencies and programs? Does the school include a consolidated school for the upper grades and to what extent is there participation in the planning and/or use of a regionalized network of health and social services?

3. *The Degree of Traditionalism in Local Institutions*

Traditionalism represents in its simplest form the degree to which current practices and decisions by persons representing local institutions are governed by beliefs about the correctness of past precedents, and it is reflected in the absence of change in practices over time. Among the conditions required to support a high of traditionalism are the exclusion of outsiders from decision-making positions and the absence of formalized procedures governing the extent to which decision-makers can exercise personal preferences in making policy.

Traditionalism can therefore be measured in terms of the extent of the incorporation of outsiders into local decision-making processes, the extent of change in practices and policies of local institutions over time, and the extent to which services, justice, and other products of such institutions are provided on the basis of personal favoritism rather than formal procedure to local residents. School boards can be evaluated, for example, on the basis of the characteristics of the membership and how members are selected as well as on the basis of their decisions about hiring and promoting teachers, setting teacher qualifications, approving teaching materials and methods, and so on.

4. *The Degree of Community-Family Stability*

Finally, community-family stability has something to do with geo-cultural remoteness. The extent of stability in community and family social structure over time dictates at least in part how insulated a locality will be, how impervious to outside influences. A major factor governing such stability is the extent of out-migration and in-migration over time. Net migration is not a good measure here because we are more interested in how many people were exchanged between localities rather than simply whether the community experienced a net gain or loss over a period of time. Low levels of population exchanges obviously enhance insularity.

A second factor is family stability. How prevalent is the 3-generation family in the community? The more prevalent the 3-generation family, the more likely that values, attitudes, and behaviors will be passed on on inter-generationally, and the greater the potential for socially reinforcing behavior conforming to local norms.

Thirdly, what is the extent of racial-ethnic homogeneity between the poor and non-poor segments of a population in a community? It may well be that a high degree of racial-ethnic homogeniety contributes to locality insularity especially when found in conjunction with other factors which contribute to a locality's remoteness.

Measuring Socio-Economic/Political Mobilizability

The extent of a locality's mobilizability is obviously influenced by the degree of its geo-cultural remoteness, but there are also socio-economic factors affecting mobilizability which bear independent consideration. Among these are the following:

1. *Economic Growth Potential*

Here it is essential to estimate the skills levels and immediate potentials among the labor force in a locality in conjunction with the current employment opportunity structure and the feasibility of creating new and/or expanded employment opportunities.

For purposes of illustration, consider a locality which is still primarily agriculturally oriented, with a major portion of the labor force engaged in farm and farm related employment. To what extent would promotion of such activities expand employment opportunities? On the other hand, how capable would the current labor force be of responding to new and different kinds of employment opportunities? Finally, to what extent might a lack of skilled labor and the distribution costs of products manufactured in remote localities inhibit the attraction of new commercial-industrial establishments?

2. *The Ratio of Dependent to Employable Population, Poor and Non-Poor*

This factor is of considerable importance since it reflects at least in part the proportion of the population in a locality which may have the vigor as well as the commitment to move it toward improvements. It is essential to make these estimates for both the poor and non-poor segments of the population in order to estimate the extent to which the two groups can act in combination, or conversely, the extent to which one group will have to shoulder leadership for the other.

Localities having high proportions of dependent persons (the elderly, the disabled, young children and their mothers) may be in the most difficult circumstances. Unchecked paternalism might prevail in localities where the majority of the dependent population also comprises the bulk of the poor population, while open hostility might be encountered in localities comprised of high proportions of employable persons in poverty facing an aging "old line" population still in control of local institutions.

3. *Degree of Racial, Ethnic, and Status Homogeniety among the Poor*

To some extent, the degree to which the poor can identify with one another by virtue of their poverty status may influence their mobilizability, and in turn, the degree to which they can affect the actions of the non-poor in their locality. Previously it was suggested that high levels of racial-ethnic homogeniety might contribute to insularity (and presumably undercut mobilizability). Here we are not simply suggesting the reverse, namely, that racial-ethnic differences separating the poor and non-poor may contribute to mobilizability. This may well play a part, but a more important aspect is the extent to which the poor perceive their poverty to have common roots or causes. If, for example, the great majority of those in poverty in a given locality are mothers with small children, or unemployed but employable adults, the likelihood is greater that they will see their plight and solutions to it in common terms. Racial-ethnic similarities may enhance the possibilities of the poor mobilizing themselves, but differences in these matters might not inhibit collective efforts if common conceptions of causes and solutions prevail. On the other hand, a mix of employables, children, the disabled, and the elderly, might well undercut mobilizability.

4. *Spacial Separation*

This factor does not require extensive comment; however, it is obvious that it is more difficult to mobilize a locality within which the population, poor and non-poor, generally lives at great distances.

5. *The Existence and Distribution of Helping Profession Personnel*

Finally, the mobilization potential of a locality rests at least in part on the contribution of helping professionals, from planners to pharmacists. The absence of such personnel, their availability to only certain segments of the population (e.g., those in official positions or those who can pay), and/or their lack of linkage with similar professionals in neighboring localities, the nearest major metropolitan center, and state and federal offices, all affect the extent of their potential usefulness in moving a locality out of lethargy and beyond dependence.

Summary Points

Two essential dimensions for the analysis of localities outside major metropolitan areas in the South have been suggested: geo-cultural remoteness and socio-economic/political mobilizability. The discussion presented on the measurement of each dimension was meant to be illustrative, not exhaustive. Nor is there any intent to conclude with the presentation of a formal analytical model.

Yet it can be suggested that analyses of target localities which yield good estimates of their current remoteness and mobilizability can be quite valuable in setting goals, developing program priorities, and establishing workable implementation methods, in addressing the problem of nonmetropolitan Southern poverty, locality by locality.

Such an analytical strategy departs in subtantial ways from the oft used one of aggregating data on individual needs among the poor in designated target localities as the first order of business. It is suggested here that such efforts are of most use following the type of analysis previously set forth. They should be carried out by personnel—the poor and the non-poor—engaged in programs aimed at alleviating poverty in localities. But the setting of realistic goals and feasible and appropriate program priorities must both precede such efforts and be based on other kinds of analyses, perhaps of the type outlined here.

Aggregating data on individual need among the poor in a given locality as to their employment, education, health, family composition, and the like may lead, and indeed often seems to have led, to the development of a battery of programs and facilities without the slightest recognition being paid to the feasibility of their implementation—that is, their potential for receptivity by localities and for utilization by the poor.

In the broadest possible way, the analysis of remoteness and mobilizability in target localities can contribute to preventing the lunacy of advocating economic independence through employment as a first order of business in localities marked by extreme remoteness and high proportions of dependent persons in poverty. Such analyses might also help prevent the waste which accompanies the implementation of an array of health and social service programs aimed at developing social self-management in localities capable of and receptive to achieving this goal as well as economic independence for the poor through the immediate creation of employment opportunities.

A "culture of poverty" may well be nourished in localities by extreme remoteness and immobility. Should this be the case, program priorities should reflect this factor as a primary cause of poverty with other program priorities set at a lower level and timed to follow upon the success of programs aimed at penetrating and altering the influence of this abiding culture. On the other hand, programs designed to achieve such a goal where cultural reinforcement of poverty cannot be demonstrated to exist are patently wasteful. Application of this line of reasoning to the other causal theses and their implications is unnecessary, the point being that any one of the causal theses can be considered an appropriate or inappropriate place to begin in clarifying goals, program priorities, and evaluation criteria, depending on the characteristics of a given target locality.

Concluding Remarks

The data marshalled in this work do not support a conclusion that any one causal thesis is the major explanation of nonmetropolitan poverty in the South. When we try to explain the size and persistence of poverty population in the nonmetropolitan areas of the region in composite form, the data will not even afford a rank ordering of the causal theses in terms of their explanatory power.

This simply means that no one explanation or rank ordering of several explanations is possible or likely to be useful—even if an ordering were achieved by force-fitting explanations to some broad theoretical overview—when the target of explanation is the whole of poverty in the nonmetropolitan South. It most certainly does not mean, on the other hand, that the entirety of the problem is adequately explained by the invention of a model proposing to show poverty to be the result of the simultaneous interaction of all causal factors. Such a conclusion borders on pure jibberish.

If we are to move planning, program, and research efforts aimed at resolving nonmetropolitan poverty in the South forward out of this morass, at least three objectives need to be achieved immediately:

1. The urban ghetto mentality of poverty theorists and planners which so pervaded the thinking of the 60's must be brought to an end. A clear vision of the nature and causes of rural Southern poverty must be acquired. The simple extrapolation of thinking about and programing for urban ghetto poverty to rural areas must cease. Such extrapolations are so thoroughgoing among some poverty theorists that they have even come to refer to the rural poor as living in rural ghettoes.

2. The fashionable view that poverty is the result of simultaneously interacting multiple factors must be challenged. Research designs and programs which subscribe to this view are not only costly and difficult to carry out, they are often impossible to evaluate. The amount of waste in such efforts may well be substantial, the amount of effect on poverty miniscule. This view must be replaced both in research and planning about poverty by realistic goals, time sequenced priorities, and clearly measurable evaluation criteria.

3. Finally, the implementation of uniform program packages and the evaluation of programs according to uniformly applicable criteria must be surplanted by programing, research and evaluation uniquely tailored to the assessed characteristics of target localities.

These have, indeed, been the aims of this work. It is hoped that it has contributed somewhat to our knowledge about the size, nature, and causes of poverty in the nonmetropolitan South, and pointed the way toward some of the things that need to be known and done.

BIBLIOGRAPHY

Abramowicz, M., and E. H. Kass.
1966 "Pathogenesis and Prognosis of Prematurity," *New England Journal of Medicine,* CCLXXV (October 20), 878-85; (October 27), 938-43; (November 3), 1001-7; (November 10), 1053-59.

Agricultural Policy Institute of North Carolina State University in Cooperation with the Tennessee Valley Authority.
1965 *Problems of Chronically Depressed Rural Areas.* Asheville, North Carolina.

Akin, J., compiler.
1970 "The Feasibility and Actuality of Modern New Towns for the Poor in the United States," Exchange Bibliography No. 167, *Journal of Planning Librarians* (December), Monticello, TU.

Albin, P. S.
1970 "Poverty, Education and Unbalanced Economic Growth," *The Quarterly Journal of Economics,* LXXXIV (February 1), 70-84.

Alcoholic Rehabilitation Program: Florida Project.
1967 *Final Report, Alcoholic Rehabilitation Program.* Avon Park, Florida.

Aldous, J., and R. Hill.
1965 "Social Cohesion Lineage Type, and Intergenerational Transmission," *Social Forces,* XLIII (May), 471-82.
1969 "Breaking the Poverty Cycle: Strategic Points for Intervention," *Social Work,* XIV (July 3), 3-12.

Alleger, D. E.
1966a "The Anomia of Rural People, Its Measurement and Correlates," *Agricultural Science Review,* IV (First Quarter), 1-9.
1966b "A Southern Rural Paradox: Social Change and Despair," *Research Report,* II (January 1) 5-8. University of Florida Agricultural Experiment Station, Gainesville, Florida.

Allen, R. C.
1970 *Legal Rights of the Disabled and Disadvantaged.* National Citizens Conference on Rehabilitation of the Disabled and Disadvantaged. U. S. Department of Health, Education, and Welfare. Social and Rehabilitation Service. Washington, D. C.

Allen, V. L.
1970a Ed., *Psychological Factors in Poverty.* Chicago: Markham.
1970b "Theoretical Issues in Poverty Research," *Journal of Social Issues,* XXVI (2), 149-67.

American Statistical Association.
1964 "The Measurement of Poverty," *1964 Proceedings of the Business and Economic Statistics Section.* Washington, D. C.

Anastasi, A.
1956 "Intelligence and Family Size," *Psychological Bulletin,* LIII, 187-210.

Anderson, C. L.
1965 "Development of an Objective Measure of Orientation Toward Public Dependence," *Social Forces,* XLIV (September), 107-12.

Anderson, W. H. L.
1964 "Trickling Down: The Relationship Between Economic Growth and the Extent of Poverty Among American Families," *Quarterly Journal of Economics,* LXXVIII (November 4), 511-24.

Ansbacher, H. L.
1967 "Life Style: A Historical and Systematic Review," *Journal of Individual Psychology,* XXIII (November 2), 191-212.

Aquizap, R. B., and E. A. Vargas.
1970 "Technology, Power and Socialization in Appalachia, *Social Casework,* LI (March 3), 131-45.

Arkansas State Board of Vocational Education. The Arkansas Rehabiliation Service.
1970 Intensive Follow-up Services to Marginal Workers. *Final Report of a Research and Development Project.* Little Rock, Arkansas.

Asbell, B.
1967 "The Case of the Wandering IQ's," Reprinted from *Redbook* (August).

Association for Research in Nervous and Mental Disease.
1954 "Genetics: and the Inheritance of Integrated Neurological and Psychiatric Patterns," *Proceedings of the Association.* New York.

Athens Banner-Herald.
1970a "Black Lawyers Remain Sparse in the Deep South" (November 26).
1970b "Senator Hollings and the Politics of Hunger," by A. Harrigan (December 29).

Athens Banner-Herald and *The Daily News.*
1971 "Promise of a Better Future in Rural Georgia," by R. Bell (January 3).

Atlanta Constitution.
1970 "S. C. Medical College Studying Intestinal Ills of Rural South" (December 25).

Atlanta Journal.
1970 "The Rural Revival: There's A Power Struggle for This Privilege," by J. Spalding (October 1).

Ausubel, D. P.
1963 "Teaching Strategy for Culturally Deprived Pupils: Cognitive and Motivational Considerations," *Scholastic Review,* LXXI, 454-63.

Ayers, G., ed.
1967 *Rehabilitating the Culturally Disadvantaged.* Proceedings of the Conference on Rehabilitating the Culturally Disadvantaged. Mankato State College, Minnesota.

Bachmura, F., and J. H. Southern.
1965 "Economic Bases and Potentials of Rural Communities," *Rural Youth in Crisis: Facts, Myth, and Social Change.* U. S. Department of Health, Education, and Welfare. Washington, D. C.

Bacon, L.
1970 "Poverty Among Inter-Regional Rural to Urban Migrants," Paper presented at the annual meeting of the Rural Sociological Society. Washington, D. C. (August 26-30).

Bajema, C. J.
1963 "Estimation of the Direction and Intensity of Natural Selection in Relation to Human Intelligence by Means of the Instrinsic Rate of Natural Increase," *Eugenics Quarterly,* X, 175-87.

Balch, B. W.
1968 "Migration-Inducing and Income-Equilibrating Factors Involved in Restructuring the Alabama Farm Labor Force, 1950-1967: A Multivariate Analysis," Dissertation, University of Alabama.

Ballas, A. C.
1968 "An Inquiry into the Sources and Extent of Poverty in the United States," Dissertation, New School for Social Research.

Baller, W. R., D. C. Charles, and E. L. Miller.
1967 "Midlife Attainment of the Mentally Retarded: A Longitudinal Study," *Genetic Psychology Monographs,* LXXV, 235-329.
Banfield, E. C.
1970 *"The Unheavenly City.* Boston: Little & Brown.
Barnett, L. D.
1970 "Achievement Values and Anomie Among Women in a Low-Income Housing Project," *Social Forces,* XLIX (September), 127-34.
Barth, M.C.
1970 "Migration and Income Maintenance," *Technical Studies.* The President's Commission on Income Maintenance Programs. Washington, D. C.: U. S. Government Printing Office
Battler, E., and J. Rotter.
1963 "Children's Feelings of Personal Control as Related to Social Class and Ethnic Group," *Journal of Personality,* XXXI, 482-90.
Baughman, E. E., and W. G. Dahlstrom.
1965 "Children of the Rural South," *Research Project Summaries No 2.* U. S. Department of Health, Education, and Welfare. Public Health Service. National Institute of Mental Health. Washington, D. C.: U. S. Government Printing Office.
Beale, C.
1966 "The Negro in American Agriculture," *The American Negro Reference Book.* Ed. J. P. Davis. Englewood Cliffs, N. J.: Prentice-Hall.
1969 "Demographic and Social Considerations for U. S. Rural Economic Policy," *American Journal of Agricultural Economics,* LI (May 2), 410-27.
1970 "Rural-Urban Migration of Blacks: Past and Future," Paper presented to the American Agricultural Economics Association Meeting, Detroit, Michigan (December 29).
Bealer, R., F. K. Willits, and W. P. Kuvlesky.
1965 "The Meaning of 'Rurality' in American Society: Some Implications of Alternative Definitions," *Rural Sociology,* XXX (September 3), 255-66
Beck, B.
1967 "Bed Bugs, Stench, Dampness and Immorality: A Review Essay on Recent Literature about Poverty," *Social Problems,* XV (Summer), 101-14.
Becker, G.
1957 *The Economics of Discrimination.* Chicago: University of Chicago Press.
Beiser, M.
1965 "Poverty, Social Disintegration and Personality," *Journal of Social Issues,* XXI (January 1), 56-78.
Bell, R. R.
1965 "Lower Class Negro Mothers' Aspirations for Their Children," *Social Forces,* XLIII (May), 493-500.
Bell, W.
1957 "Anomie, Social Isolation and the Class Structure," *Sociometry,* XX (June 2), 105-16
Bender, L. D., D. J. Hobbs, and J. F. Golden.
1967 "Congruence Between Aspirations and Capabilities of Youth in a Low-Income Rural Area," *Rural Sociology,* XXXII (September 3), 278-89.
Bennett, F.
1966 "The Condition of Farm Workers," *Poverty in America.* Ed. L. A. Ferman. Ann Arbor, Michigan: University of Michigan Press.
1969 *The Condition of Farm Workers and Small Farmers in 1969.* U. S. Congress. Senate. Sub-Committee Report on Migratory Labor. 91st Congress, 1st Session.
Ben-Rubin, J.
1968 *An Economic Evaluation of the Southwestern North Carolina Rural Renewal Area,* ERS-387. U. S. Department of Agriculture. Economic Research Service. Washington, D. C.: U. S. Government Printing Office.
Bentz, W. K., J. W. Edgerton, and M. Kherlopian.
1969 "Perceptions of Mental Illness Among People in a Rural Area," *Mental Hygiene,* LIII (July 3), 459-65.
Bereford, J. C., *et al.*
1963 "Family Formation and Family Composition: Trends and Prospects," *Source Book in Marriage and the Family.* 2nd ed. Ed. M. B. Sussman. Boston: Houghton-Mifflin.
Berelson, B., and G. S. Steiner, eds.
1964 *Human Behavior: An Inventory of Scientific Findings.* New York: Harcourt, Brace & World.
Bernard, J.
1966 *Marriage and Family Among Negroes.* Englewood Cliffs, New Jersey: Prentice-Hall, Inc.
Bernard, S. E.
1964 *Fatherless Families: Their Economic and Social Adjustment.* Brandeis University Papers in Social Welfare, No. 7. Waltham, Massachusetts: The Florence Heller Graduate School for Advanced Studies in Social Welfare.
Berry, B. J. L.
1967 *Strategies, Models and Economic Theories of Development in Rural Regions.* Agricultural Economic Report 127. U. S. Department of Agriculture. Economic Research Service. Washington, D. C.: U. S. Government Printing Office.
Berry, C. A.
1968 "Measurement of the Economic Impact of Public Investment on Regional Economic Growth in Appalachia," Dissertation, University of Cincinnati.
Besner, A.
1965 "Economic Deprivation and Family Patterns," *Welfare in Review,* II (September 9), 20-28.
Billingsley, A.
1969 "Family Functioning in the Low-Income Black Community," *Social Casework,* L(December 12), 563-72.
Birch, H. G., ed.
1964 *Brain Damage in Children: The Biological and Social Aspect.* New York: Williams & Wilkins.
Birch, H., and J. D. Gussow.
1970 *Disadvantaged Children: Health, Nutrition, and School Failure.* New York: Grune & Stratton.
Bird, A. R., and J. L. McCoy.
1964 *Poverty in Rural Areas of the United States.* Agricultural Economics Report 63, U. S. Department of Agriculture. Economics Research Service. Washington, D. C.: U. S. Government Printing Office.
1967 *White Americans in Rural Poverty.* Agricultural Economic Report 124. U. S. Department of Agriculture. Economic Research Service. Washington, D. C.: U. S. Government Printing Office.
Birren, J. E., and R. D. Hess.
1968 "Influence of Biological, Psychological and Social Deprivation upon Learning and Performance," *Perspectives on Human Deprivation: Biological, Psychological and Sociological.* U. S. Department of Health, Education, and Welfare. Washington, D. C.: U. S. Government Printing Office.
Blank, M.
1970 "Implicit Assumptions Underlying Preschool Intervention Programs," *Journal of Social Issues,* XXVI (2), 15-33.
Blardwood, R.
1968 "The Southern Roots of Urban Crises," *Fortune,* LXXCIII (August 18), 80-87 and 151-56.
Blau, P. N., and O. D. Duncan.
1967 *The American Occupational Structure,* New York: John Wiley & Sons, Inc.

Blewett, D. R.
1954 "An Experiment Study of the Inheritance of Intelligence," *Journal of Mental Science*, C, 922-33.

Block, C. E., C. S. Cope, J. T. Kunce, and D. Harston.
1970 *The Badge of Poverty*. Research Series No. 4. (Columbia, Missouri: Regional Rehabilitation Research Institute. University of Missouri at Columbia).

Blum, Z. G., and P. H. Rossi.
1969 "Social Class Research and Images of the Poor: Bibliographic Review," *On Understanding Poverty*. Ed. D. Moynihan. New York: Basis Books.

Bollman, A. D., H. W. Demone, and A. W. Stearns.
1951 "Does Failure Run in Farm Families: A Further Study of 1,000 Unsuccessful Careers," *Journal of Psychiatry*, CVII (March), 107, 667-76.

Bonnen, J. T.
1966 "Rural Poverty: Programs and Problems," *Journal of Farm Economics*, XLVIII (May 2), 452-65.

Book, J. A.
1961 "Genetical Etiology in Mental Illness," *Causes of Mental Disorders: A Review of Epidemiological Knowledge, 1959*. Proceedings of a Round Table Held at Arden House, Harriman, New York, October 27-28. New York: Milbank Fund.

Booth, E. J. R.
1969 "The Economic Dimensions of Rural Poverty," *American Journal of Agricultural Economy*, LI (May 2), 428-47.

Borgaonkor, D. S., and S. A. Shak.
1970 "Advances in Human Genetics and Their Impact on Society," *Science*, CLXX (October 16), 347-48.

Boulding, K. E.
1966 "The Economics of the Coming Spaceship Earth," *Environmental Quality in a Growing Economy*. Ed. H. Jarrett. Baltimore: Johns Hopkins Press for Resources for the Future, Inc.

Bowdoin, M. H.
1969 "Poverty and Education in the South," *Atlanta Economic Review*, XIX (February), 14-16.

Bowerman, C. E.
1959 "Changes in Family and Peer Orientations of Children between the Fourth and Tenth Grades," *Social Forces*, XXXVII, 206-11.

Bowlby, J.
1951 *Maternal Care and Mental Health*. Geneva: World Health Organization Monograph Series No. 2.

Bowles, G.
1970 "A Profile of the Incidence of Poverty among Rural Urban Migrants and Comparative Populations", Paper presented at the annual meeting of the Rural Sociological Society, Washington, D. C. (August 26-30).
1965 *Net Migration of the Population, 1950-1960 by Age, Sex and Color*. Population-Migration Report II U. S. Department of Agriculture. Economic Research Service. Washington, D. C.: U. S. Government Printing Office.

Boxley, R. F.
1965 *White and Non-White Owners of Rural Land in the Southeast*, ERS-238. U. S. Department of Agriculture. Economic Research Service. Washington, D. C.: U. S. Government Printing Office.

Brager, G. A.
1965 "Organizing the Unaffiliated in a Low-Income Area," *Poverty in America*. Ed. L. A. Ferman, *et. al.* Ann Arbor, Michigan: University of Michigan Press.

Brainin, S., and H. C. Yeager.
1964 *An Examination of the Concept of "Culture of Poverty" and Its Relationship to Ethnic Cultural Definitions*. New York: Mobilization for Youth, Inc.

Bramhall, D. F., and H. J. Brice.
1969 "Interstate Migration of Labor-Force Age Population," *Industrial and Labor Relations Review*, XXII (July), 576-83.

Bredemeier, H. C.
1967 "New Strategies for the War on Poverty: a Plan to Enlist Private Enterprise in the Management of Social Welfare," *Combating Social Problems: Techniques of Intervention*. Ed. H. Gold and F. R. Scarpetti. New York: Holt, Rinehart & Winston.

Briar, S.
1966 "Welfare from Below: Recipients' Views of the Public Welfare System," *Law and the Poor*. Ed. J. ten Broek. San Francisco: Chandler.

Britt, R. D.
1966 "New Jobs and Labor Mobility in Depressed Areas," Dissertation. University of Colorado.

Bronfenbrenner, U.
1958 "Socialization and Social Class Through Time and Space," *Readings in Social Psychology*, 3rd ed. Ed. E. Maccoby, T. Newcomb, and E. Hartley. New York: Holt, Rhinehart & Wilson.
1967 "Early Deprivation in Mammals and Man," *Early Experience and Behavior*. Ed. N. Grant. Springfield, Illinois: C. C. Thomas.
1970 "The Psychological Costs of Quality and Equality in Education," *Psychological Factors in Poverty*. Ed. V. L. Allen. Chicago: Markham.

Brooks, M. P.
1964 *The Dimensions of Poverty in North Carolina*. Durham, North Carolina: The North Carolina Fund.

Brown, J. S., H. K. Schwarzweller, and J. J. Mangalam.
1963 "Kentucky Mountain Migration and the Stem Family: An American Variation on a Theme by Le Play," *Rural Sociology*, XXVIII (September 3), 48-69.

Bryan, C. H.
1968 "Breaking the Poverty Cycle: An Investigation into the Correlates of Propensity for Change among the Rural Impoverished in the Mississippi Delta," Dissertation, Louisiana State University.

Bryan, C. H., and A. L. Bertrand.
1970 *Propensity for Change among the Rural Poor in the Mississippi Delta: A Study of the Roots of Social Mobility*. Agricultural Economic Report 185. U. S. Department of Agriculture. Economic Research Service. Washington, D. C.: U. S. Government Printing Office.

Buell, B.
1952 *Community Planning for Human Services*. New York: Columbia University Press.

Bultena, G. L.
1969 "Rural-Urban Differences in the Familial Interaction of the Aged," *Rural Sociology*, XXXIV March 1), 5-15.

Burchinal, L. G.
1960 "What About Your Daughter's Future?" *Iowa Farm Science*, XIV (12), 9-10.
1961 Differences in Educational and Occupational Aspirations of Farm, Small-Town and City Boys," *Rural Sociology*, XXVI (2), 114.
1963 "How do Farm Families Adjust to City Life?" *Iowa Farm Science*, XVII (10), 6-8.

Burchinal, L. G. and H. Siff.
1964 "Rural Poverty," *Journal of Marriage and the Family*, XXVI (November 4), 399-405.

Burden, C. A.
1970 "After Mental Illness—An Examination of Work and Worth," *Atlanta Economic Review*, XX (November), 8-14.

Bureau of Business and Economic Research. University of Georgia.
1968 *Georgia Statistical Abstract 1968*. Athens, Georgia.

Burgess, E.
1964 "Some Implications of Social Change for Dependency among Lower Class Families," *American Journal of Orthospsychiatry,* XXXIV, 895-906.
Burgess, E., and D. D. Price.
1963 *An American Dependency Challenge.* Chicago: American Public Welfare Association.
Burkhart, J. M., Project Director.
1969 *Regional Demonstration of Comprehensive Rehabilitation Services in a Rural, Mountainous, Economically Depressed Area.* Frankfort, Kentucky: Kentucky Department of Education. Bureau of Rehabilitation Services.
Burt, C.
1958 "The Inheritance of Mental Ability," *American Psychologist,* XIII, 1-15.
1961 "Intelligence and Social Mobility," *British Journal of Statistical Psychology,* XIV (March 24).
1963 "Is Intelligence Distributed Normally?" *British Journal of Statistical Psychology,* XVI (November 2), 175-90.
1966 "The Genetic Determination of Differences in Intelligence: A Study of Monozygotic Twins Reared Together and Apart," *British Journal of Psychology,* LVII, 137-53.
Caplovitz, D.
1963 *The Poor Pay More.* New York: Free Press.
1965 "The Merchant and the Low-Income Consumer," *Poverty in America.* Ed. L. A. Ferman, *et al.* Ann Arbor, Michigan: University of Michigan Press.
Carson, G. L.
1967 "The Self-Concept of Welfare Recipients," *Personnel and Guidance Journal,* XLV, 424-28.
Carter, G. W.
1970 *Review of Research Findings in Public Welfare: A Five-Year Analysis.* Los Angeles: Regional Research Institute for Social Welfare: University of Southern California.
Cattell, R. B.
1960 "The Multiple Abstract Variance Analysis Equations and Solutions: For Nature-Nurture Research on Continuous Variables," *Psychology Review,* LXVII, 353-72.
Cazden, C. B.
1970 "The Situation: A Neglected Source of Social Class Differences in Language Use," *Journal of Social Issues,* XXVI (2), 35-59.
Center for Business and Economic Research. University of Tennessee.
1969 *Personal Income Trends in Tennessee 1929-1967.* Knoxville, Tennessee.
Chalmers, W. E., and N. W. Dorsey.
1962 "Research on Negro Job Status," *Journal of Intergroup Relations III* (Autumn), 344-59.
Chamberlain, R. M.
1969 "Participation in Voluntary Associations and Heterogeneous Social Characteristics of Rural-Urban Fringe Residents," Dissertation. University of Missouri.
Chilman, C. S.
1965 "Child-Rearing and Family Relationship Patterns of the Very Poor," *Welfare in Review,* III (January 1), 3-19.
1966 *Growing up Poor.* U. S. Department of Health, Education, and Welfare. Welfare Administration. Washington, D. C.: U. S. Government Printing Office.
Chilman, C. S., and M. B. Sussman.
1964 "Poverty in the United States in the Mid-Sixties," *Journal of Marriage and the Family,* XXVI (November 4), 391-95.
Chilton, R. J.
1968 *Consequences of a State Suitable Home Law for AFDC Families in Florida.* Tallahassee, Florida: Institute for Social Research. Florida State University.
Clark, F.
1970 "Trends in Food Consumption in the South," *The Food Problem in Georgia.* Ed. G. G. Dull. ICON. Athens, Georgia.
Clausen, J. A., and J. R. Williams.
1968 "Sociological Correlates of Child Behavior," *Children and Poverty.* Ed. N. Y. Glazer and C. F. Creedon. Chicago: Rand McNally.
Clawson, M.
1967 "Rural Poverty in the United States," *Journal of Farm Economics,* XLIX (December 5), 1227-33.
Cleland, C. L.
1969 "Changes and Trends in Rural Communities in Tennessee," *Tennessee Planner,* XXVIII (Summer), 114-21.
Cleland, C. C., and J. D. Swartz.
1968 "Deprivation, Reinforcement and Peer Support as Work Motivators: A Paradigm for Habilitation of Older Retardates," *Community Mental Health Journal,* IV (April 2), 120-28.
Clements, H. A., J. A. Duncan, and R. E. Hardy.
1967 *The Unfit Majority, A Research Study of the Rehabilitation of Selective Service Rejectees in South Carolina.* Final Report. Columbia, South Carolina: Vocational Rehabilitation Department.
Cloward, R. A., and F. F. Piven.
1968 "Migration, Politics, and Welfare," *Saturday Review* (November 16), 31-5.
Cochran, C.
1971 "Our Rural Scandal: Two-Thirds of the Nation's Bad Housing Is Out There," *South Today,* II March 7), 5-8.
Coffey, J. D.
1968 "Personal Distribution of Farmers' Income by Source and Region," *American Journal of Agricultural Economy,* L (December 5), 1383-96.
Cohen, A. K.
1955 *Delinquent Boys.* Glencoe, Illinois: Free Press.
Cohen, A. K., and H. M. Hodges, Jr.
1963 "Characteristics of the Lower-Blue-Collar-Class," *Social Problems,* X (Spring), 303-34.
Cohen, J.
1964 "Social Work and the Culture of Poverty," *Mental Health of the Poor.* Ed. F. Riessmen, *et al.* New York: Free Press.
Cohen, J., and W. S. Murphy.
1966 *Burn, Baby, Burn!* New York: Dutton.
Coles, R.
1969 "Rural Upheaval: Confrontation and Accommodation," *On Fighting Poverty: Perspectives from Experience.* Ed. J. Sundquist. New York: Basis Books.
Coles, R., and H. Huge.
1969 "A Cry from the Delta," *South Today,* I (July 1), 5-6.
Coll, B. D.
1965 "Deprivation in Childhood: Its Relation to the Cycle of Poverty," *Welfare in Review,* III (March 3), 1-10.
Collins, J. A.
1970 *Springfield Federal Offender Rehabilitation Project.* Final Report. Springfield, Illinois: Illinois Division of Vocational Rehabilitation.
Comer, J. P.
1967 "The Social Power of the Negro," *Scientific American,* CCXVI, 21-27.
Community Service Society of New York. Institute of Welfare Research.
1969 *Annual Report 1968-1969.* New York.
Conference on Social Issues.
1966 *Poverty: Four Approaches/Four Solutions.* Proceedings of the First Annual Conference on Social

Issues. University of Oregon, Eugene, Oregon (January 27-28).

Conklin, D. J., and R. A. Quesinberry.
1969 *Selected South Carolina Economic Data.* Columbia South Carolina: Bureau of Business and Economic Research. University of South Carolina .

Contes, G., and D. L. Brown.
1970 "Industry, Labor and the Federal Government's Role in Family Planning Programs," Paper presented at the International Conference on Population Priorities and Options for Commerce and Industry. University of North Carolina, Chapel Hill, North Carolina (October 22-23).

Copp, J. H., ed.
1964 *Our Changing Rural Society: Perspectives and Trends.* Ames, Iowa: Iowa State University Press.

Corwin, R. G.
1965 *A Sociology of Education.* New York: Appleton-Century-Crofts.

Coser, L. A.
1965 "The Sociology of Poverty: To the Memory of George Simmel," *Social Problems,* XIII (Fall), 140-48.

Costello, E. T.
1966 "An Empirical Investigation of the Singer-Prebisch Thesis: The Terms of Trade of the Southeastern United States, 1947-1958," Dissertation, University of Tennessee.

Cowhig, J. D., and C. L. Beale.
1964 "Socioeconomic Differences Between White and Non-white Farm Populations of the South," *Social Forces,* XLIII (March), 354-62.

Crandell, V. C., *et al.*
1965 "Children's Beliefs in Their Own Control of Reinforcements in Intellectual-Academic Achievement Situations," *Child Development,* XXVI, 91-109.

"Creating a Doctor Corps."
1971 *Time* (January 18).

Crecink, J. C., and H. Hoover.
1960 *Incomes and Resources of Rural Families in the Clayhills Area of Mississippi.* Mississippi Agricultural Experiment Station Bulletin 604 (September).

Crecink, J. C., and R. Steptoe.
1970 *Human Resources in the Rural Mississippi Delta—with Emphasis on the Poor.* Agricultural Economic Report 170. U. S. Department of Agriculture. Economic Research Service. Washington, D. C.: U. S. Government Printing Office.

Crosswhite, W. M., ed.
1970 *People in Poverty: Selected Case Studies.* Raleigh, North Carolina: Agricultural Policy Institute of North Carolina State University.

Crow, J. F.
1970 "Do Genetic Factors Contribute to Poverty?" *Psychological Factors in Poverty.* Ed. V. L. Allen. Chicago: Markham.

Cully, W. J.
1965 "Nutrition and Mental Retardation," *Medical Aspects of Mental Retardation.* Ed. C. H. Carter. Springfield, Illinois: C. C. Thomas.

Cumming, R.
1969-70 "Which Exit for the Rural Poor?" *Interplay,* III (October-January), 42-5.

Daft, L. M.
1969 "Income Maintenance in Rural Areas," *Agricultural Policy Review,* IX (October-December), 4-6.

Dailey, J. T.
1964 "Education and Emergence from Poverty," *Journal of Marriage and the Family,* XXVI (November 4). 430-4.

Darlington, G. D.
1970 *The Evolution of Man and Society.* New York: Simon & Schuster.

David, M.
1964 "Income and Dependency in Coming Decades," *The American Journal of Economics and Sociology,* XXIII (July), 249-68.

David, M., *et al.*
1961 *Educational Achievement—Its Causes and Effects.* Ann Arbor, Michigan: Survey Research Center.

Davis, A., and J. Dollard.
1964 *Children of Bondage.* New York: Harper & Row.

Davis, J. H., and B. R. Miller.
1970 "Trends in the Growth of the Property Tax Base in Georgia and other Southeastern States," *Atlanta Economic Review* XX (November 4), 22-5.

Davis, K.
1966 "Sociological Aspects of Genetic Control," *Genetics and the Future of Man.* Ed. J. D. Roslansky. New York: Appleton-Century-Crofts.

Davis, W. A.
1948 *Social-Class Influences Upon Learning.* Cambridge. Massachusetts: Harvard University Press.

Davis, W. A., and R. J. Havighurst.
1946 "Social Class and Color Differences in Child Rearing," *American Sociological Review,* XI, 698-710.

Dean, D. G.
1961 "Alienation: Its Meaning and Measurement," *American Sociological Review,* XXVI (October 5). 753-58.

Deutermann, W.
1970 "Educational Attainment of Workers, March 1969. and 1970," *Monthly Labor Review,* XCIII (October 10), 9-17.

Deutsch, M.
1960 *Minority Group and Class Status as Related to Social and Personality Factors in Scholastic Achievement.* Society for Applied Anthropology, Monograph No. 2. Ithaca, New York.
1965 "The Role of Social Class in Language Development and Cognition," *American Journal of Orthopsychiatry,* XXXV, 77-88.
1966 "The Disadvantaged Child and the Learning Process," *Poverty in America.* Ed. L. A. Ferman, *et al.* Ann Arbor, Michigan: University of Michigan Press.

Deutsch, M., and B. Brown.
1964 "Social Influences in Negro-White Intelligence Difference," *Journal of Social Issues,* XX (2), 24-35.

Dixion, D. F., and D. J. McLaughlin, Jr.
1970 "Low Income Consumers and the Issue of Exploitation: A Study of Chain Super Markets," *Social Science* LI (September 2), 320-28.

Dobzhansky, T.
1968 "On Genetics, Sociology, and Politics," *Prospectives Quarterly in Biological Medicine,* II, 544-54.

Doherty, N.
1970 *Rurality, Poverty, and Health: Medical Problems in Rural Areas.* Agricultural Economic Report 172. U. S. Department of Agriculture. Economic Research Service. Washington, D. C.: U. S. Government Printing Office.

Dotson, F.
1951 "Patterns of Voluntary Association Among Urban Working Class Families," *American Sociological Review,* XVI (October 5), 687-93.

Dreger, R. M., and K. S. Miller.
1960 "Comparative Psychological Studies of Negroes and Whites in the United States," *Psychological Bulletin,* LVII (September 5), 361-402.
1968 "Comparative Psychological Studies of Negroes and Whites in the United States," *Psychological Bulletin Monograph Supplement,* LXX (September 3), 1-58.

Drucker, P. F., D. C. Miller, and R. N. Dahl.
1961 *Power and Democracy in America.* South Bend, Indiana: University of Notre Dame Press.

Duncan, B., and O. D. Duncan.
1969 "Family Stability and Occupation Success," *Social Problems,* XVI (Winter), 273-85.

Duncan, O. D.
1969 "Inheritance of Poverty or Inheritance of Race?" *On Understanding Poverty.* Ed. D. Moynihan. New York: Basic Books.

Dunkelberger, J. E.
1965 "Anomie and Aspiration Among Male Household Heads in Low-Income Rural Areas," *Proceedings of the Association of Southern Agricultural Workers, Inc., Agricultural Economics and Rural Sociology Section.* 62nd Annual Convention. Paper 3. Dallas, Texas.

Dunmore, C. J.
1969 "Social-Psychological Factors Affecting the Use of an Educational Opportunity Program by Families Living in a Poverty Area," Dissertation, Brandeis University.

Dunn, J. H.
1970 "Total Rehabilitation in Wood County," *Rehabilitation Record* (September-October), 29-30 and 32-33.

Durbin, E. F.
1969 "Welfare Income and Employment: An Economic Analysis of Family Choice," *Labor Economics and Urban Studies,* Vol. I. New York: F. A. Praeger.

Echols, F. H.
1961 *An Evaluation Survey of the Medical, Social and Rehabilitation Factors in Work Adjustment of 5,836 Persons Discharged from State Tuberculosis Hospitals in Florida.* Final Report. Research Reports in Social Science. Tallahassee, Florida: Institute for Social Research. Florida State University.

Echland, B. K.
1967 "Genetics and Sociology: A Reconsideration," *American Sociological Review,* XXXII (April 2), 173-94.

Eckstein, O., ed.
1967 *Studies in the Economics of Income Maintenance.* Washington, D. C.: Brookings Institution.

Edgerton, J. W., and W. K. Bentz.
1969 "Attitudes and Opinions of Rural People About Mental Illness and Program Services," *American Journal of Public Health,* LIX (March 3), 470-77.

Ehrlich, P. R., and H. A. Ehrlich.
1970 *Population, Resources, Environment: Issues in Human Ecology.* San Francisco: Freeman.

Ehrlich, P. R., and J. P. Holdren.
1971 "Impact of Population Growth," *Science,* CLXXI (March), 1212-17.

Eisenstadt, S. N.
1956 *From Generation to Generation.* Glencoe, Illinois: Free Press.

Elder, G. H.
1962 "Structural Variations in the Child Rearing Relationship," *Sociometry,* XXV, 241-62.

Ellis, R. A., and W. C. Lane.
1963 "Structural Supports for Upward Mobility," *American Sociological Review,* XXVIII, 743-56.

Emery, A. E. H.
1968 *Heredity, Disease, and Man.* Berkeley, California: University of California Press.

Empey, L. H.
1956 "Social Class and Occupational Aspirations: A Comparison of Absolute and Relative Measurements," *American Sociological Review,* XXI (December 6), 703-9.

Epstein, L. A.
1961 "Some Effects of Low Income on Children and Their Families," *Social Security Bulletin,* XXIV (February 2), 12-17.
1963 "Unmet Need in a Land of Abundance," *Social Security Bulletin,* (May 5), 3-11.

Erlenmeyer-Kimling, L., and L. F. Jarvik.
1963 "Genetics and Intelligence: A Review," *Science,* CXLII, 1477-79.

Eyre, L. A.
1970 "Three Million New Southerners: Depopulation and Migration in Five Southeast States, 1950-1968," *Florida Planning and Development,* XXI (February), 1ff.

Fantl, B.
1958 Integrating Psychological, Social, and Cultural Factors in Assertive Casework," *Social Work,* III, 30-37.

Feagin, J. R., and H. Hahn.
1970 "The Second Reconstruction: Black Political Strength in the South," *Social Science Quarterly,* LI (June 1), 42-56.

Ferman, L. A., *et al.*
1966 *Poverty in America.* Ann Arbor, Michigan: University of Michigan Press.

Fisher, J. L.
1966 "Poverty and Resource Utilization," *Poverty Amid Affluence.* Ed. L. Fishman. New Haven, Connecticut: Yale University Press.

Fishman, L., ed.
1966 *Poverty Amid Affluence.* New Haven, Connecticut: Yale University Press.

Fleisher, B. M.
1966 *The Economics of Delinquency.* Chicago: Quadrangle Book.

Floyd, R. H.
1970 "Federal Aid: A Boost to the Southeastern Economy," *The Monthly Review* (August), Research Department, Federal Reserve Bank of Atlanta.

Folkman, W. S., and J. D. Cowhig.
1963 "Intergenerational Occupational Mobility in a Rural Area," *Rural Sociology,* XXVIII (December 4), 405-7.

Ford, T. R.
1965 *The Effects of Prevailing Values and Beliefs on the Perpetuation of Poverty in Rural Areas.* 19. Raleigh, North Carolina: Agricultural Policy Institute of North Carolina State University.

Ford, T. R., ed.
1962 *The Southern Appalachian Region: A Survey.* Lexington, Kentucky: University of Kentucky Press.

Franks, B. B.
1967 "Some Social Determinants of Academic Success Among Culturally Disadvantaged Negro Children," Dissertation, Pennsylvania State University.

Frazier, F.
1950 "Problems and Needs of Negro Children and Youth Resulting from Family Disorganization," *Journal of Negro Education,* XIX (Summer 3), 269-77.
1966 *The Negro Family in the United States.* Chicago: University of Chicago Press.

Fried, M.
1969 "Deprivation and Migration: Dilemmas of Casual Interpretation," *On Understanding Poverty.* Ed. D. Moynihan. New York: Basic Books.

Friedman, R. D.
1965 *Poverty—Definition and Perspectives.* Washington, D. C.: American Enterprise Institute for Public Policy.

Frumkin, R. M.
1961 "Rural Families in an Urban Setting: A Study in Persistence and Change," *Journal of Human Relations,* IX (Summer), 494-503.

Fuchs, V. R.
1965 "Toward a Theory of Poverty," *The Concept of Poverty.* 1st Report of the Task Force on Economic Growth and Opportunity. Washington, D. C.: U. S. Chamber of Commerce.

Fuller, J. L., and W. R. Thompson.
1960 *Behavior Genetics.* New York: John Wiley & Sons.

Fuller, V.
1965 "Rural Poverty and Rural Area Development," *Poverty in America*. Ed. M. S. Gordon. San Francisco: Chandler.

Furman, S. S., ed.
1962 *Reaching the Unreached*. New York: New York City Youth Board.

Galantry, E.
1968 "Black New Towns: The Fourth Alternative," *Progressive Architecture,* XLIX (August), 126-31.

Galbraith, J. K.
1958 *The Affluent Society*. Boston: Houghton Mifflin.
1962 "The Cause of Poverty: A Clinical View," *Population Review,* VI (July), 62-66.

Galloway, L. E.
1966 "On the Importance of 'Picking One's Parents,'" *Quarterly Review of Economics and Business,* VI (Summer), 7-15.
1967 "The Negro and Poverty," *The Journal of Business,* XL (January), 27-35.
1969 "A Note on the Incidence of Hidden Unemployment in the United States," *Western Economic Journal,* VII (March), 71-83.

Gans, H. J.
1966 "Subculture and Class," *Poverty in America*. Ed. L. A. Ferman, *et al.* Ann Arbor, Michigan: University of Michigan Press.
1967 "Income Grants and 'Dirty Work'?" *The Public Interest* (Winter), 110-113.
1969 "Culture and Class in the Study of Poverty: An Approach to Anti-Poverty Research," *On Understanding Poverty*. Ed. D. Moynihan. New York: Basic Book.

Garin, P.
1966 "Some Characteristics of Students from Poverty Backgrounds Attending Predominantly Negro Colleges in the Deep South," *Social Forces,* XLV (September), 27-40.

Garza, J. M.
1969 "Race, the Achievement Syndrome, and Perception of Opportunity," *Phylon,* XXX (Winter), 338-54.

Geismar, L. L.
1957 *Families in Trouble*. St. Paul, Minnesota: Family-Centered Project.

Georgia Department of Family and Children Services. Division of Research and Publications.
1969 *The AFDC Family in Georgia*. Atlanta, Georgia.

Gerson, W. M.
1966 "Mass Media Socialization Behavior: Negro-White Differences," *Social Forces,* XLV (September), 40-50.

Gilliland, A. R.
1951 "Socio-Economic Status and Race as Factors in Infant Test Scores," *Child Development,* XXII, 271-73.

Ginsberg, L. H.
1969a "Social Problems in Rural America," *Social Work Practice, 1969*. New York: Columbia University Press for the National Conference on Social Welfare, Columbus, Ohio.
1969b "Education for Social Work in Rural Settings," Paper presented to the Council on Social Work Education Seventeenth Annual Program Meeting, Cleveland, Ohio.

Gittell, M.
1965 "A Pilot Study of Negro Middle Class Attitudes Toward Higher Education," *Journal of Negro Education,* XXXIV (Fall), 384-95.

Gladwin, T.
1961 "The Anthropologist's View of Poverty," *Social Work Forum, 1961*. New York: Columbia University Press.

Glass, B.
1966 "The Effect of Changes in the Physical Environment on Genetic Change," *Genetics and the Future of Man*. Ed. J. D. Roslansky. New York: Appleton-Century-Crofts.

Glass, D. C.
1967 "Genetics and Social Behavior," *Social Science Research Council Items,* XXI (1), 1-12.

Goldin, G. J.
1970 "Rehabilitation and Poverty," Paper Presented at the National Conference on the Psychological Aspects of Disability, Monterey, California (October 26-28).

Goldin, G. J., *et al.*
1967 *Dependency and Its Implication for Rehabilitation*. Monograph 1. Boston, Massachusetts: New England Rehabilitation Research Institute. Northeastern University.

Goldman, R.
1969 Ethical Considerations in Longer Life Span," *Geriatric Focus,* VIII (October 1), 1-6.

Good, P.
1968a *The American Serfs*. New York: G. P. Putnam's Sons.
1968b *Cycle to Nowhere*. United States Commission on Civil Rights. Clearinghouse Publication No. 14. Washington, D. C.: U. S. Government Printing Office.
1968c "Poverty in the Rural South," *New South,* XXIII (Winter), 2-119.
1969 "Farmer: The Genesis of the Chicago Riot May be Traced to the Cotton Field," from *Cycle to Nowhere* in *South Today*, I (5), 4.

Goodchilds, J.D., and E. E. Smith.
1963 "The Effects of Unemployment as Mediated by Social Status," *Sociometry,* XXVI, 287-93.

Goode, W. J.
1951 "Economic Factors and Marital Stability," *American Sociological Review,* XVI (December 6), 802-12.
1961 "Illegitimacy, Anomie, and Cultural Penetration," *American Sociological Review,* XXVI (December 6), 910-25.
1962 "Marital Satisfaction and Instability," *International Social Science Journal,* XIV, 507-26.

Goodstein, M. E.
1970 "A Note on Urban and Non Urban Employment Growth in the South, 1940-1960," *Journal of Regional Science,* X (3), 397-401.

Gordon, E. W.
1965 "Characteristics of Socially Disadvantaged Children," *Review of Educational Research,* XXXV, 377-88.

Gordon, E.
1970 "Race, Ethnicity, and Social Disadvantagement," Paper presented at the National Conference on Psychological Aspects of Disability, Monterey, California (October 26-28).

Gordon, M.
1947 "The Concept of the Sub-Culture and Its Application," *Social Forces,* XXVI, (October), 40-43.

Gottliek, D.
1967 "Poor Youth Want to be Middle-Class but It's Not Easy," *Personnel and Guidance Journal,* XLVI, 116-22.

Gouldner, A. W.
1963 "The Secrets of Organizations," *The Social Welfare Forum,* 1963, Proceedings of the National Conference on Social Welfare. New York: Columbia University Press.

Graham, J. J.
1970 *The Enemies of the Poor*. New York: Columbia University Press.

Green, C.
1967 *Negative Taxes and the Poverty Problem*. Washington, D. C.: Brookings Institution.
1970 A Macroeconomic Analysis of the Economic Impact of Negative Income Tapes. *Technical Papers*. President's Commission on Income Maintenance Pro-

grams. Washington, D. C.: U. S. Government Printing Office.

Green E.
1970 "Race, Social Status, and Criminal Arrest," *American Sociological Review,* XXXV (June 3), 476-90.

Grossack, M. M., ed.
1963 *Mental Health and Segregation.* New York: Springer.

Grotberg, E. H.
1965 "Learning Disabilities and Remediation in Disadvantaged Children," *Review of Educational Research,* XXXV, 413-25.

Gurin, G., and P. Gurin.
1970 "Expectancy Theory in the Study of Poverty," *Journal of Social Issues,* XXVI (2), 83-104.

Guttentag, M.
1970a "Introduction," *Journal of Social Issues,* XXVI (2), 1-13.
1970b "Group Cohesiveness, Ethnic Organization, and Poverty," *Journal of Social Issues,* XXVI (2), 105-32.

Gwartney, J.
1970 "Discrimination and Income Differentials," *The American Economic Review,* LX (June 3), 396-407.

Haber, A.
1966 "Poverty Budgets: How Much is Enough?" *Poverty and Human Resources Abstracts,* Vol. I (May-June), 5-14.

Haggstrom, W. C.
1964 "The Power of the Poor," *Mental Health of the Poor.* Ed. F. Reissman, *et al.* New York: Free Press.

Hahn, A. J.
1970 "Planning in Rural Areas," *American Institute Planners Journal,* XXXVI (January), 44-9.

Haller, A. O., and C. Ellis.
1962 "Personality Orientations of Farm, Village, and Urban Boys," *Rural Sociology,* XXVII (September 3), 275-93.

Haller, A. O., and W. H. Sewell.
1957 "Farm Residents and Levels of Educational and Occupational Aspiration," *American Journal of Sociology,* LXII (4), 407-11.

Hamilton, D.
1967 "The Political Economy of Poverty: Institutional and Technological Dimensions," *Journal of Economic Issues,* I (December), 309-20.

Handel, G., and L. Rainwater.
1961 Working-Class People and Family Planning," *Social Work,* VI (April 2), 18-25.

Hansen, N. M.
1970 *Rural Poverty and the Urban Crisis: A Strategy of Regional Development.* Bloomington: Indiana University Press.

Hardin, G.
1968 "The Tragedy of the Commons," *Science,* CLXVII (December 13), 1243-48.

Harmeling, M. B.
1961 "Social and Cultural Links in the Urban Occupational Adjustment of Southern Appalachian Migrants," Dissertation, Fordham University.

Harper, G. L.
1961 "A Comprehensive Case Program for Migrant Farm Workers," *Public Health Reports* (August), 690-6.

Hathaway, D. E., J. A. Beegle, and W. K. Bryant.
1968 *People of Rural America.* U. S. Department of Commerce. Bureau of the Census. Washington, D. C.: U. S. Government Printing Office.

Hausman, L. J.
1969 *The Potential for Work Among Welfare Parents.* Manpower Research Monograph No. 12. U. S. Department of Labor. Washington, D. C.: U. S. Government Printing Office.
1970 'The Impact of Welfare on the Work Effort of AFDC Mothers," *Technical Studies.* The President's Commission on Income Maintenance Programs. Washington, D. C.: U. S. Government Printing Office.

Haywood, C. F.
1966 "The Unemployed Poor, Labor Mobility and Poverty," *The Disadvantaged Poor: Education and Employment.* 3rd Report of Task on Economic Growth and Opportunity. Washington, D. C.: U. S. Chamber of Commerce.

Heilbroner, R. L.
1959 *The Future as History.* New York: Grove Press.

Heineman, B. W.
1969 "Guaranteed Annual Income: A Placebo or a Cure?" *The Conference Board Record,* VI (May), 26-31.

Hellmuth, J., ed.
1967 *Disadvantaged Child,* Vol. I. Seattle: Special Child Publications of the Seattle Sequin School, Inc.
1968 *Disadvantaged Child,* Vol. II: Head Start and Early Intervention. Seattle: Special Child Publications, Inc.

Henderson, G.
1966 "Occupational Aspirations of Poverty-Stricken Negro Students," *Vocational Guidance Quarterly,* XIV, 41-45.

Henderson, H. A.
1960 *Resources and Incomes of Rural Upper East Tennessee People.* Tennessee Agricultural Experiment Station Bulletin 312 (March).

Henderson, V. W.
1963 *The Economic Status of Negroes: In the Nation and in the South.* Toward Regional Realism Series, No. 3. Atlanta, Georgia: Southern Regional Council.

Hendrix, W. E.
1959 "Income Improvement in Low-Income Areas," *Journal of Farm Economics,* XLI (December 5), 1065-75.
1967 "Relation of Chronic Low Farm Incomes to Major National Economic Problems," *Major American Social Problems.* Ed. R. A. Dentler. Chicago: Rand McNally.

Hersey, J.
1964 "Our Romance with Poverty," *The American Scholar,* XXXIII (Autumn), 525-36.

Herzog, E.
1963 "Some Assumptions About the Poor," *Social Service Review* XXXVII (December 4), 389-402.
1966 "Is there a Culture of Poverty?" *Poverty in the Affluent Society.* Ed. H. H. Meissner. New York: Harper & Row.
1967 *About the Poor: Some Facts and Fictions.* Children's Bureau Publication 451. U. S. Department of Health, Education, and Welfare, Social and Rehabilitation Service. Washington, D. C.: U. S. Government Printing Office.

Herzog, E., and H. Lewis.
1970 "Children in Poor Families: Myths and Realities," *American Journal of Orthopsychiatry,* XL (April 3), 375-87.

Herzog, E., and C. E. Sudia.
1968 "Fatherless Homes, a Review of Research," *Children,* XV, 177.

Hess, R. D.
1964 "Educability and Rehabilitation: The Future of the Welfare Class," *Journal of Marriage and the Family,* XXVI (November 4), 422-29.

Higgins, J., *et al.*
1962 "Intelligence and Family Size: A Paradox Resolved," *Eugenics Quarterly,* IX, 84-90.

Hill, A. C., and F. S. Jaffe.
1966 "Negro Fertility and Family Size Preferences: Implications for Programming of Health and Social Services," *The Negro American.* Ed. T. Parsons and B. Clark. Boston: Houghton.

Hines, F., and L. Tweeten.
1968 "Push-Pull and Schooling Investment," *American*

Journal of Agricultural Economics, L (December 5), 1426-31.

Hines, R. H.
1964 "Social Expectations and Cultural Deprivation," *Journal of Negro Education,* XXXIII (Spring), 136-42.

Hoffman, M. L., and L. W. Hoffman, eds.
1964 *Review of Child Development Research,* Vol. II. New York: Russell Sage Foundation.

Hofley, J. R.
1969 "Lower Class Religion: The Moral Basis of a Backward Society," Dissertation, University of North Carolina.

Hollingshead, A. B., and F. C. Redlich.
1958 *Social Class and Mental Illness: A Community Study.* New York: John Wiley & Sons.

Honigmann, J. J.
1965 "The Middle-Class View of Poverty Culture, Sociocultural Disintegration and Mental Health," Paper presented at the University of Kentucky Conference on Cross-Cultural Psychiatry and Psychoethnology, Lexington, Kentucky.

Hooever, H., and J. C. Crecink.
1962 *Rural Non-farm Families in the Clay Hills of Mississippi—Incomes and Resources.* Mississippi Agricultural Experiment Station Bulletin 648 (July).

Houston, D. G., and J. Finely.
1969 *Rehabilitation versus Poverty.* Final Report. Jefferson City, Missouri: Missouri State Department of Education. Section of Vocational Rehabilitation.

Hughes, C. C., *et al.*
1960 *People of Cone and Woodlot.* New York: Basic Books.

Hunt, E. P.
1967 "Infant Mortality and Poverty Areas," *Welfare in Review,* V (August-September), 1-12.

Hunt, J. M.
1965 "Traditional Personality-Theory in the Light of Recent Evidence," *American Scientist,* LIII, 80-96.
1969 *The Challenge of Incompetence and Poverty.* Urbana, Illinois: University of Illinois Press.

Hunter, R.
1965 *Poverty-Social Conscience in the Progressive Era.* New York: Harper & Row.

Hurley, R. L.
1969 *Poverty and Mental Retardation: A Casual Relationship.* New York: Random House.

Hutchison, B. R.
1967 "Money Can't Buy Maturity," *International Journal of Psychiatry,* IV (October), 312-13.

Hyman, H.
1953 "The Value Systems of Different Classes: A Social Psychological Contribution to the Analysis of Stratification," *Class, Status and Power.* Ed. R. Bendix and S. M. Lipsett. Glencoe, Illinois: Free Press.

Institute for Rural American. Spindletop Research.
1969 *Poverty, Rural Poverty, and Minority Groups Living in Rural Poverty: An Annotated Bibliography.* Lexington, Kentucky.

Irelan, L. M.
1965 "Health Practices of the Poor," *Welfare in Review,* III (October 10), 1-9.
1966 *Low-Income Life Styles.* Publication No. 14. U. S. Department of Health, Education, and Welfare. Welfare Administration. Washington, D. C.: U. S. Government Printing Office.

Irelan, L. M., and A. Besner.
1965 "Low-Income Outlook on Life," *Welfare in Review,* III (September 9), 13-19.

Irelan, L. M., *et al.*
1969 "Ethnicity, Poverty, and Selected Attitudes: A Test of the 'Culture of Poverty' Hypothesis," *Social Forces,* XLVII (June), 405-13.

Jackson, L. P.
1966 *Poverty's Children.* U. S. Department of Health, Education, and Welfare. Washington, D. C.: U. S. Government Printing Office.

Jaffe, F. S.
1964 "Family Planning and Poverty," *Journal of Marriage and the Family,* XXVI (November 4), 467-70.

Jaffee, F., and S. Polgar.
1968 "Family Planning and Public Policy: Is the 'Culture of Poverty' the New Cop-Out?" *Journal of Marriage and the Family,* XXX, 228-35.

James, G.
1961 "The Epidemiology of Mental Disorder Associated with Damage to the Brain After Birth," *Causes of Mental Disorder: A Review of Epidemiological Knowledge.* Proceedings of a Round-Table held at Arden House, Harriman, N. Y. (October 27-28, 1959), New York: Milbank Fund.

Janssen, M. R.
1963 *Summaries of Selected Studies on Training of Workers and Migration from Low-Income Rural Areas.* U. S. Department of Agriculture in cooperation with Purdue University Agricultural Experiment Station (February).

Jensen, A. R.
1968 "Social Class, Race and Genetics: Implications for Education," *American Educational Research Journal,* V, 1-42.
1969 "How Much Can We Boost IQ and Scholastic Achievement?", *The Harvard Educational Review,* XXXIX (Winter), 1-123.
1970 "Learning Ability, Intelligence and Educability," *Psychological Factors in Poverty.* Ed. V. L. Allen. *et al.* Chicago: Markham.

Jerome, N. W.
1967 "Food Habits and Acculturation: Dietary Practices and Nutrition of Families Headed by Southern-Born Negroes Residing in a Northern Metropolis," Dissertation, University of Wisconsin.

Johnson, C. L.
1971 *Adolescent Pregnancy-Intervention into the Poverty Cycle.* Athens, Georgia: Regional Institute of Social Welfare Research. School of Social Work. University of Georgia.

Johnson, C. S.
1967 *Growing Up in the Black Belt: Negro Youth in the Rural South.* Washington, D. C.: American Council on Education.

Joiner, C. L.
1968 "An Analysis of the Employment Patterns of Minority Groups in the Alabama Economy, 1940-1960," Dissertation. University of Alabama.

Jones, W. C., *et al.*
1962 "Social and Psychological Factors in Status Decision of Unmarried Mothers," *Marriage and Family Living,* XXIV (August), 224-30.

Jordan, J. E.
1968 *Attitudes Toward Education and Physically Disabled Persons in Eleven Nations.* East Lansing, Michigan: Latin American Studies Center. Michigan State University.

Jordan, M. F., J. F. Golden, and L. D. Bender.
1967 "Aspirations and Capabilities of Rural Youth," Agricultural Experiment Station Bulletin 772. University of Arkansas and U. S. Department of Agriculture (May).

Kahn, T., ed.
1966 "The Economics of Inequality," *Poverty in America.* Ed. L. A. Ferman, *et al.* Ann Arbor, Michigan: University of Michigan Press.

Kain, J. F., and J. J. Persky.
1968 "The North's State in Southern Rural Poverty," *Rural Poverty in the United States.* Report of the President's National Advisory Commission on Rural

Poverty. Washington, D. C.: U. S. Government Printing Office.

Kain, J. F., and J. R. Meyer.
1970 "Transportation and Poverty," *The Public Interest*, XVIII (Winter), 175-78.

Kampe, R. E., and W. A. Lindamood.
1969 *Underemployment Estimates by County, United States, 1960*. Agricultural Economic Report 166. U. S. Department of Agriculture. Economic Research Service. Washington, D. .C: U. S. Government Printing Office.

Kantor, M, *et al.*
1958 "Socioeconomic Level and Maternal Attitudes Toward Parent-Child Relations," *Human Organization*, XVI (Winter), 44-48.

Kaplan, B.
1954 "Environment and Human Plasticity," *American Anthropologist*, LVI, 780-800.

Kaplan, B. H.
1965 "Lower Class Religious Groups," *Journal of Social Issues*, XXI (1), 126-41.

Kappelman, M. M., E. Kaplan, and R. L. Ganter.
1969 "A Study of Learning Disorders Among Disadadvantaged Children," *Journal of Learning Disabilities*, II (5), 262-68.

Karlsson, J. L.
1966 *The Biologic Basis of Schizophrenia*. Springfield, Illinois: C. C. Thomas.

Kaufman, H. F., K. P. Wilkinson, and L. W. Cole.
1966 *Poverty Programs and Social Mobility*. Preliminary Report No. 13. State College, Mississippi: Social Science Research Center. Mississippi State University.

Keith-Lucas, A.
1957 *Decisions About People in Need*. Chapel Hill, North Carolina: University of North Carolina Press.

Keller, S.
1968 *The American Lower Class Family: A Survey of Selected Facts and Their Implications*. Research Document, 4th Printing. New York State Division for Youth.

Kelly, T. F.
1970 "Factors Affecting Poverty: A Gross Flow Analysis," *Technical Studies*. The President's Commission on Income Maintenance Programs, Washington, D. C.: U. S. Government Printing Office.

Keniston, K.
1968 *The Young Radicals*. New York: Harcourt, Brace, & World.

Kennedy, W. A.
1965 *A Follow-Up Normative Study of Negro Intelligence and Achievement*. Tallahassee, Florida: Florida State University Human Development Clinic.

Kentucky Department of Education. Bureau of Rehabilitation Services.
1969 *Regional Demonstration of Comprehensive Rehabilitation Services in a Rural Mountainous, Economically Depressed Area*. Frankfort, Kentucky.

Keyserling, L. H.
1964 *Progress of Poverty; The United States at the Crossroads*. Proceedings of a Conference on Economic Progress. Washington, D. C.

Kidneigh, J. C.
1967 "The People We Serve," Paper presented at the School of Social Welfare, Florida State University, Tallahassee, Florida (April 19), Mimeographed.

Killingsworth, C. C.
1966 "Automation, Jobs, and Manpower," *Poverty in America*. Ed. L. A. Ferman, *et al.* Ann Arbor, Michigan: University of Michigan Press.

Klingman, D.
1970 "On Affluence and Economic Conflict," *American Journal of Economics and Sociology*, XXIX (January), 55-58.

Knobloch, H., and B. Pasamanick.
1953 "Further Observations on the Behavioral Development of Negro Children," *Journal of Genetic Psychology*, LXXXIII, 137-57.

Knobloch, H., and B. Pasamanick, eds.
1959 "Distribution of Intellect Potential in an Infant Population," *Epidemiology of Mental Disorders*. Washington, D. C.: American Association for the Advancement of Sciences.

Kohn, M. L.
1959 "Social Class and Parental Values," *American Journal of Sociology*, LXIV, 337-51.
1964 "Social Class and Parent-Child Relationships: an Interpretation," *Mental Health of the Poor*. Ed. F. Reissman, *et al.* New York: Free Press.

Kohn, M. L., and E. E. Carroll.
1960 "Social Class and the Allocation of Parental Responsibilities," *Sociometry*, XXIII (December 4), 389.

Komarovsky, M.
1964 *Blue Collar Marriage*. New York: Random House.

Komisar, D., H. L. Leonhardt, and A. S. Weitz.
1960 *A Follow-Up Study of Patients Discharged from a Community Rehabilitation Center*. Final Report. Hartford, Connecticut: Hartford Rehabilitation Center.

Kosa, J., A. Antonovsky, and I. K. Zola, eds.
1969 *Poverty and Health: A Sociological Analysis*. Cambridge, Massachusetts: Harvard University Press.

Krakowski, M., *et al.*
1968 *Availability and Use of Health Services—Rural Urban Comparison*. Agricultural Economic Report 139. U. S. Department of Agriculture. Economic Research Service. Washington, D. C.: U. S. Government Printing Office.

Kriesberg, L.
1963 "The Relationship Between Socio-economic Rank and Behavior," *Social Problems*, X (Spring), 334-53.
1967 "Rearing Children for Educational Achievement in Fatherless Families," *Journal of Marriage and the Family*, XXIX, 288-301.
1968 "Intergenerational Patterns of Poverty," Paper presented at the Annual Meeting of the Eastern Sociological Society, Boston (April 6).
1970 *Mothers in Poverty*. Chicago: Aldine.

Kringler, E.
1964 "Discordance with Respect to Schizophrenia in Monozygotic Twins," *Journal of Nervous and Mental Disease*, CXXXVIII, 26-31.
1966 "Schizaphrenia in Twins: An Epidemiological-Clinical Study," *Psychiatry*, XXIX, 172-84.

Kunce, J. T., R. J. Mahoney, R. R. Campbell, and J. Finley.
1969 *Rehabilitation in the Concrete Jungle*. Research Series No. 3 Columbia, Missouri: Regional Rehabilitation Research Institute. University of Missouri at Columbia.

Kunstadter, P.
1963 "A Survey of the Consanguine or Matrifocal Family," *American Anthropologist*, LXV (1), 56-66.

Kurtz, N. R.
1968 "Gatekeepers: Agents in Acculturation," *Rural Sociology*, XXXIII (March 1), 64-79.

Kutner, B.
1970 "The Social Psychology of Disability," Paper presented at the National Conference on Psychological Aspects of Poverty, Monterey, California (October 26-28).

Lamale, H. H.
1960 "Methodology and Appraisal of Consumer Expenditure Studies," *Consumption and Savings II*, University of Pennsylvania, Philadelphia, Pennsylvania.

1965 "Poverty: The Word and the Reality," *Monthly Labor Review*, LXXXVIII, 822-27.

Lampman, R. J.
1966a "How Much Does the American System of Transfers Benefit the Poor?" *Economic Progress and Social Welfare*. Ed. L. H. Goodman, New York: Columbia University Press.
1966b "Population, 1947-1975, Change and Poverty Education," *Poverty Amid Affluence*. Ed. L. Fishman. New Haven, Connecticut: Yale University Press.
1969 "Expanding the American System of Transfers to Do More for the Poor," *Wisconsin Law Review*, II. 549.

Landes, W. M.
1966 "The Effect of State Fair Employment Legislation on the Economic Position of Non-White Males," Dissertation, Columbia University. April), 10-21.

Langner, T. S., *et al.*
1969 "Psychiatric Impairment in Welfare and Non-Welfare Children," *Welfare in Review*, VII (March-April), 10-21.

Larson, O. F.
1965 "Income and Welfare of Rural People—Agricultural Research Significant to Public Policy, Public Welfare, and Community Improvement," *Rural Sociology*, XXX (December 4), 452-61.

Lassiter, R. L., Jr.
1965 "The Association of Income and Education for Males by Region, Race, and Age," *Southern Eocnomics Journal*, XXXII (July), 15-22.

Lawson, S.
1970 "A 'New Town' Planned for the Urban and Rural Poor," *City*, IV (June-July), 35-38.

Leary, T. J.
1969 "Exports of the South: Observations on the Movement of Manufactured Products: 1960-1966," *Atlanta Economic Review*, XIX (July), 26-28.

Lee, E. S.
1951 "Negro Intelligence and Selective Migration: A Philadelphia Test of Klireberg's Hypothesis," *American Sociological Review*, LXI, 227-33.

Lee, E. S., and J. Mervine.
1968 "Our Disappearing Rural Population: What are the Consequences?" *Vital Issues*, XVII (April 8).

Lefcowitz, M.
1965 "Poverty and Negro-White Family Structures," *Background Papers*. White House Conference: To Fulfill These Rights. Washington, D. C.

Leighton, A. H.
1959 *My Name is Legion*. New York: Basic Books.
1965 "Poverty and Social Change," *Scientific American*. CCXII (May 5), 21-27.

Leighton, D., *et al.*
1963 *The Character of Danger*. New York: Basic Books.

Leckachman, R.
1967 "Can 'More Money' End Poverty?" *Dissent*, XIV (September-October), 556-64.

Lenski, G.
1966 *Power and Privilege: A Theory of Social Stratification*. New York: McGraw-Hill.

Leo, P. A., and G. Rosen.
1969 "A Bookshelf on Poverty and Health," *American Journal of Public Health*, LIX (April), 591-607.

Lerner, M.
1969 "Social Differences in Physical Health," *Poverty and Health: A Sociological Analysis*. Ed. J. Kosa, *et al.* Cambridge, Massachusetts: Harvard University Press.

Le Shan, L. L.
1952 "Time Orientation and Social Class," *Journal of Abnormal and Social Psychology*, XLVII, 589-92.

Lesser, G. S., G. Fifer, and D. H. Clark.
1965 "Mental Abilities of Children from Different Social-Class and Cultural Groups," *Monographs of the Society for Research in Child Development*, XXX (4), 1-115.

Levinson, P.
1964 "Chronic Dependency: A Conceptual Analysis," *The Social Service Review*, XXXVIII (December 4), 371-81.
1961 "The Next Generation: A Study of Children in AFDC Families," *Welfare in Review*, VII (March-April), 1-9.
1970 "How Employable are AFDC Women? "*Welfare in Review*, VIII (July- August), 12-16.

Levitan, S. A.
1965 "Area Redevelopment: A Tool to Combat Poverty," *Poverty in America*. Ed. M. S. Gordon. San Francisco: Chandler.
1969 *The Great Society Poor Law*. Baltimore: Johns Hopkins Press.

Lewis, H.
1958 *Blackways of Kent*. Chapel Hill, North Carolina: University of North Carolina Press.
1960 "The Changing Negro Family," *Nation's Children*, Vol. I: Family and Social Change. Ed. E. Ginzberg. New York: Columbia University Press.
1961 "Child Rearing Practices Among Low-Income Families in the District of Columbia," Paper presented at the National Conference on Social Welfare, Minneapolis, Minnesota (May).
1963 "Culture, Class, and the Behavior of Low-Income Families," Paper presented at the Conference on Lower Class Culture. New York (June 27-29).
1966 "Child Rearing Among Low-Income Families," *Poverty in America*. Ed. L. A. Ferman, *et al.* Ann Arbor, Michigan: University of Michigan Press.
1967 "Culture, Class, and Family Life Among Low-Income Urban Negroes," *Employment, Race and Poverty*. Ed. A. M. Ross and H. Hill. New York: Harcourt, Brace & World.

Lewis, O.
1961 *The Children of Sanchez*. New York: Random House.
1963 "The Culture of Poverty," *Trans-Action*, I (November 1), 17-19.
1969 "The Culture of Poverty," *On Understanding Poverty*. Ed. D. Moynihan. New York: Basic Books.

Leyburn, G.
1937 "Urban Adjustments from the Southern Appalachian Plateaus," *Social Forces*, XVI, 238-46.

Lieberson, S. and G. V. Fuquitt.
1967 "Negro-White Occupational Differences in the Absence of Discrimination," *American Journal of Sociology*, LXXIII, 188-200.

Lindberg, R. E.
1958 "Hard to Reach: Client or Casework Agency?" *Social Work*, III, 23-29.

Lindsley, D., and A. Riesen.
1968 "Biological Substrates of Development and Behavior," *Perspectives on Human Deprivation: Biological, Psychological, and Sociological*. U. S. Department of Health, Education, and Welfare. Washington, D. C.: U. S. Government Printing Office.

Lofquist, L. H., and R. V. Davis.
1970 *Assessing the Work Personality of Mentally Retarded Adults*. Final Report. Minneapolis, Minnesota: Department of Psychology. University of Minnesota.

Lonsdale, R. E.
1969 "Deterrents to Industrial Location in the Rural South," *Research Previews*, XVI (April 1), 1-7.

Lorenz, K.
1952 *King Solomon's Ring*. London: Methuen.

Lurie, I.
1969 "An Economic Evaluation of Aid to Families with Dependent Children," Dissertation, University of California at Berkeley.

Lustig, M., and Reiner, J. S.
1968 "Local Government and Poverty in Rural Areas," *Rural Poverty in the United States.* The President's Advisory Commission on Rural Poverty. Washington, D. C.: U. S. Government Printing Office.

Lyday, J.
1970 "New Jersey Experiment," *Background Papers.* The President's Commission on Income Maintenance Programs. Washington, D. C.: U. S. Government Printing Office.

McCall, J. J.
1969 "Analysis of Poverty: Some Preliminary Findings," Memo RM-6133. OEO. Rand Corporation (December).

McCall, R. B.
1970 "Intelligence Quotient Pattern over Age: Comparisons among Siblings and Parent-Child Pairs," *Science,* CLXX (November 6), 644-48.

McCann, G.
1966 "Appalachians: Less Poverty-Stricken Than You Think," *Research and Farming,* XXIV (Winter), 4-5.

McClelland, D. C., and D. G. Winter.
1969 *Motivating Economic Achievement.* New York: Free Press.

McCoy, J. L.
1970a *Rural Poverty in Three Southern Regions: Mississippi Delta, Ozarks, Southeast Coastal Plain.* Agricultural Economic Report 176. U. S. Department of Agriculture. Economic Research Service. Washington, D. C.: U. S. Government Printing Office.
1970b "Rural Dimensions of Poverty," Paper presented at the Annual Meeting of the Rural Sociological Society, Washington, D. C. (August 26-30).

McDaniel, A. C.
1965 "Attack on Poverty," *Rehabilitation Record* (January-February), 10-12.

MacDonald, D.
1963 *Our Invisible Poor.* New York: Sidney Hillman Foundation.

McElveen, J. V.
1969 *Characteristics of Human Resources in the Rural Southeast Coastal Plain . . . with Emphasis on the Poor.* Agricultural Economic Report 155. U. S. Department of Agriculture. Economic Research Service. Washington, D. C.: U. S. Government Printing Office.

McFarland, D. D.
1970 "Intragenerational Social Mobility as a Mark or Process: Including a Time-Stationary Markovian Model That Explains Observed Declines in Mobility Rates Over Time," *American Sociological Review,* XXV, (June 3), 463-76.

McGee, L. R.
1967 *Income and Employment in the Southeast: A Study in Cyclical Behavior.* Lexington Kentucky: University of Kentucky Press.

McGill, R. E.
1967 "The South and the Southerner," *Seminar on Manpower Policy and Program.* U. S. Department of Health, Education and Welfare. Office of Manpower Policy, Evaluation, and Research. Washington, D. C.: U. S. Government Printing Office.

Mack, D. E.
1971 "Where the Black-Matriarchy Theorists Went Wrong," *Psychology Today,* IV (January 8), 24-35.

MacMahon, B., and J. M. Sowa.
1961 "Physical Damage to the Fetus," *Causes of Mental Disorders: A Review of Epidemilogical Knowledge.* Proceedings of a Round-Table Held at Arden House, Harriman, New York: Milbank Fund.

McPhee, W. M.
1969 "Rehabilitation in a Rural Poverty Setting," *Research Utilization Conference on Rehabilitation in Poverty Settings.* Ed. R. J. Margolin and G. J. Goldin. Boston, Massachusetts: New England Rehabilitation Research Institute. Northeastern University.

McPherson, W. W.
1964a "Overview of Southern Economic Growth," *Optimizing Institutions for Economic Growth.* Raleigh, North Carolina: Agricultural Policy Institute of North Carolina State University.
1964b "Programs to Alleviate Rural Poverty," *Rural America Looks to the Future.* Raleigh, North Carolina: Agricultural Policy Institute of North Carolina: State University.
1968 "An Economic Critique of the National Advisory Commission Report on Rural Poverty," *American Journal of Agricultural Economy,* L (December 5), 1362-72.

Maddox, J. G., *et al.*
1967 *The Advancing South: Manpower Prospects and Problems.* New York: The Twentieth Century Fund.

Mahoney, R. J., C. Cope, and R. Campbell, eds.
1969 *Rehabilitation and the Culturally Disadvantaged: A Digest.* Research Series No. 2. Columbia, Missouri: Regional Rehabilitation Research Institute. University of Missouri at Columbia.

Maitland, S. T., and S. M. Knebel.
1968 "Rural to Urban Transition," *Monthly Labor Review,* XCI (June), 28-32.

Manning, S. W.
1960 "Cultural and Value Factors Affecting the Negro's Use of Agency Services," *Social Work,* V (October 4), 3-14.

Marans, A. E., and R. Lourie.
1967 "Hypotheses Regarding the Effects of the Child-Rearing Patterns on the Disadvantaged Child," *Disadvantaged Child,* Vol. I. Ed. J. Hellmuth. Seatttle: Special Child Publications of the Seattle Sequin School, Inc.

March, M. S.
1967 "Public Programs for the Poor: Coverage, Gaps, and Future Directions," Paper presented to the Conference of the National Tax Association. Atlanta, Georgia (October).

Marckwardt, A. M.
1968 "Differentials of Recent Internal Migration in the U. S.," Dissertation, University of Michigan.

Margolis, R. J.
1969 "The Rural Poor—Broken Promises, Broken Lives," *Think* (September-October), 27-32.
1970 "Sheriffs North and South," *The New Leader,* LIII (November 30), 9-10.

Marris, P., and M. Rein.
1969 *Dilemmas of Social Reform.* New York: Atherton Press.

Marsh, C. P., and M. M. Brown.
1965 "Facilitative and Inhibitive Factors in Training Program Recruits Among Rural Negroes," *Journal of Social Issues,* XXI (1), 110-25.

Marshall, D. G.
1968 "Family Adjustment in Selected Low-Income Areas of Northern Wisconsin," Population Series 13, Special Report. Madison, Wisconsin: Institute for Research on Poverty.

Martin, L. R.
1966 "Effects of Alternative Federal Policies on Welfare of Rural People," *Journal of Farm Economics,* XLVIII (December 5), 1267-78.

Maxwell, N.
1970 "Paternalism Dies in the Delta," *South Today,* I (March 8), 8.

Meenach, L.
1969 "Vocational Rehabilitation Needs and Resources in a Depressed Area of Appalachia Located in Eastern Kentucky," *Research Utilization Conference on Re-*

habilitation in Poverty Settings. Ed. R. J. Margolin and G. J. Goldin. Boston, Massachusetts: New England Rehabilitation Research Institute. Northeastern University.

Menkin, J. A., and M. C. Sheps.
1970 "On Relationships between Longitudinal Characteristics and Cross-sectional Data," *American Journal of Public Health,* LX (October), 1506-14.

Metzler, W. H.
1959 "Socioeconomic Aspects of Manpower Adjustments: Low-Income Rural Areas," *Rural Sociology,* XXIV (September 3), 226-35.

Meyers, S. M., and J. McIntyre.
1969 *Welfare Policy and Its Consequences for the Recipient Population: A Study of AFDC Programs.* U. S. Department of Health, Education, and Welfare. Social and Rehabilitation Service. Washington, D. C.: U. S. Government Printing Office.

Michelson, S. E.
1968 "Income of Racial Minorities," Dissertation, Stanford University.

Michiellatte, R. L.
1966 "Structural Correlates of Economic Inequality: A Study of White—Non-White Economic Differentials," Dissertation, Florida State University.

Middleton, R., and C. M. Grigg.
1959 "Rural-Urban Differences in Aspiration," *Rural Sociology,* XXIV (December 4), 347-54.

Miller, H.
1965 "Characteristics of AFDC Families," *Social Service Review.* XXXIX (December 4), 399-409.

Miller, H. M.
n.d. "The Definition of Poverty: Social and Economic Considerations," Department of Anthropology, University of Georgia, Athens, Georgia.

Miller, H. P.
1966 "Poverty and the Negro," *Poverty in America.* Ed. L. A. Ferman, *et al.* Ann Arbor, Michigan: University of Michigan Press.

Miller, H. P., ed.
1966 *Poverty: American Style.* Belmont, Massachusetts: Wadsworth.

Miller, J.
1964 *The Problems of Dependency.* Selective Reading Series No. 2. Sacramento, California: California State Department of Social Welfare.

Miller, S. M.
1964 "The American Lower Class: A Typological Approach," *Social Research,* XXXI (Spring), 1-22.
1966 "Poverty and Self-Indulgence: A Critique of the Now-Deferred Gratification Pattern," *Poverty in America.* Ed. L. A. Ferman, *et al.* Ann Arbor, Michigan: University of Michigan Press.
1970 "Poverty Research in the Seventies," *Journal of Social Issues,* XXVI (2), 169-73.

Miller, S. M., M. Rein, P. Roly, and B. M. Gross.
1967 "Poverty, Inequality, and Conflict," *The Annuals of the American Academy of Political and Social Science,* CCLXXIII (July), 16-52.

Miller, S. M., and F. Reissman.
1961 "The Working Class Subculture: A New View," *Social Problems,* IX (Summer), 86-97.

Miller, S. M., and P. Roly.
1970 *The Future of Inequality.* New York: Basic Books.

Miller, W. B.
1958 "Lower-Class Culture as Generating Milieu of Gang Delinquency," *Journal of Social Issues,* XIV (3), 5-19.
1959 "Implications of Urban Lower-Class Culture for Social Work," *Social Service Review,* XXXIII (September 3), 219-36.
1966 "Focal Concerns of Lower-Class Culture," *Poverty in America.* Ed. L. A. Ferman, *et al.* Ann Arbor, Michigan: University of Michigan Press.

Mingione, A.
1965 "Need for Achievement in Negro and White Children," *Journal of Consulting Psychology,* XXIX, 108-11.

Minturn, L., and W. W. Lambert.
1964 *Mothers of Six Cultures.* New York: John Wiley & Sons.

Mishan, E. J.
1967 *The Costs of Economic Growth.* New York: Praeger.

Moles, O. C.
1970 "Up from Poverty: Intergenerational Movement Out of Low-Income Occupation," *Welfare in Review,* VIII (May-June), 8-16.

Monahan, T. P.
1960 "Premarital Pregnancy in the U. S.: A Critical Review and Some New Findings," *Eugenics Quarterly,* VII, 133-47.

Moody, P. A.
1967 *Genetics of Man.* New York: Norton.

Moons, S. G.
1963 "A Study of Factors in the Adjustment of Rural Families in Low Income Areas," Dissertation, North Carolina State University.

Moore, E. J., *et al.*
1964 *Economic Factors Influencing Educational Attainments and Aspirations of Farm Youth.* Agricultural Economic Report 51. U. S. Department of Agriculture. Economic Research Service. Washington, D. C.: Government Printing Office.

Morgan, C. A., and V. A. Boyd.
1966 *Annotated Bibliography of Publications and Reports Resulting from Southern Regional Cooperative Research Project S-44: Factors in the Adjustment of Families and Individuals in Low-Income Rural Areas of the South.* Clemson, South Carolina: Clemson University.

Morgan, J. N., and J. D. Smith.
1968 *A Panel Study of Income Dynamics; 1968 Interviewing Year (Wave 1).* Ann Arbor, Michigan: Surveys Research Center. Institute for Social Research. University of Michigan.
1969 *A Panel Study of Income Dynamics: 1969 Interviewing Year (Wave 2).* Ann Arbor, Michigan: Survey Research Center. Institute for Social Research. University of Michigan.

Morgan, J. N., *et al.*
1962 *Income and Welfare in the United States.* New York: McGraw-Hill.

Morrison, P. A.
1967 "Duration of Residence and Prospective Migration: The Evaluation of a Stochastic Model," Dissertation. Brown University.

Moynihan, D. P.
1965 *The Negro Family: The Case for National Action.* U. S. Department of Labor. Office of Policy Planning and Research. Washington, D. C.: U. S. Government Printing Office.
1969a Ed. *On Understanding Poverty:* Perspectives from the Social Sciences. New York: Basic Books.
1969b *Maximum Feasible Misunderstanding.* New York: Free Press.

Munk, M.
1967 *Rural Youth Work Programs: Problems of Size and Scope.* Manpower Training Series. New York: Center for the Study of Unemployed Youth. Graduate School of Social Work. New York University.

Murth, R. F.
1966 "The Structural Change Hypothesis for Employment Among Youth, Aged, and Minorities: A Critical Analysis" (Unpublished Research Paper), p. 275. Institute for Defense Analysis.

Myrdal, G.
1962 *Challenge to Affluence.* New York: Pantheon.

Nam, C. B., and M. G. Powers.
1965 "Variations in Socio-Economic Structure by Race, Residence, and the Life Cycle," *American Sociological Review*, XXX (February 1), 97-103.

National Advisory Committee on Farm Labor.
1965 *Poverty on the Land*. New York.

"Negro American, The."
1965 *Daedalus*, XLIV (Fall).

Nelson, H. M., and S. E. Storey.
1969 "Personality Adjustment of Rural and Urban Youth: The Formation of a Rural Disadvantaged Subculture," *Rural Sociology*, XXXIV (March 1), 43-55.

Newman, D. K.
1965 "The Negro's Journey to the City," Part I, *Monthly Labor Review*, LXXXVIII, 644-49.

Newsweek.
1970 "The Cities: Poverty: A Losing War," (November 23). New York City: New York City Youth Board, Research Department.
1957 "A Study of Some of the Characteristics of 150 Multiproblem Families," (Mimeographed).

New York *Times Sunday Magazine*
1970 "When You Just Give Money to the Poor," by F. J. Cook (May 3).

New York *Times*
1971a "Mississippi Gets Legal Aid Grant: O.E.O. Backs Disputed Plan for Services to Poor," by J. Rosenthal (January 17).
1971b "Negro Aid by U. S. Get Poor Marks: Two Professors are Critical of Federal Efforts in Past," (January 17).
1971c "Negro Migration to North Found Steady Since '40's," by J. Rosenthal (March 4).

Nix, H. L.
1962 "Opportunities for and Limitations of Social and Economic Adjustments in an Alabama Rural County, Alabama Agriculture Experiment Station Bulletin 338 (January).

Nixon, J. W., and H. Thompson.
1970 "Rural Industrialization: Prospects for Resolving Rural Income Problems in the Coastal Plains," *Atlanta Economic Review*, XX (November), 8-12.

Olson, M.
1964 "Agriculture and Depressed Areas," *Journal of Farm Economics*, XLVI (December 5), 984-88.

O'Reilly, C. T.
1968 *Locked in Poverty: The Rural Poor Family in Dave County*. Monograph. Madison, Wisconsin: University of Wisconsin. School of Social Work.

O'Reilly, C. T., W. E. Downing, and S. T. Pflanczer.
1965 *The People of the Inner Core-North* Milwaukee, Wisconsin: University of Wisconsin.

Ornati, O.
1965 "The Convergence of Poverty-Linked Characteristics," *Poverty in Affluence*. Ed. R. E. Will and H. G. Vatter. New York: Harcourt, Brace & World.
1966 *Poverty Amid Affluence*. New York: Twentieth Century Fund.

Orshansky, M.
1965a "Counting the Poor: Another Look at the Poverty Profile," *Social Security Bulletin*, XXVIII (January 1), 3-29.
1965b "Measuring Poverty," *Social Welfare Forum*. New York: Columbia University Press.
1966a "More About the Poor in 1964," *Social Security Bulletin*, XXIX (May 5), 3-38.
1966b "Counting the Poor," *Poverty in America*. Ed. L. A. Ferman, *et al*. Ann Arbor, Michigan: University of Michigan Press.
1968 "The Shape of Poverty in 1966," *Social Security Bulletin*, XXXI (March 3), 3-32.
1969 "How Poverty is Measured," *Monthly Labor Review*, XCII (February), 37-41.

Osburn, D. D.
1968 "Returns to Investment in Human Migration," Dissertation. University of North Carolina at Raleigh.

Osofsky, H. J.
1969 "Antenatal Malnutrition: Its Relationship to Subsequent Infant and Child Development," *American Journal of Obstetrics and Gynecology*, CV (December 1), 1150-59.

Park, T. H.
1968 "Non-Local Job Information in a Low-Income Rural Area: The Tennessee Upper Cumberland," Dissertation. Vanderbilt University.

Pasamanick, B.
1946 "A Comparative Study of the Educational Development of Negro Infants," *Journal of Genetic Psychology*, LXIX, 3-44.

Palvick, A. L.
1964 "West Virginia: Economic Opportunities and Limitations in Rural Development," U. S. Department of Agriculture. Economic Research Service. Washington, D. C.: U. S. Government Printing Office.

Pearce, J. F.
1966 "Human Resources in Transition: Rural Alabama Since World War II," Dissertation, University of Alabama.

Pearl, A.
1970 "The Poverty of Psychology—An Indictment," *Psychological Factors in Poverty*. Ed. V. L. Allen. Chicago: Markham.

Pearman, J. R.
1970 "Survey of Unmet Medical Needs of Children in Six Counties of Florida," *Public Health Report*, LXXXV (March 3), 189-95.

Pender, D. R.
1969 *Strategic Hamlets in America: An Approach to the Problems of the Urban and Rural Poor*. Columbia, South Carolina: University of South Carolina Press.

Penrose, L. S.
1948 "The Supposed Threat of Declining Intelligence," *American Journal of Mental Deficiency*, LIII, 114-18.
1950 "Propagation of the Unfit," *The Lancet*, CCLIX (September 30), 425-27.

Persky, J. J., and J. F. Kain.
1970 "Migration, Employment, and Race in the Deep South," *Southern Economic Journal*, XXXVI (January 3), 268-76.

Peters, D. L.
1970 "Critical Issues in Research Related to Disadvantaged Children," *Science*, CLXX (October 2), 102-22.

Peterson, R. A.
1967 "Rehabilitation of the Culturally Different, A Model of the Individual in Cultural Change," *Personnel and Guidance Journal* (June), 1001-7.

Petras, J. W., and J. E. Curtis.
1968 "The Current Literature on Social Class and Mental Disease in America: Critique and Bibliography," *Behavioral Science*, XIII (September 5), 382-98.

Pettigrew, T. F.
1964 *A Profile of the Negro American*. Princeton, New Jersey: D. Van Nostrand.

Planned Parenthood-World Population. Center for Family Planning Program Development.
1968 *Need for Subsidized Family Planning Services: U. S., Each State and County, 1968*. Report for the Office of Economic Opportunity. Washington, D. C.

Polansky, N. A.
1970 *The Apathy-Futility Syndrome in Child Neglect*. (March 1), Mimeographed.

Polansky, N. A., *et al.*
1969 "Verbal Accessibility of Appalachian Mother: A Casework Challenge," *Social Work Practice, 1969*. New York: Columbia University Press for the

National Conference on Social Welfare, Columbus, Ohio.

Pomeroy, R., in a collection with R. Lejeune and L. Podell.
1969 *Studies in the Use of Health Services by Families on Welfare: Utilization by Publicly-Assisted Families.* New York: The Center for the Study of Urban Problems. Graduate Division, Bernard M. Baruch College. The City University of New York.

Pratt, L.
1971 "The Relationship of Socioeconomic Status to Health," *American Journal of Public Health,* LXI (February), 281-91.

Prentice, N. M.
1961 "Ethnic Attitudes Toward Neuroticism and Culture," *The Journal of Social Psychology,* LIV (June), 75-82.

President's Commission on Income Maintenance Programs, The.
1970 *Background Papers.* Washington, D. C.: U. S. Government Printing Office.

President's Committee on Mental Retardation, The.
1969 *MR 69: Toward Progress: The Story of the Decade.* Third Report. Washington, D. C.: U. S. Government Printing Office.

President's National Advisory Commission on Rural Poverty, The.
1967a *The People Left Behind.* Report. Washington, D. C.: U. S. Government Printing Office.
1967b *Rural Poverty Hearings,* Vols. 2, 3. Washington, D. C.: U. S. Government Printing Office.
1968 *Rural Poverty in the United States.* Report. Washington, D. C.: U. S. Government Printing Office.

Pruitt, W. A., and R. L. Castle.
1962 "Dependency Measures and Welfare Chronicity," *Journal of Consulting Psychology,* XXVI, 559-60.

Query, W. T.
1969 *Illness, Work, and Poverty.* San Francisco: Jossey-Bass.

Radin, N., and P. H. Glasser.
1965 "The Use of Parental Attitude Questionnaires with Culturally Deprived Families," *Journal of Marriage and the Family,* XXVII (August 3), 373-82.

Radomski, A. L., and A. U. Mills.
1964 "Family Income in Low-Income States and Counties," *Welfare In Review,* II (October), 16-24.

Rainwater, L.
1960 *And the Poor Get Children.* Chicago: Quadrangle Books.
1964 "Marital Sexuality in Four Cultures of Poverty," *Journal of Marriage and the Family,* XXVI (November), 457-66.
1969 "The Problem of Lower Class Culture and the Poverty-War Strategy," *On Understanding Poverty.* Ed. D. Moynihan. New York: Basic Books.
1970 "The Problem of Lower Class Culture," *Journal of Social Issues,* XXVI (2), 133-48.

Rainwater, L., and W. L. Yancey.
1967 *The Moynihan Report and the Politics of Controversy.* Cambridge, Massachusetts: Massachusetts Institute of Technology Press.

Ramsey, C. E., R. A. Polson, and G. E. Spencer.
1959 "Values and the Adoption of Practices," *Rural Sociology,* XXIV, 35-47.

Rasmussen, D. W.
1969 "The Determinants of Non-White/White Income Ratio," Dissertation. Washington University of St. Louis.

Read, P. B.
1970 "Migration and Mobility: The Myth of a Northern Haven for Blacks," *The Cornell Journal of Social Relations* (Spring), 57-78.

Reed, S. C.
1966 "The Normal Process of Genetic Change in a Stable Physical Environment," *Genetics and the Future of Man.* Ed. J. D. Roslansky. New York: Appleton-Century-Crofts.

Regional Economics Division Staff.
1970 "Personal Income in Metropolitan and Non-Metropolitan Areas," *Survey of Current Business,* L (May), 22-36.

Reid, H.
1967 "Rehabilitating the Culturally Disadvantaged in a Rural Setting—A Psychiatric Approach," *Rehabilitating the Culturally Disadvantaged.* Ed. G. E. Ayers. Proceedings of a Regional Conference on Rehabilitating the Culturally Disadvantaged, Mankato State College, Mankato, Minnesota (August 16-17).

Reid, O., P. Arnaudo, and A. White.
1968 "The American Health-Care System and the Poor: A Social Organizational Point of View," *Welfare in Review,* VI (November-December), 1-12.

Rein, M.
1965 "The Strange Case of Public Dependency," *Trans-Action,* II (March-April), 16-23.
1966 "Problems in the Definition and Measurement of Poverty," *Poverty in America.* Ed. L. A. Ferman, *et al.* Ann Arbor, Michigan: University of Michigan Press.
1967 "Social Science and the Elimination of Poverty," *American Institute of Planners Journal,* XXXIII (May), 146-63.

Reissman, L.
1954 "Class, Leisure, and Social Participation," *American Sociological Reviews,* XIX (February 1), 76-84.

Report of the National Advisory Commission on Civil Disorders.
1968 New York: E. P. Dutton.

Reul, M. R.
1969a "Culture of the Rural Disadvantaged," Paper presented at the Division of Federal Assistance Conference, Columbus, Ohio (April 26).
1969b "The Migrant Child," Paper presented at the Ohio Conference on Migrant Education, Bowling Green, Ohio (July 31).
1970 "Needs of the Migrant Farm Worker," Paper presented at the Annual National Farm Labor Rural Manpower Conference, Las Vegas, Neveda (January).

Reuss, L. A., and K. M. Gilbraith.
1962 *Income, Resources, and Adjustment Potentials Among Rural Families in North and West Florida.* Florida Agricultural Experiment Station Bulletin 649 (December).

Ribich, T. I.
1968 *Education and Poverty.* Washington, D. C.: Brookings Institution.

Rice, E. P., M. C. Ekdahl, and L. Miller.
1971 *Children of Mentally Ill Parents.* New York: Behavioral Publications.

Richardson, S. A., and A. F. Guttmacher, eds.
1967 *Childbearing: Its Social and Psychological Aspects.* Baltimore: Williams & Wilkins.

Richmond, J. B., and H. L. Weinberger.
1970 "Program Implications of New Knowledge Regarding the Physical, Intellectual, and Emotional Growth and Development and the Unmet Needs of Children and Youth," *American Journal of Public Health,* LX (April), 23-67.

Rider, R. V., M. Taback, and H. Knobloch.
1955 "Associations Between Premature Birth and Socioeconomic Status," *American Journal of Public Health,* XLV (August 8), 1022-28.

Riessman, F.
1962 *The Culturally Deprived Child.* New York: Harper & Row.
1964 "Low-Income Culture: The Strength of the Poor," *Journal of Marriage and the Family,* XXVI (November 4), 417-21.

Riessman, F., J. Cohen, and A. Pearl.
1964 *Mental Health of the Poor.* New York: Free Press.

Ritchey, P. N.
1970 "Poverty Among Rural-Urban Migrants to Metropolitan Areas," Paper presented at the Annual Meeting of the Rural Sociological Society, Washington, D. C. (August 26-30).

Roach, J. L.
1965 "Sociological Analysis and Poverty," *American Journal of Sociology,* LXXI (7), 69-70.

Roach, J. L., and O. R. Gursslin.
1965 "The Lower Class, Status Frustration and Social Disorganization," *Social Forces,* XLIII (May), 501-10.
1967 "An Evaluation of the Concept 'Culture of Poverty,'" *Social Forces,* XLV, 383-91.

Robertson, N. L.
1968 "Higher Education and Economic Growth: A Regional Study," Dissertation, Indiana University.

Robinson, T. E., H. Bronfin, and J. O. Balswick.
1970 "Nursing Home Resources and Rural and Urban Needs," *Journal of Health and Social Behavior,* XI (June 2), 146-51.

Rodman, H.
1959 "On Understanding Lower-Class Behavior," *Social and Economic Studies,* VIII (December 4), 441-50.
1963 "The Lower-Class Value Stretch," *Social Forces,* XLII (December), 205-15.

Rogers, T. W., and G. L. Wilbur.
1964 *School Drop-Outs in Mississippi.* Mississippi Agricultural Experiment Station Information Sheet 838 (February).

Rokeach, M., and S. Parker.
1970 "Values as Social Indicators of Poverty and Race Relations in America," *The Annals of the American Academy of Political and Social Science,* CCCLXXXVIII (March), 97-111.

Roman, P. M., and H. M. Trice.
1967 *Schizophrenia and the Poor.* Ithaca, New York: New York School of Industrial and Labor Relations. Cornell University, Cayuga Press.

Rosen, B. C.
1956a "The Achievement Syndrome: A Psychocultural Dimension of Social Stratification," *American Sociological Review,* XXI, 203-14.
1956b "Race, Ethnicity, and the Achievement Syndrome," *American Sociological Review,* XXI, 214-27.
1964 "Family Structure and Value Transmission," *Merrill-Palmer Quarterly,* X (January), 59-76.

Rosenstock, I. M.
1969 "Prevention of Illness and Maintenance of Health," *Poverty and Health: A Sociological Analysis.* Ed. J. Kosa, *et al.* Cambridge, Massachusetts: Harvard University Press.

Rosenthal, D., and S. Kety, eds.
1968 *The Transmission of Schizophrenia.* New York: Pergamon Press.

Rubin, M.
1960 "Migration Patterns of Negroes from a Rural Northeastern Mississippi Community," *Social Forces,* XXXIX (October), 59-66.

Rushing, W. A.
1968 "Objective and Subjective Aspects of Deprivation in a Rural Poverty Class," *Rural Sociology,* XXXIII (September 3), 269-84.
1970 "Class Differences in Goal Orientations and Aspirations in Rural Patterns," *Rural Sociology* XXXV (September 3), 377 ff.

Russell, J. L.
1966 "The Negro's Occupational Progress," *Occupational Outlook Quarterly,* X (December 4), 8-13. U. S. Department of Labor. Bureau of Labor Statistics.

Samuelson, C. O.
1962 "The Unemployed Rehabilitant," Rehabilitation Counseling Bulletin (December).

Sarbin, T. R.
1970 "The Culture of Poverty, Social Identity, and Cognitive Outcomes," *Psychological Factors in Poverty.* Ed. V. L. Allen.. Chicago: Markham.

Sazama, G. W.
1970 "State Industrial Development Loans: A General Analysis," *Land Economics,* CLVI (May 2), 171-80.

Scheerenberg, R. C.
1965 "Genetic Aspects of Mental Retardation," *Mental Retardation Abstracts,* II (October-December), 463-81.

Scheff, T., and E. Sundstron.
1970 "The Stability of Deviant Behavior Over Time: A Reassessment," *Journal of Health and Social Behavior,* XI (March 1), 37-43.

Schlesinger, B.
1966 *Poverty in Canada and the United States: Overview and Annotated Bibliography.* Toronto: University of Toronto Press.

Schorr, A. L.
1964 "The Nonculture of Poverty," *The American Journal of Orthopsychiatry,* XXXIV (October), 907-12.
1966 "The Family Cycle and Income Development," *Poverty in America.* Ed. L. A. Ferman, *et al.* Ann Arbor, Michigan: University of Michigan Press.

Schneder, L. S., and S. Lysgaard.
1953 "The Deferred Gratification Pattern: A Preliminary Study," *American Sociological Review,* XVIII, 142-49.

Schneiderman, L.
1964 "Value Orientations Preferences of Chronic Relief Recipients," *Social Work,* IX (July 3), 13-18.

Schultz, T. W.
1964 "Our Welfare State and the Welfare of Farm People," *Social Service Review,* XXXVIII (June 2), 123-29.
1965 "Investing in Poor People: An Economist's View," *American Economic Review,* LV (May), 510-20.

Schwartz, J. L.
1970 *1,000 Poor Families: Socio-Demographic Profile of Enrollees in a Rural Health Project (King City, California).* Research Report No. 1, King City.

Schwarzweller, H. K.
1959 "Value Orientations in Education and Occupational Choices," *Rural Sociology,* XXIV (September 3), 246-56.
1964 "Education, Migration and Economic Life Chances of Male Entrants to the Labor Force from a Low-Income Rural Area," *Rural Sociology,* XXIX (June 2), 152-67.

Schwarzweller, H. K., and J. S. Brown.
1962 "Education as a Cultural Bridge Between Eastern Kentucky and the Great Society," *Rural Sociology,* XXVII (December 4), 357-73.
1967 "Social Class Origins, Rural-Urban Migration, and Economic Life Chances: A Case Study," *Rural Sociology,* XXXII (March 1), 5-19.

Scott, E. M., and J. D. Nisbet.
1955 "Intelligence and Family Size in an Adult Sample," *Eugenics Review,* XLVI, 233-35.

Scrimshaw, N. S.
1969 "Early Malnutrition and Central Nervous System Function," *Merrill-Palmer Quarterly,* XV (April), 375-88.

Seagull, A. A.
1964 "The Ability to Delay Gratification," Dissertation, Syracuse University.

Seligman, B. B.
1968 *Permanent Poverty: An American Syndrome.* Chicago: Quadrangle Books.

Sewell, W. H.
1961 "Social Class and Childhood Personality," *Sociometry,* XXIV (August), 352.
1963 "Some Recent Developments in Socialization Theory and Research," *The Annals of the American Academy of Political and Social Science,* CCXLIX (September), 163-81.

Shaffer, H. B.
1964 "Persistence of Poverty," *Editorial Research Report,* I (February 5), 81-100.

Shanas, E., and G. F. Streik.
1965 *Social Structure and the Family: Generational Relations.* Englewood Cliffs, New Jersey: Prentice Hall.

Sharansky, I.
1967 "Government Expenditures and Public Services in the American States," *American Political Science Review,* LXI (December 4), 1066-77.

Sharp, L. M., and G. B. Peterson.
1967 *The Cleveland Southern In-Migrant Study: An Overview.* Washington, D. C.: Bureau of Social Science Research, Inc.

Sheldon, H.
1969 "Distribution of the Rural Aged Population," *Older Rural Americans: A Sociological Perspective.* Lexington, Kentucky: University of Kentucky Press.

Shockley, W.
1966 "Population Control or Eugenics," *Genetics and the Future of Man.* Ed. J. D. Rolansky. New York. Appleton-Century-Crofts.
1969 *Human Quality Problems and Research Taboos: New Concepts and Directions.* Greenwich, Connecticut: Educational Records Bureau.
1970 "A 'Try Simplest Cases' Approach to the Heredity-Poverty-Crime Problems," *Psychological Factors in Poverty.* Ed. V. L. Allen. Chicago: Markham.

Shontz, F. B.
1970 "Physical Disability and Personality," Paper presented at the National Conference on Psychological Aspects of Disability, Monterey, California (October 26-28).

Shuey, Q. M.
1958 *The Testing of Negro Intelligence.* Lynchburg, Virginia: J. P. Bell.
1966 *The Testing of Negro Intelligence.* 2nd ed. New York: Social Science Press.

Shulz, D. A.
1968 "Variations in Complete and Incomplete Families of the Negro Lower Class," Dissertation, Washington University of St. Louis.

Silberman, C. E.
1967 *The Myths of Automation.* New York: Harper & Row.

Sinler, N. J.
1964 "Long-Term Unemployment, the Structural Hypothesis, and Public Policy," *American Economic Review,* LIV (December), 985-1001.

Simpson, R. L., and M. Miller.
1963 "Social Status and Anomia," *Social Problems,* X (Winter), 256-64.

Sizer, T. R.
1970 "Low-Income Families and the Schools for Their Children," *Public Administration Review,* XXX (July-August), 340-46.

Skeels, H. M., R. Updegraff, B. Wellman, and H. M. Williams.
1938 *A Study of Environmental Stimulation: An Orphanage Preschool Project.* University of Iowa Studies: Studies in Child Welfare, Vol. XV, No. 4. Iowa City, Iowa: University of Iowa.

Slocum, W.
1962 *Agricultural Sociology: A Study of Sociological Aspects of American Farm Life.* New York: Harper & Row.
1967 *Aspirations and Expectations of the Rural Poor—A Guide to Research.* Agricultural Economic Report 122. U. S. Department of Agriculture. Economic Research Service. Washington, D. C.: U. S. Government Printing Office.

Smith, P. M.
1961 "Personal and Social Adjustment of Negro Children in Rural and Urban Areas in the South," *Rural Sociology,* XXVI (March 1), 73-77.

Smith, T. L.
1969 "A Study of Social Stratification in the Agricultural Sections of the U. S.: Nature, Data, Procedures and Preliminary Results," *Rural Sociology,* XXXIV (December 4), 496-509.

Smolensky, E.
1966 "Investment in the Education of the Poor: A Pessimistic Report," *American Economic Review,* LVI (May), 370-78.

Sneden, L. E.
1968 "Factors Involved in Upward Social Mobility from the Culture of Poverty," Dissertation, Michigan State University.

Snyder, E. M.
1956 "Validity of Field Survey Data for Low-Income Groups," *Proceedings of a Conference on Research in Income and Wealth.* National Bureau of Economic Research. New York.

Somers, G.
1968 *Retraining the Unemployed.* Madison, Wisconsin: University of Wisconsin Press.

South Today, II.
1971 (January 2).

Southern Regional Conference on Urbanization.
1967 *Proceedings.* Athens, Georgia.

Southern Regional Council.
1962 *A Study of Negro Farmers in South Carolina.* Atlanta, Georgia.
1966 *Cooperatives, Credit Unions, and Poor People.* Special Report from the Southern Regional Council. Atlanta, Georgia.
1971 *The South and Her Children: School Desegregation, 1970-71.* Atlanta, Georgia.

Spady, W. G.
1967 "Educational Mobility and Access: Growth and Paradoxes," *American Journal of Sociology,* LXXIII (November), 272-86.

Spencer, G.
1967 *A Comparative Study of the Reduction of Dependency in Four Low-Income Housing Projects: A Descriptive and Conceptual Introduction.* Monograph 4. Boston, Massachusetts: New England Rehabilitation Research Institute. Northeastern University.

Spitz, R.
1946 "Hospitalization: A Follow-Up Report on the Investigation Described in Vol. I, 1954," *The Psychoanalytic Study of The Child,* Vol. II. New York: International Universities Press.

Stein, C. S.
1967 *Toward New Towns for America.* Cambridge, Massachusetts: Massachusetts Institute of Technology Press.

Steiner, G. Y.
1966 *Social Insecurity: The Politics of Welfare.* Chicago: Rand McNally.

Steinman, D.
1970 "Health in Rural Poverty: Some Lessons in Theory and from Experience," *American Journal of Public Health,* LX (September 9), 1813-23.

Stiles, L. A.
1968 "Aiding the Poor: The Negative Income Tax," *Business Conditions* (September 9-15), Federal Reserve Bank of Chicago.

Stinner, W. F., and G. F. DeJong.
1969 "Southern Negro Migration: Social and Economic

Components of an Ecological Model," *Demography*, VI (November 4), 455-69.

Stinson, T. F.
1968 "Drawing a Poverty Line for Government Services: An Initial Attempt," *American Journal of Agricultural Economy*, L (December 5), 1416-20.

Stoch, N. B., and P. M. Smythe.
1963 "Does Undermalnutrition During Infancy Inhibit Brain Growth and Subsequent Intellectual Development?" *Archives of Disease of Childhood*, XXXVIII, 546-52.

Stone, P. S.
1969 "Analysis of Economic Relationships and Employment Changes in the Northeastern Region of North Carolina," Dissertation, North Carolina State University at Raleigh.

Stone, R. C., and F. Y. Schlamp.
1965 "Characteristics Associated with Receipt or Nonreceipt of Financial Aid from Welfare Agencies," *Welfare in Review*, III (July 7), 1-11.

Strauss, M. A.
1962 "Deferred Gratification. Social Class and the Achievement Syndrome," *American Sociological Review*, XXVII, 326-35.
1964 "Societal Needs and Personal Characteristics in the Choice of Farm, Blue-Collar, and White-Collar Occupations by Farmers' Sons," *Rural Sociology*, XXIX (December 4), 408-25.

Strauss, R.
1965 "Poverty As an Obstacle to Health Progress in Our Rural Areas," *American Journal of Public Health*. LV (November), 1772-79.

Street, P., and L. Meenach.
1967 *Vocational Rehabilitation Needs and Resources in Eastern Kentucky*. Final Report. Frankfort, Kentucky: Bureau of Rehabilitation Services. State Department of Education.

Strodtbeck, F.
1965 "Family Communication and Child Development," *Research Project Summaries*, No. 2 U. S. Department of Health, Education, and Welfare. Public Health Service. Washington, D. C.: U. S. Government Printing Office.

Su, T. Y.
1970 *The South Carolina Economy: An Input-Output Study*. Columbia, South Carolina: Bureau of Business and Economic Research. University of South Carolina.

Sutton, G. F.
1967 "Poverty in the Rural Population of the United States," *Proceedings of Social Statistics Section, American Statistical Association*. Washington, D. C.

Swinehart, J. W.
1963 "Socioeconomic Level. Status Aspiration and Maternal Role," *American Sociological Review*, XXVIII, 391-99.

Symonds, J. D.
1969 *Cultural Differences and Social Class in the Negro Community*. Technical Report No. 1. Illinois Studies of the Culturally Disadvantaged. University of Illinois.

Szasy, T.
1970 *Ideology and Insanity*. New York: Doubleday.

Tadros, H. R.
1968 "Return Migration to Selected Communities in the Ozarks: A Predominantly Rural, Economically Depressed Region," Dissertation, University of Missouri.

Tallahassee *Democrat*
1969 "Negro Genetically Inferior? Study is Asked," (September 4).

Tang, A. M.
1959 "Economic Development and Changing Consequence of Race Discrimination in Southern Agriculture," *Journal of Farm Economics*, XLI (December), 1113-26 and 1134-40.

Tarver, J. D., and C. L. Beale.
1969 "Relationship of Changes in Employment and Age Composition to the Population Changes of Southern Nonmetropolitan Towns," *Rural Sociology*, XXXIV (March 1), 16-28.

Taylor, L., and C. W. Glasgow.
1963 *Occupations and Low-Income Rural People: A Southern Regional Study*. Southern Cooperative Series Bulletin 90. Florida, North Carolina, Kentucky, Louisiana, Mississippi, Tennessee and Texas Agricultural Experiment Station (December).

ten Broek, J., ed.
1966 *The Law of the Poor*. San Francisco: Chandler.

Terjen, K.
1970 "Uneasy Peace Reigns in Delta Schools; Gimmickry Starves Welfare Programs," *South Today*, II (November 4), 2.

Theobald, R.
1965 *Free Men and Free Markets*. Garden City, New York: Doubleday.

Thiessen, D. D.
1971 "Reply to Wilcock on Gene Action and Behavior," *Psychological Bulletin*, LXXV (February 2), 103-5.

Thoday, J. M., and A. S. Parkes, eds.
1968 *Genetics and Environmental Influences on Behavior*. A Symposium Held by the Eugenics Society (September 1967). New York: Plenum Press.

Thomas, E. J.
1966 "Psychological Dependency and Its Relationship to Economic Deprivation," *The Social Welfare Forum*, 1966. New York: Columbia University Press.

Thomas, E. J., and R. D. Carter.
1967 "Social Psychological Factors in Poverty," *Organizing for Community Welfare*. Ed. M. N. Zald. Chicago: Quadrangle Books.

Thomas, G.
1971 "Just Above Welfare: The Plight of Domestics in a Southern City" (Mimeographed).

Thompson, C. P., and N. W. Bell.
1969 "Evaluation of a Rural Community Mental Health Program," *Archives of General Psychiatry*, XX (4), 448-56.

Thurow, L. C.
1967 "The Causes of Poverty," *The Quarterly Journal of Economics*, LXXXI (February), 39-57.
1969 *Poverty and Discrimination*, Washington, D. C.: Broolings Institution.

Tienari, P.
1964 "Psychiatric Illness in Identical Twins," *Acta Psychiatrica Scandinavica*, XXXIX (supp. 171), 46-121.

Tiffany, D. W.
1969 "Understanding the Problem in Employment of the Hard-Core Poor—Whose Responsibility?" Ed. C. E. Curran. *Midwest Review of Public Administration*. III (February 1), 20-23.

Tinbergen, N.
1965 *Social Behavior in Animals*. 2nd ed. New York: Wiley.

Tobin, J.
1966 "On Improving the Economic Status of the Negro," *The Negro American*. Ed. T. Parsons and K. B. Clark. Boston: Houghton.
1968 "Raising the Income of the Poor," *Agenda for the Nation*. Washington, D. C.: Brookings Institution.

Tolley, G. S., and H. W. Hjort.
1963 "Age-Mobility and Southern Farmer Skill—Looking Ahead for Area Development," *Journal of Farm Economy*, XLV (February 1), 31-46.

Trahan, J. E.
1958 "Future Time Perspective. Optimism and Academic Achievement," *Journal of Abnormal and Social Psychology*, LVII (November), 379-80.

Troobaff, B. M.
1968 "Employment Experience after MDTA Training: A Study of the Relationship Between Selected Trainee Characteristics and Post Training Experience," Dissertation, Georgia State College.
Truett, D. B.
1969 "Negro Employment in Dade County," *Business and Economic Dimensions* (December), 1-9.
Tucker, M. A.
1970 "Effects of Heavy Medical Expenditures on Low-Income Families," *Public Health Reports,* LXXXV (May), 419-25.
Turner, R. H.
1958 "Life Situation and Subculture," *British Journal of Sociology,* IX (December), 299-320.
Turner, R. J., and M. Wagenfield.
1967 "Occupational Mobility and Schizophrenia: An Assessment of the Social Causation and Social Selection Hypotheses," *American Sociological Review,* XXXII, 104-13.
Tweeten, L. G.
1967 *The Role of Education in Alleviating Rural Poverty.* Agricultural Economic Report 114. U. S. Department of Agriculture. Economic Research Service. Washington, D. C.: U. S. Government Printing Office.
1968 *Rural Poverty: Incidence, Causes, and Cures.* Oklahoma State University Agricultural Experiment Station, Stillwater, Oklahoma (July).
Udry, J. R., K. E. Bauman, N. M. Morris, and C. L. Chase. "Social Class, Social Mobility and Prematurity: A Test of the Childhood Environment Hypothesis for Negro Women," *Journal of Health and Social Behavior,* XI (September 3), 190-95.
U. S. Advisory Commission on Intergovernmental Relations.
1966 *Intergovernmental Relations in the Poverty Program.* Commission Report. Washington, D. C.: U. S. Government Printing Office.
1968 *Urban and Rural America: Policies for Future Growth.* Commission Report. Washington, D. C.: U. S. Government Printing Office.
U. S. Advisory Commission on Intergovernmental Relations and Council of State Governments.
1970 *The Gap Between Federal Aid Authorization and Appropriations.* Joint Report. Washington, D. C.: U. S. Government Printing Office.
U. S. Bureau of the Budget. Office of Statistical Standards.
1964 *Family Income Distribution Statistics Published by Federal Agencies.* Statistical Evaluation Report 5.
U. S. Chamber of Commerce.
1961 *Rural Poverty and Regional Progress in an Urban Society.* 4th Report of the Task Force on Economic Growth and Opportunity. Washington, D. C.
U. S. Congress.
1970 *Semi-Annual Report of the Director of Selective Service to Congress of the United States, July 1-December 31, 1969.* Washington, D. C.: U. S. Government Printing Office.
U. S. Congress. Commission on Civil Rights.
1968 *Staff Report.* Hearings on Income Maintenance Programs Before the Subcommittee on Fiscal Policy of the Joint Economic Committee. (June 11-27), Vol. II, Appendix Materials. 90th Congress, 2nd Session.
U. S. Congress. House. Agriculture Committee.
1968 *Hunger Study.* 90th Congress, 2nd Session.
U. S. Congress. Senate. Committee on Labor and Public Welfare.
1969 *The Migratory Farm Labor Problem in the United States.* Report No. 91-83, 91st Congress, 1st Session.
U. S. Congress. Senate Select Committee on Nutrition and Human Needs.
1970 *Nutrition and Human Needs*—1970. Hearings Before the Select Committee and Nutrition and Human Needs, Senate, 91st Congress, 2nd Session.
1971 *Promises to Keep: Housing Need and Federal Failure in Rural America.* 92nd Congress, 1st Session.
U. S. Council of Economic Advisors.
1964 *Economic Report of the President, 1964.* Washington, D. C.: U. S. Government Printing Office.
U. S. Department of Agriculture. Economic Research Service.
1965 *Economic Survey of the Appalachian Region.* ERS 67. Washington, D. C.: U. S. Government Printing Office.
1966 *Rural People in the American Economy.* Agricultural Economic Report 101. Washington, D. C.: U. S. Government Printing Office.
1969a *Farm Income: State Estimates, 1949-1968* ERS 214 Supp. Washington, D. C.: U. S. Government Printing Office.
1969b *The Poor: A Selected Bibliography.* Washington, D. C.: U. S. Government Printing Office.
U. S. Department of Commerce. Bureau of the Census.
1960a *1960 Census of Population.* Washington, D. C.: U. S. Government Printing Office.
1964 "Lifetime Occupational Mobility of Adult Males: March 1962," Current Population Reports, Series P-23, No. 11. Washington, D. C.: U. S. Government Printing Office.
1966a *Population Characteristics.* Current Population Reports, Series P-20, No. 154. Washington, D. C.: U. S. Government Printing Office.
1966b *America at Mid-Decade.* Current Population Reports. Series P-23, No. 16. Washington, D. C.: U. S. Government Printing Office.
1966c "Characteristics of Families Residing in 'Poverty Areas,'" Current Population Reports, Series P-23, No. 19. Washington, D. C.: U. S. Government Printing Office.
1966d *Statistical Abstract of the United States, 1966.* 87th ed. Washington, D. C.: U. S. Government Printing Office.
1968 *Technical Studies.* Current Population Reports. Series P-23, No. 25. Washington, D. C.: U. S. Government Printing Office.
1970a *Special Studies.* Current Population Reports, Series P-23, No. 33. Washington, D. C.: U. S. Government Printing Office.
1970b *Consumer Income.* Current Population Report, Series P-60, No. 73. Washington, D. C.: U. S. Government Printing Office.
1970c *Consumer Income.* Current Population Reports, Series P-60, No. 76. Washington, D. C.: U. S. Government Printing Office.
1970d *1967 Census of Manufactures.* Areas Series MC67 (3), Series 1, 10, 11, 18, 25, 34, 41, 43, and 47. Washington, D. C.: U. S. Government Printing Office.
1970e *1970 Census of Population.* Washington, D. C.: U. S. Government Printing Office.
1971 *Population Characteristics.* Current Population Reports, Series P-20, No. 210. Washington, D. C.: U. S. Government Printing Office.
U. S. Department of Commerce. U. S. Economic Development Administration.
1970 *Economic Development Districts: Composition and Status as of December 31, 1969.* Washington, D. C.: U. S. Government Printing Office.
U. S. Department of Health, Education and Welfare.
1967 *Delivery of Health Services for the Poor.* Program Analysis No. 12. Washington, D. C.: U. S. Government Printing Office.
U. S. Department of Health, Education and Welfare. Bureau of Family Service.
1965 *Study of Recipients of Aid to Families with Dependent Children, November-December 1961: Na-*

tional Tabulations. Washington, D. C.: U. S. Government Printing Office.

U. S. Department of Health, Education, and Welfare. Office of Economic Opportunity. Information Center.
1967 *County Community Profiles.* Washington, D. C.: U. S. Government Printing Office.

U. S. Department of Health, Education, and Welfare. Office of Juvenile Delinquency and Youth Development.
1966 *Neighborhood Legal Services—New Dimensions in the Law.* Washington, D. C.: U. S. Government Printing Office.

U. S. Department of Health, Education, and Welfare. Public Health Service.
1965 *Health and Manpower Source Book.* Washington, D. C.: U. S. Government Printing Office.
1970a *Health Resources Statistics: Health Manpower and Health Facilities, 1969.* Washington, D. C.: U. S. Government Printing Office.
1970b *Natality Statistics Analysis: U. S., 1965-1967.* National Center for Health Statistics Series 21, No. 19. Washington, D. C.: U. S. Government Printing Office.
1971 *Monthly Vital Statistics Report,* XIX (11), National Center for Health Statistics. Washington, D. C.: U. S. Government Printing Office.

U. S. Department of Health, Education, and Welfare. Public Health Service. Health Services and Mental Health Administration.
1971 *Chronic Conditions and Limitation of Activity and Mobility, United States—July 1965-June 1967.* Vital and Health Statistics: Data from the National Health Survey. Publication No. 1000, Series 10, No. 61. Washington, D. C.: U. S. Government Printing Office.

U. S. Department of Health, Education, and Welfare. Public Health Service, National Institutes of Health, National Institute of Child Health and Human Development.
1968 *Perspectives on Human Deprivation: Biological, Psychological and Sociological.* Washington, D. C.: U. S. Government Printing Office.

U. S. Department of Health, Education, and Welfare. Public Health Service. National Institute of Mental Health.
1965 *Research Project Summaries,* No. 2. Washington, D. C.: U. S. Government Printing Office.

U. S. Department of Health, Education, and Welfare. Social and Rehabilitation Service. National Center for Social Statistics.
1969 *Public Assistance—Annual Statistical Data: Calendar Year 1969.* Washington, D. C.: U. S. Government Printing Office.
1970a *Public Assistance Statistics.* Report A-2. Washington, D. C.: U. S. Government Printing Office .
1970b *Assessments Completed and Referrals to Manpower Agencies by Welfare Agencies Under Work Incentive Programs for AFDC Recipients, January-March 1970.* Report E-5. Washington, D. C.: U. S. Government Printing Office.
1970c *Findings of the 1969 AFDC Study: Data by Census Division and Selected States.* Washington, D. C.: U. S. Government Printing Office.

U. S. Department of Health, Education, and Welfare. Social Security Administration. Office of Research and Statistics.
1970 *Poverty Studies in the Sixties—A Selected, Annotated Bibliography.* Washington, D. C.: U. S. Government Printing Office.
1971 "Health Insurance for the Aged: Professional and Technical Employees of Participating Facilities, July 1969," *Health Insurance Statistics.* HI-22. Washington, D. C.: U. S. Government Printing Office.

U. S. Department of Labor.
1966 *Manpower Report of the President and A Report on Manpower Requirements, Resources, Utilization and Training.* Washington, D. C.: U. S. Government Printing Office.
1967 *Manpower Report of the President.* Washington, D. C.: U. S. Government Printing Office.
1969 *Handbook of Labor Statistics, 1969.* Washington, D. C.: U. S. Government Printing Office.

Valentine, C. A.
1968 *Culture and Poverty.* Chicago: University of Chicago Press.

Vanderberg, S. G.
1965 "The Genetics of Human Behavior," *Research Project Summaries, No. 2.* U. S. Department of Health, Education and Welfare. Public Health Service. Washington, D. C.: U. S. Government Printing Office.
1968 "Inheritance in Families," *Heredity, Disease, and Man.* Ed. A. E. H. Emery. Berkeley, California: University of California Press.
1970 "Genetic Factors in Poverty: A Psychologist's Point of View," *Psychological Factors in Poverty.* Ed. V. L. Allen. Chicago: Markham.

van Es, J., and E. Wilkening.
1970 "Response Stability in Survey Research: A Cross-Cultural Comparison," *Rural Sociology,* XXXV (June 2), 191-205.

Verba, S.
1961 *Small Groups and Political Behavior: A Study of Leadership.* Princeton, New Jersey: Princeton University Press.

"Vicious Cycle of Poverty, The."
1964 *Business Week* (February) 38-43.

Wagar, J. A.
1970 "Growth Versus the Quality of Life," *Science,* CLXVIII (June 5), 1179-84.

Walls, R. T., and J. J. Miller
1970 "Perception of Disability by Welfare and Rehabilitation Clients," *Perceptual and Motors Skills,* XXXI, 793-94.

Warren, M., and S. Berkowitz.
1969 "The Employability of AFDC Mothers and Fathers," *Welfare in Review,* VII (July- August), 1-7.

Warren R.
1960 *Multi-Problem Families: A New Name or a New Problem.* New York: State Charities Aid Association.

Wasserman, H. L.
1968 "Father Absent and Father Present Lower Class Negro Families: A Comparative Study of Family Functioning," Dissertation, Brandeis University, F. Heller Graduate School for Advanced Studies in Social Welfare.

Watters, P.
1969 "Atlanta and the Urban South," *Atlanta Magazine,* XI (December), 57-63.
1970 "Atlanta and the Urban South," *Atlanta Magazine,* X (January), 81-84.

Watts, H.
1967 "The Iso-Prop Index: An Approach to the Determination of Differential Poverty Income Threshholds," *Journal of Human Resources,* II (Winter), 3-18.
1969a "Graduated Work Incentives: An Experiment in Negative Taxation," *American Economic Review,* LIX (May), 463-92.
1969b "An Economic Definition of Poverty," *On Understanding Poverty.* Ed. D. Moynihan. New York: Basic Books.

Weaver, T.
1969 *Poverty: New Interdisciplinary Perspectives.* San Francisco: Chandler.

Welch, F.
1967 "Labor-Market Discrimination: An Interpretation of Income Differences in the Rural South," *The*

Journal of Political Economy, LXXV (June 3), 225-40.

Wender, P. H.
1969 "The Role of Genetics in the Etiology of the Schizophrenias," *American Journal of Orthopsychiatry,* XXXIX (April 3), 447-58.

Wendlend, M. M.
1968 "Self-Concept in Southern Negro and White Adolescents as Related to Rural-Urban Residence," Dissertation, University of North Carolina.

"What FIND Found: A Tarnished Myth."
1970 *Aging* (September-October), 9 and 34-35.

Whelpton, P., *et al.*
1966 *Fertility and Family Planning in the U. S.* Princeton. New Jersey: Princeton University Press.

White, R. A.
1969 "Estimating Small-Area Unemployment in Rural States," *Business and Economic Dimensions* (June), 1-7.

Whitney, V. H.
1960 "Changes in the Rural-Nonfarm Population, 1930-1950," *American Sociological Review,* XXV (June 3), 363-68.

Wilensky, H., and H. Edwards.
1959 "The Skidder: Ideological Adjustment of Downward Mobile Workers," *American Sociological Review,* XXIV (April 2), 215-31.

Willerman, L., A. F. Naylor, and N. C. Myrianthropoulos.
1970 "Intellectual Development of Children from Interracial Matings," *Science,* CLXX (December 18), 1329-1331.

Williams, T. T., and R. B. Glasgow.
1968 "Developing Estimates of Economic Underemployment for the Rural Labor Force of Seven Southern States," *American Journal of Agricultural Economy,* L (December 5), 1431-36.

Willie, G. V.
1970 *Family Structure, Poverty, and Race.* Syracuse University, Syracuse, New York.

Willie, C. V., and J. Weinandy.
1963 "The Structure and Composition of 'Problem' and 'Stable' Families in a Low-Income Population," *Marriage and Family Living,* XXV (November). 439-47.

Willits, F. K., and R. C. Bealer.
1967 "An Evaluation of a Composite Definition of 'Rurality,'" *Rural Sociology,* XXXII (June 2), 165-77.

Wilson, J. W.
1968 "The Urban Unease: Community Versus City," *The Public Interest,* XII (Summer), 25-39.

Wiltse, K. T.
1958 "The 'Hopeless' Family," *Social Work,* III (October), 12-22.

Wolfe, A. W., *et al.*
1967 "Progress Report into Adaptation by Urban White *Families to Poverty"* (Mimeographed).

Wright, B.
1960 *Physical Disability: A Positive Approach.* New York: Harper & Row.

Wright, C. R., and H. H. Hyman.
1958 "Voluntary Association Memberships of American Adults: Evidence from National Sample Surveys," *American Sociological Review,* XXIII (June 3), 284-94.

Wright, M. W.
1964 "Public Assistance in the Appalachian South," *Journal of Marriage and the Family,* XXVI (November 4), 406-9.

Yancy, W. L.
1965 *"The Culture of Poverty: Not so Much Parsimony,"* Washington University at St. Louis (Mimeographed).

Yeager, J. H.
1962 *Rural Housing.* Alabama Agricultural Experiment Station Report (May).

Yinger, M.
1960 "Contraculture and Subculture," *American Sociological Review,* XXV (October 5), 625-35.

Youmans, E. G., ed.
1967 *Older Rural Americans; A Sociological Perspective.* Lexington, Kentucky: University of Kentucky Press.

Youmans, E. G., S. E. Grigsky, and H. King.
1969 "Social Change, Generation, and Race," *Rural Sociology,* XXXIV (September 3), 305-12.

Yuker, H. E., J. R. Block, J. H. Young, and N. Y. Albertson.
1967 *The Measurement of Attitudes Toward Disabled Persons.* Human Resources Studies, Graduate School of Business, University of Colorado.

Zdyislaw, P., and J. W. Wesoloski.
1970 "The Impact of Automation on the Nature and Level of Employment," *Atlanta Economic Review,* XX (November), 32-34.

Zimbalist, S. E.
1964 "Drawing the Poverty Line," *Social Work,* IX (July 3), 19-26.

Zimmer, J. M.
1967 "Expenditures for Public Elementary and Secondary Education in Counties Classified by the Relative Poverty Status of Their Rural Populations," *Journal of Farm Economics,* XLIX (December 5), 1204-08.

Zola, I., and J. Kosa.
1969 *Poverty and Health: A Sociological Analysis.* Cambridge, Massachusetts: Harvard Press.

Zurcher, L. A.
1970 *Poverty Warriors.* Austin, Texas: University of Texas Press.